Discovering
Wine

Discovering
Wine

Joanna Simon

For Robin

Discovering Wine

Edited and designed by Mitchell Beazley,
an imprint of Reed Consumer Books Ltd,
Michelin House, 81 Fulham Road, London SW3 6RB
and Auckland, Melbourne, Singapore and Toronto

A CIP catalogue record for this book is
available from the British Library.

ISBN 1 85732 264 9

The author and publishers will be grateful for
any information which will assist them in keeping
future editions up to date. Although all reasonable
care has been taken in the preparation of this book,
neither the publishers nor the author can accept
responsibility for any consequences arising from the
use thereof or from the information
contained herein.

Executive Editor: Anne Ryland
Art Director: Tim Foster
Art Editor: Paul Tilby
Editor: Susan Keevil
Picture Research: Anna Smith
Indexer: Ann Barrett
Production: Michelle Thomas

Photographers: James Johnson,
    Anita Corbin/John O'Grady, Simon Wheeler
Maps: Lovell Johns
Illustrations: Conny Jude

Typeset in Gill Sans and Perpetua
Production by Mandarin Offset
Printed and bound in China

Contents

PART THREE

Where the best wines are made

Foreword and
introduction

Foreword

What: another book on wine? Yes, but this I think neatly bridges various important aspects of a fascinating subject. It is sensible, logical, unpretentious and, above all, helpful and informative.

It is the sort of book you can read from start to finish and be very much the wiser, no matter how well you thought you knew your wine. Or you can dip into it by subject: practical tips on tasting, the wines of Alsace neatly summed up, common sense about that tricky question 'when to drink'.

As refreshing as a *flûte* of champagne, as deeply satisfying as a glass of the finest claret. Read on.

Michael Broadbent
Christie's London

Introduction

A generation ago books about wine could confine themselves to the classic wines of Europe. There were so few other wines of more than local significance. The modern California wine industry was only just getting under way. Australia was predominantly a fortified wine producing country until the seventies: its first commercial vintage of Chardonnay was as recent as 1973. The export effort on behalf of Bulgarian wines did not begin until 1980. South African wine exports were mostly fortified 'sherry' types until the mid-eighties. New Zealand, another fortified wine producer, did not make enough table wines to export significantly until the eighties. And the great progress in Chilean wines is largely a phenomenon of the nineties.

As for the traditional European wine producing countries, they each had numerous regional wine styles of their own, but it was only the famous names of France – claret, burgundy, Chablis, champagne, Sauternes et al – and the hocks (Rhines) and Mosels of Germany, sherry and port, and perhaps Hungarian Tokay, that really impinged on the mass of wine drinkers and producers in other countries. Most other wines were very basic (wicker covered flasks of Chianti, Laski Rizling, anonymous *vins de table* etc) or they were household brands – often one and the same anyway.

Of course, there were *cognoscenti* – Italophiles and Hispanophiles who knew all about the wines of Barolo or Rioja and who knew how to distinguish the best from the dross (of which there was a great deal more two decades ago) – but wines such as these were not universally considered to be 'classics'. They did not dominate restaurant wine lists; they were not given pride of place by wine merchants; they were seldom laid down in private cellars; they did not change hands at high prices at auction; and – the crucial point so far as the modern international wine industry is concerned – they were not the wines and styles copied by the world's new producers in America, Australasia and South Africa (which, for simplicity's sake, I refer to collectively in this book as the New World). It was this eruption of activity, starting in California in the sixties, that marked the start of a completely new era in the history of wine – an era of more rapid and radical change than ever before.

To the wine drinker standing before ranks of bottles in a shop in the nineties, probably the most obvious and enveloping change wrought by the rise of the New World is the emphasis now placed on grape varieties. Twenty-five years ago few people had heard of Chardonnay – let alone Sauvignon Blanc, Cabernet Sauvignon and Merlot – and fewer still could name the classic wines which they produce. Today, wines labelled Chardonnay come from every wine-producing country, old and new. More excitingly, the interest in grape varieties is beginning to move on a stage. Unusual, esoteric and even distinctly odd varieties, which not long ago looked as if they might sink under a tidal wave of Chardonnay and Cabernet, are quietly being revived and nurtured.

But the climb to prominence of grape varieties is not by any means the only change to penetrate the entire winemaking world – nor is it even the most dramatic. More fundamental is the improvement in quality and reliability of wine – at all levels, but especially at the bottom. The word 'plonk', which used to signify something undrinkable (and if you drank it the consequences could be dire), is now more likely to be applied to something cheap but cheerful. It might be rather bland or neutral, but it is unlikely to be truly awful. If it is, there is a high chance that it has been spoiled by a tainted cork or unsuitable storage conditions. There are still undeniably badly-made wines, but there is so much choice among good wines that the really poor ones find it ever harder to gain an entrée into markets outside their immediate locality (which means that it is when you are on holiday in a village in the backwoods of Europe that you are most likely to find the unpalatable).

The improvements came about through technical advances in cellars and wineries – and these came via the New World. Unencumbered by preconceptions and dyed-in-the-wool older generations, the new producers studied, questioned, travelled and applied their new knowledge using the latest equipment. In no time at all their wines were competing with some of the best of the Old World. The tables were turned; it was time for the Old World to take something from the New. Gradually (and often grudgingly) winemakers in the traditional areas of Europe began to absorb and apply lessons learned from visiting Californian, Australian and New Zealand winemakers – winemakers who had originally come to Europe to learn from the old order.

It is not just that wine today is better, it is different. Few New World wines need to be laid down to improve for years before they are ready to be drunk and many of the European classics are

deliberately being made in such a way that they can be enjoyed sooner – so that they can compete, in fact, with the new. Moreover, wine is drunk by more people and in more varied circumstances than ever before. Enjoyment of, and interest in, wine is no longer the preserve of those greeted at birth with a pipe of port and schooled in claret appreciation from the cradle on. Appreciation of wine is open to anyone today; the aim of this book is to show the way.

Joanna Simon

How to get the most out of
every glass

Wine is for drinking, not for worshipping, but there is a world of difference between drinking without thinking and making the most of every mouthful. Knowing how to taste wine to appreciate all its flavours and nuances, knowing about serving temperatures, wine-friendly glasses and the purpose of decanting, being confident about matching food and wine and confident about which wines to lay down and which to drink tomorrow are the keys to a lifetime's fun and appreciation.

Why and how
to taste

Unless you have aspirations to become a wine taster by trade, you will know that you wouldn't want to be seen dead going through that extraordinary contortionist tasting ritual of sipping (or slurping), sucking in air (far from soundlessly), chewing as if battling with a piece of tough steak, then spitting.

And you wouldn't want to get into that habit of writing reports of every wine (usually littered with references to fruit and vegetables) and grandly calling them your tasting notes, would you? It all seems so pretentious, doesn't it?

In fact, it is pretentious to do all that outside the environs of a wine tasting. It is not only that you don't spit out wine when you are drinking it for pleasure. It is simply that you don't need to make a noisy spectacle of yourself to get a lot more pleasure out of every sip than you would if you simply knocked it back without thinking. And that's the point. You can treat wine simply as the unobtrusive stage set for the important action – whether food, conversation or a good book – or you can let the wine play the title role. Give it your attention, concentrate on it – and you will be duly rewarded.

The middle route – between drinking without taking any interest and the painstaking (and painful-looking) ritual of the professional in the tasting room – is simply the one which delivers most pleasure. (The aim of the professional, after all, is not personal enjoyment, but assessment of whether wines will give enjoyment at the right time and right price to those who are destined to drink them.)

To get more out of every sip, glass and bottle, you simply need to consider the wine in three stages: look, smell, then taste. Then, if you want a record for the future, you write down what you sensed in the same order, giving an overall impression at the end. (It is, I'm afraid, a mistake to rely on memory alone, especially if you are tasting or drinking more than one wine.) Lavishly-bound cellar books look the part – provided you fill them in – but I've never managed more than a few entries in one of these before I've returned to my infinitely less glamorous, but always accessible, common-or-garden notebooks. I start each entry by writing the date, the place (if it's not home), details on the wine label (of which more in a moment), where I bought it, the price and size of bottle. On the whole labels are getting easier to understand (German and expensive Italian designer labels are the main exceptions), but it can still be difficult to work out which are the pertinent details. Label-reading is explained in the last section of the book, but, as a guide, look for the name of the wine and of the property and producer, the name of a region or appellation, a vintage, and a grape variety and/or style (for example blanc de blancs or moelleux). You are now ready for the fun.

Look

Begin by looking at the wine, preferably in a reasonably good, but not fluorescent light, and against a plain, pale background (a sheet of white paper is ideal if you're at home). If you are doing the pouring, don't fill the glass too full: it makes the tasting process far easier if you don't. Hold the glass by the base or the stem and tip it away from you at an angle of about 45 degrees (if the glass was too full, there will now be wine everywhere). Look down on it and you should be able to see how clear the wine is – whether it has any minute bubbles or foreign bodies, how deep the colour is, what sort of hue it is, and how much the colour graduates from the centre to the rim. (With white wines it isn't actually so necessary to tilt the wine – you can hold the glass up and look at it at eye level – but it's a good habit to get into.)

(*Top left*) **Your first move is to check that the wine looks clean and bright:** with white wine you can usually do this at eye level.

(*Left*) **To see what the colour** – particularly of red wine – tells you, tilt the glass away from you against a plain, pale background, such as a piece of white paper or a tablecloth, and look at the surface of the wine.

(*Above*) **Hold the glass either by the stem** (*above left*) or, if you have a steady hand, **by the base** (*above right*). This not only gives you an unimpeded view of the wine, but also stops your hand from warming it. (Cupping your hands around the bowl is a useful trick for quickly raising the temperature of a wine, if it's too cold.)

Wine should always be clear and bright, never cloudy or hazy. At best the latter is caused by sediment that has been shaken up. At worst it suggests some kind of contamination. Sediment is less common in white wine than red, but if it is present, apart from indicating that the wine is quite mature (probably seven or more years), it shows that it has not been over filtered – which is a point in its favour. Of course, as with red wine (where a deposit may begin to appear within a couple of years), the sediment should remain in the bottle and not be tipped carelessly into the glass, because it muddies both the taste (it is often bitter) and texture, as well as the appearance. Small colourless crystals at the bottom of a glass or bottle of white

wine are harmless tartrate deposits and are a sign that the wine has not been over treated.

Bubbles in still wines can be a danger sign, indicating an unwanted re-fermentation, but a few tiny bubbles in a white wine – especially a pale, young, light one for drinking young – may be deliberate: wines such as Portugal's Vinho Verde are bottled with a little carbon dioxide to give a bit more zip to the palate (which you experience as a slight, refreshing prickle on the tongue). Bad – secondary fermentation – bubbles, on the other hand, give a vinegary sharpness to both smell and flavour.

Although colour is less indicative for white wine than red, it still varies from almost colourless, with perhaps a hint of green in a Mosel or a Chablis, to

(*Left*) **Most of the world's greatest sweet wines are made from grapes affected by botrytis (aka noble rot), a mould which attacks the grapes on the vine and dehydrates them. This concentrates both flavour and colour, giving the typically deep yellow to this Sauternes.**

(*Left*) **Warm climates give deeper coloured wines – both red and white – than cool climates. On colour alone, it would be hard to confuse this sunny-hued Australian Chardonnay with a Chardonnay from Chablis.**

(*Left*) **Age and production methods affect colour in several ways: this vin de pays from the south of France owes its paleness to youth, to cold fermentation and to early bottling.**

deep yellow. Once you see brownish tinges, however, it means that things are not looking good: white wines go darker with age (the reverse of reds) and by the browning stage they are usually heavily oxidised, or maderised, which gives them an increasingly sherry-like, or 'rancio', off-taste. Broadly speaking, paler wines come from cooler climates and deeper yellow ones come from warmer, especially southern hemisphere, regions, but sweet botrytis-affected wines (*see* page 92), including northern German ones, and oak-aged whites have more colour too.

The colour in red wine gives more away – in terms of age, quality and provenance. Red wines gradually shed their colour (eventually as sediment),

which means they become paler with age, changing from a deep purple-red, through to ruby, to brick-red and finally to an over-the-hill tawny. The place to look to get a feel for a wine's age is the rim: the paler and browner it is (and the greater the graduation of colour from the centre of the glass), the more mature the wine. And generally speaking a red wine of some quality that is intended to be aged, rather than drunk within two or three years, needs to have considerable colour to start with – because colour is closely linked to tannin content, and tannin is a major life-giver in red wines.

Inevitably, though, some grape varieties and climates produce more colour than others. As with white wines, warmer regions produce deeper

(*Right*) **Ageing in wood has the opposite effect on the colour of red wines to whites: whites become deeper, while oak-matured reds, such as this Rioja, lose colour.**

(*Right*) **Cabernet Sauvignon, the main component of 1983 Château Cos d'Estournel, typically gives deep-coloured wines, but after more than a decade this has mellowed to a ruby-garnet red.**

(*Right*) **In 1990 Château Léoville-Las-Cases the dense, vibrant purple colour indicates a top class, still young Cabernet Sauvignon-based Bordeaux.**

colours, but Cabernet Sauvignon grapes, for example, should produce a good strong-coloured wine everywhere. The same, only more so, goes for Syrah (or Shiraz) and Nebbiolo, although Syrah is basically only grown in reasonably warm climates anyway and Nebbiolo is pretty well a one-region (Piedmont) wine. Nebbiolo, though dark, also turns browner more quickly than most wines, as does Grenache. Pinot Noir, on the other hand, is naturally paler than wines such as Cabernet Sauvignon and Syrah.

The way red wine is aged also affects colour. Wines matured in wood lose more colour than those matured predominantly in the bottle: wood-aged tawny port versus bottle-aged vintage port is the archetypal example. Rioja is another: although Tempranillo grapes produce well-coloured wines, top quality Gran Reservas and Reservas can be relatively pale because of their long oak maturation.

(*Below*) **After swirling, look to see if there are 'legs' or 'tears' of wine down the inside of the glass: these can be a clue to the wine's alcohol and sugar content.**

(*Right*) **Watching as you do it, gently twirl the glass round so that wine and air interact to bring out the aromas.**

Swirl

Now for the first swirl. Either put the glass on the table, or continue to hold it by the stem or base (the base is more difficult), then twirl it round to get the wine moving – and do practice at home with water first, rather than drench your neighbouring taster. The main point of doing this is to aerate the wine so that it releases its volatile compounds – that's to say its smells, or aromas – but, before you plunge your nose into the glass, take a look.

The way the wine clings to the glass and then trickles down may tell you something. A wine that trickles back only slowly and in distinct streams, or 'legs', is fairly viscous, which means that it is high in alcohol, sugar or both. A wine with an edge that breaks quickly and raggedly may be old, very light and dry, or you may have a not very well-rinsed glass! (Detergent and cloth residues interfere with the surface tension of the wine.)

Nose

Put your nose down to the glass and sniff. Then give your glass its second twirl, put your nose further into it and sniff more deeply. Most people find one deep sniff more rewarding than several short sharp ones, but the important thing is to do what is most effective for you.

The first thing you learn is that wine, with the exception of wine made from the Muscat grape, doesn't smell of grapes. In fact it smells of wine. And wine smells of... if you weren't afraid of sounding like one of those wine writers with what you had always assumed was chronic Purple Prose syndrome, you would say it reminded you of blackcurrants, gooseberries, grass, vanilla, petrol, linoleum, sweat – and you would be right. You would be right because your brain's interpretation of any aroma is what counts. It is useless to pretend that a wine smells of pineapple, butter and vanilla, because that is what you think it is supposed to smell of, when it actually reminds you of nothing so much as stale stair carpet, cardboard and cabbage. You won't kid yourself or anyone else.

The other reason you are right to trust your own senses is that, however outlandish your identification of a smell seems, you might well have hit the scientific bull's-eye. Wines smell of strawberries, bananas, blackcurrants, peaches, green peppers and an extraordinary number of other familiar non-wine substances, precisely because they share the same volatile chemical compounds. Some 500 aromatic compounds have been identified in wine to date (*see* next page for further details), variously derived from the grapes themselves, the fermentation process and the maturation process (although some wines are drunk before they have had a chance to develop any real aromas at this third stage, either because they are so delicious or because they are simple wines with no development potential).

The most obvious and fruity aromas (the so-called primary aromas) come from the grapes – especially from the skin and flesh just beneath. The fermentation process yields more complex aromas, which at their most easily identifiable include yeast, butter, freshly sawn oak and other oak-derived aromas such as vanilla, spice and toast. The complicated and still partly mysterious chemical and physical changes that take place as wine matures produce the so-called tertiary aromas – the most subtle and difficult to describe and identify, but ulti-

mately perhaps the most rewarding. In white wines, both sweet and dry, the most obvious is usually honey, with toast or brioche in champagne (but not, incidentally, derived from oak) and petrol in Riesling. Red wine maturation aromas are even harder to pinpoint, except that the fruit character becomes mellower and the good wines simply become richer (sometimes it is a gamey richness) and more profound. Together, the secondary and tertiary aromas are called the 'bouquet', although the word tends to be loosely used – often for the smell as a whole. The less euphonious but succinct 'nose' is also used for the overall smell.

So, that's the science, but how does it shape up in practice? Assuming that the wine is in prime condition (without specific faults and not getting too old), it should always smell clean and fresh rather than stale or baked – although, with a wine of some age, it isn't the invigorating freshness of youth. It should also smell in some way fruity, although not all grape varieties have the strong, fruity identity of, say, Cabernet Sauvignon (blackcurrants) or Gewürztraminer (lychees), and in older wines the vivid, youthful fruit is replaced by mellower, more

Wines and grapes mentioned in this chapter are described in more detail in the final part of the book (pages 94–157) and in 'The importance of Grapes' (pages 50–59).

(*Below*) **Having swirled your glass to release the aromas, don't be afraid to sniff deeply and decisively.**

complex, less clearly defined fruit aromas – sometimes with more of the character of dried fruit and autumnal fruit compotes.

On the whole you should feel that the aromas are attractive, but there are some honourable exceptions, especially among old wines. Mature burgundy, for example, can smack of farmyards and well-patronised stables, while other old reds, especially claret, can be oddly mushroomy. Red wines from the Syrah (Shiraz) grape can be quite leathery, or tarry, and in the Hunter Valley in Australia, Shiraz commonly used to have a pungent pong of sweaty saddles; nowadays, though, this is considered to come from a fault occurring in the winemaking process. Among white wines, the strong petrol or kerosene smell acquired by the Riesling grape can come as a shock to the uninitiated and both young Sauvignon Blanc and Müller-Thurgau are sometimes enthusiastically described as having a smell of cat's pee.

If you do encounter an off-putting smell, but one which is not positively bad, and if you sense that there is more to the wine than this one particular pong, think of it as a kindred spirit to one of those awe-inspiringly smelly, but wonderfully tasty cheeses.

So far as positively bad smells are concerned, all you will really need to know about are the few easily recognised ones. A musty, dank, mouldy smell indicates a 'corked' wine, one irredeemably tainted by infected cork (frustratingly this is an increasing problem – affecting perhaps one in 20 bottles worldwide). The corked smell always gets worse rather than better when the wine is in the glass and exposed to air, but occasionally you find a slightly similar stale smell that disappears quickly when the wine is poured. This is called 'bottle stink' and is harmless stale air that was caught in the bottle beween wine and cork.

A wine that smells of vinegar is almost certain to be beyond hope. The same goes for a wine smelling of cheap, tired sherry; but oxidation or maderisation – the problem in this case – takes a while to reach such a stage. On its way it may give a flat, stale, cardboardy smell to white wines, or a stewed, sharp, tomato purée aroma to reds, but it isn't always the most obvious of off-smells. A whiff of bad eggs, struck matches, blocked drains, old overcooked cabbage or burnt rubber is. These are all caused by sulphur-related problems. Sometimes they rather unexpectedly recover with a spot of rough handling – pouring the wine into a jug and swirling it around for example – but this is only potentially a solution at home. In a restaurant, the rule is reject it.

There is one final scenario: you put your nose down, inhale deeply, and get more or less nothing from the glass. It could be because your nose is begging for a few moments' rest after a period of concentrated sniffing. If you think that's the case, then do oblige. But if you are sure your faculties are in full working order you may have a wine in your glass that is going through a 'dumb' phase. This is as mysterious as it sounds. The scientists don't know why, but many good wines that need maturing suddenly seem to batten down the hatches after their first flush of exuberant youth. The fruit goes into retreat and not much else seems to be there. (On the palate they are equally withdrawn: red wines display rather pugnacious tannins, whites show acidity, both hide behind oak.) This moody adolescent phase often starts after about two to four years and goes on for as long as a piece of string. Maybe two years, maybe five. If the wine is yours, you just have to sit it out patiently and bravely.

The Flavour Connection

Around 500 chemical compounds have so far been identified in wine, many of them shared with fruits, vegetables and some rather more surprising common substances. To give you just a few examples: pyrazines give the green pepper aroma to Cabernet Sauvignon and Cabernet Franc; ethyl caprylate gives Chardonnay a pineapple aroma; ethyl acetate gives a pear aroma which is present in many young wines (including Beaujolais Nouveau); both piperonal and one of the deltalactones can give a peach aroma; another deltalactone is responsible for coconut smells; terpenes give Muscat its unmistakeable grapey scent; ionones give flowery aromas; cyanohydrin benzaldehyde is responsible for cherry aromas; isoamyl acetate gives Pinotage, for example, a smell of bananas; and the oxidation of certain fatty acids results in grassy, herbaceous smells.

The chemical compounds that give aromas – pong would be more apt in some cases – of garlic, goat, camphor, carnations, mouse, butter, honey, horse sweat and numerous others have all been found in wine. I could go on, but I'm sure you've got the picture – and the point, which is to have confidence in your own interpretations, by all means using prompts. My aromas and flavours crib (see pages 20 and 21) helps link common and distinctive aromas with wines in which they are often found.

Taste

Take a sip – a generous sip, but not a mouth so full that the reflex is to swallow immediately. Savour the flavours, rolling the wine gently around your mouth so that it reaches every tastebud. Then, if you're on your own, or feeling brave in sympathetic company, open your lips and draw in some air. (Yes, the slurping sound is you.) This aerates the wine, just as the earlier twirl of the glass did, and helps send the volatile compounds up from the back of your mouth to your olfactory bulb, the all-important organ at the top and back of your nose. Swallow (or spit) only when you have really got a sense of the flavours and feel of the wine. Then pay attention to the taste that is left – known as the finish or aftertaste. It should be pleasant and it should linger (try counting the seconds).

The first thing you usually learn is that your nose was right. You smelt blackcurrants, cedar wood and tobacco, or melon, vanilla and honey, and those are the flavours you taste. The mouth, by sending these volatile compounds up to the olfactory bulb, largely confirms what bulb and brain have already told you about the aromas. But the emphasis may be different: you may find their relative intensity has changed now you are experiencing them with other flavours and sensations. And taste reveals other facets of a wine's make-up, quality and constitution.

Although tastebuds on their own only pick up a few basic, non-volatile flavours, they play a crucial role in that they 'feel' the wine, with certain groups of tastebuds having particular strengths. Those at the tip of the tongue are especially sensitive to sugar. Those at the sides are more alert to acid sharpness, and those at the back are often acutely aware of bitterness (a feature of tannin, the dry, mouth-coating substance of cold tea fame). The tastebuds also register astringency (from tannin or acid), roughness or harshness (from tannin), smoothness (glycerol) and three other very important aspects of any wine – its 'weight', its balance of flavours and its length or aftertaste.

Weight (light-, medium- or full-bodied) is perceived through alcohol, glycerol, tannin, sugar and all the other non-water elements that together are called 'extract'. It is basically a matter of style. The question of balance (harmony of sugar, acid, tannin and alcohol levels) and the length of time the flavours last (which is usually allied to their

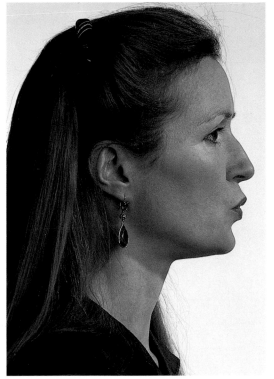

(*Above*) **Now taste the wine – take enough to be able to roll the wine all around your mouth, so that it reaches all the tastebuds. Think about texture as well as flavour.**

(*Left*) **Nose and mouth work in tandem – so, if you're feeling brave, open your mouth slightly and draw in some air to help aerate the wine and send aromas from the back of your mouth up to your olfactory bulb (a very perceptive organ).**

concentration) are aspects more related to quality. The greater the wine, the more harmonious all the elements appear to be and the longer and more intensely the taste lingers.

But balance can be difficult to assess, particularly in young wines that need cellaring for some years before they are drinkably mature. Red wines for laying down will have a certain amount of acidity and rather more tannin. Tannin is the inherent red wine preservative that gradually softens as the wine matures, but it is not in itself very pleasant, either in flavour or feel. What the expert looks for in a young red wine is sufficient (ie, a balance of) ripe fruit flavour behind the tannin – *see* page 90 for more details on how winemakers manipulate tannins. Then, by the time the wine is fully mature, the tannin should be mellow and seemlessly blended with the other flavours and textures.

It is much less prominent in white wines (although certainly not absent), but it is the acid levels in whites intended to age that need to be high – sometimes raspingly so. The effect of age is to soften acidity to the taste (although it doesn't actually reduce it). Again, the key is to have sufficient fruit at the outset, so that it does not 'dry out', or fade, before the acidity has softened. The acid balance is also very important, and particularly precarious, in sweet wines. If lacking, as it tends to be in cheaper wines, they simply become cloying.

The taste of new oak offers another area of potential imbalance. It gives dimension and complexity of texture to a wine, as well as contributing its own seductive flavours, but it shouldn't be intrusive – and certainly it should not be so assertive that you feel you might as well be chewing toothpicks. You will have no trouble spotting an old wine with too much oak: it will be dry, sawdusty and fruitless. But in a young wine you may have to delve behind the oaky exterior to a fruity core: the fruit must be there if the wine is to develop well.

Finally, when you have swallowed or spat out the wine, you should be left with a taste that is undeniably clean and pleasant. It shouldn't, for example, be predominantly tart or bitter. And this pleasant 'aftertaste' should linger. If it disappears in an instant, you have a very ordinary, simple wine (so I should go on to the next), but if it lasts more than about 30 seconds you probably have something rather good. So take another sip.

All this may have read as if tasting a wine takes an inordinately long time. It really doesn't – a minute or two, and I can assure you they will be minutes well and pleasurably spent.

PS Spitting

The other thing you need to get to grips with, if you are going to taste a lot of wines in earnest, is spitting. I know it goes against the grain to spit out good wine and against what you always thought was good manners, but spitting is the done thing. Fortunately it isn't difficult and you don't have to be aim-perfect from a great distance, but, if you take the time to have a few private practise runs, you are less likely to spatter fellow tasters and less likely to be embarassed by your spitting image. Take a little time to practise when you are cleaning your teeth, spit in the bath, or practise with water and a bucket in the kitchen. And so that you don't learn the hard way, can I point out that, as you spit, the following need to be held, pinned or tucked out of the way: ties, long hair (I learnt the hard way years ago), strings of beads, pendants and dangling scarves. You would also be well-advised to eschew pale colours and hard-to-clean silks, cashmeres, kid shoes and so on. And please note that, even if you can't see a sign, you shouldn't smoke. You may argue that you are so used to tobacco fumes they don't interfere with your tasting, but other people are unlikely to have developed a similar inbuilt filtration system.

(*Above*) **Spitting is not a pretty sight, but at least the Spittoo, a nifty portable spittoon designed by Hugh Johnson, looks attractive.**

(*Below*) **Spitting is essential at a large tasting, if you are to keep a clear head, but rest assured there is no great virtue in being able to spit from great distances. Practise first in the bathroom if you feel hesitant.**

Tasting terms

The following terms are in common usage and are mostly fairly self-explanatory:

Aggressive (said of young wine or older wine that hasn't mellowed as it should have done)

Aromatic (plenty of aromas and flavours – often the spicy or flowery grape varieties)

Astringent (mouth-puckering tannin)

Austere (rather tough and ungiving – maybe because the wine is too young)

Baked (as if the wine or grapes have been baked in the sun – so there is a lack of freshness)

Beefy (full-bodied, strapping, flavoursome – usually red wine)

Coarse (rough-and-ready – so should be cheap)

Creamy (wines of quality, especially champagne, can develop a creamy richness, which is half flavour and half texture)

Crisp (fresh and positively refreshing – especially whites)

Dense (solid colour and/or densely packed with flavour – usually positive)

Dried-out (a wine that is over-the-hill because the fruit flavours have faded away)

Earthy (an earthy, gravelly, minerally smell that seems to come straight from the soil, eg in fine Graves, as well as some more rustic wines)

Elegant (self-explanatory – and much used)

Fat (full-bodied with high glycerol – maybe sweet)

Finesse (high quality – self-explanatory)

Firm (good tannin and/or acid)

Flabby (lacking acidity)

Flat (lacking freshness and acid)

Fleshy (generously flavoured, round with no edges)

Forward (more mature than you would expect)

Fragrant (attractive, usually flowery)

Green (young and raw – may develop or the grapes may simply have been unripe)

Grip (a young wine with grip has the tannin and/or acid potential to develop)

Hard (too much tannin or acid – but can be a question of youth and time)

Heavy (full-bodied and alcoholic – usually used to indicate imperfect balance, although not in the case of fortified wines)

Herbaceous or herby (reminiscent of grass, herbs and leaves)

Hollow (wine that has an initial taste and an end-taste, but a disappointing lack of flavours in between)

Hot (high, out-of-balance alcohol – usually in wines from warm climates)

Jammy (jam rather than fresh fruit flavours – from hot climates)

Lean (lacking breadth of flavours)

Long (wine the taste of which lasts – a very positive feature)

Meaty (richly flavoured, full-bodied wine – sometimes literally savoury meat flavours)

Mouth-filling (wine with a satisfying richness of texture and flavours that fill the whole mouth)

Neutral (short on aroma and flavour – very common among inexpensive dry whites)

Oily (some grapes have an oily character in the mouth – Gewürztraminer is one, Viognier another; Sauternes can also have a rich, slightly oily texture, but otherwise not usually a quality sign)

Penetrating (intense aromas and flavours)

Perfumed (fragrant, scented, often flowery)

Rich (having depth and breadth of flavour)

Robust (full-bodied, sturdy wine, usually red)

Rough (coarse, basic wine)

Round (no hard edges – ready to drink)

Scented (fragrant, perfumed, often floral)

Sharp (a sharp, acid flavour that may simply need time to soften – mostly whites)

Short (no aftertaste – can't be a high quality wine)

Silky (smooth texture – high quality)

Simple (sound, drinkable wine of no great distinction)

Smooth (applies to texture – no tannin or acid getting in the way)

Soft (sometimes interchangeable with smooth, but often refers to soft, mellow flavours rather than texture)

Solid (plenty of substance, usually full-bodied)

Sour (irredeemably acidic or vinegary)

Spritz (prickle on the tongue of carbon dioxide in young, light-bodied whites)

Stalky (bitter aroma and taste of stalks and stems)

Steely (hard to describe: firm, sinewy character, usually allied to quite high acid, found in Chablis and some other good quality young French whites)

Stewed (coarse, cooked flavours from overripe grapes and/or over-hot fermentation)

Stringy (thin, mean wine)

Structure (as in good, firm structure or poor, weak structure – the balance and strength of the basic components, ie acid, tannin, fruit, alcohol and maybe sugar)

Supple (round and smooth)

Tangy (a lively aftertaste, in white wines, sherry and madeira)

Thin (lacking flavour and body)

Tough (too much tannin)

Vegetal (brassica, rather than leafy and herbaceous – often in mature burgundy, red and white)

Velvety (similar to silky, but richer)

Watery (feeble, thin, weak)

Woody (smell of old, dirty casks instead of clean, young ones)

Zesty (fresh, crisp and lively – usually young white wine)

(*Right*) **A silver tastevin – still used as a tasting tool by a few producers, especially in Burgundy. It is specially dimpled to catch the light and show the colour.**

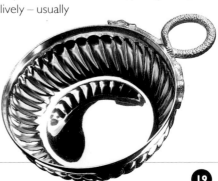

Aromas and flavours crib

Almond – usually Italian, especially Soave and Valpolicella

Apple – many dry white wines, sweet Loires, and, when particularly aromatic, maybe German Riesling

Apricot – Condrieu, and good sweet Loires eg Coteaux du Layon and Vouvray

Asparagus – Sauvignon Blanc, eg Sancerre, New Zealand Sauvignon, California Fumé Blanc

Banana – young, inexpensive whites and Beaujolais

Biscuit – champagne

Blackcurrant – Cabernet Sauvignon, including claret, and less pronounced in Merlot and Cabernet Franc

Bread (fresh baked, yeasty) – champagne

Brioche – champagne

Bubblegum – Beaujolais Nouveau

Butter – Chardonnay, including white burgundy

Cabbage – mature burgundy, both red and white

Cat's pee – Sauvignon Blanc from France and Müller-Thurgau

Cedar or cigar box – claret, above all, but also other Cabernet Sauvignons

Cherry – burgundy, Beaujolais and a lot of Italian reds

Chocolate – many medium- and full-bodied reds (New World and Old), claret and burgundy

Clove – young Cabernet Sauvignon

Coffee (fresh ground) – various reds, usually top quality, fairly young

Currant leaf – Sauvignon Blanc

Eucalyptus – New World Cabernet, some claret, some Shiraz

Flint and wet stones – Pouilly-Fumé, Chablis

Floral – German Riesling

Game – northern Rhône (Hermitage), Shiraz, mature red burgundy

Gooseberry – Sauvignon Blanc, especially Loire and New Zealand

Grape – Muscat

Grapefruit – Scheurebe grape (English and German wines)

Grass – Sauvignon Blanc

Green pepper – Cabernet Sauvignon and Cabernet Franc, eg Chinon and Bourgueil

Honey – lots of sweet wines, especially botrytis affected ones; also mature dry whites including burgundy

Lanolin – Sauternes

Leather – Syrah/Shiraz

Lemon – many young whites

Lime – Australian Riesling

Liquorice – many reds, especially young, tannic, full-bodied ones

Lychee – Gewürztraminer

Marzipan – sweet white Loires, eg Coteaux du Layon, Quarts de Chaume, Bonnezeaux

Melon – New World Chardonnay

Mint – Cabernet Sauvignon, especially New World, and Coonawarra Shiraz

Nivea or Pond's Cold Cream – Gewürztraminer

Nut (hazelnut or walnut) – white burgundy, champagne and other Chardonnays

Oak – any wine, red or white, that has been fermented and/or aged in oak (or has been aged with oak chips)

Olive – Cabernet Sauvignon and Cabernet Franc

Orange – many sweet whites, including fortified

Peach – many whites, including New World Chardonnay and sweet whites

Pear/pear-drop – many young whites, especially inexpensive ones for drinking young, also Beaujolais Nouveau

Pepper (fresh ground) – red southern Rhônes, eg Châteauneuf-du-Pape and Côtes du Rhône, and also Austrian Grüner Veltliner

Petrol or kerosene – a good sign in mature Riesling, especially German and some Australian

Plum – a less pronounced fruit smell in many red wines

Potato peelings – Cabernet Franc in Chinon, Bourgueil and Saumur-Champigny

Raisins – sweet fortified wines

Raspberry – red Rhônes, red burgundy and New World Pinot Noir, Beaujolais, and red Loires in good vintages

Rose – dry Alsace Muscat, Gewürztraminer; some red burgundy

Salt – *manzanilla* sherry

Smoke – full-bodied reds, especially Syrah; Pouilly-Fumé and Alsace Tokay-Pinot Gris

Spice – many reds, especially Rhônes; Alsace whites and any wine that has been oak-aged, especially in American oak

Strawberry – Beaujolais, red burgundy and Rioja

Tar – Barolo especially, but also northern Rhônes

Toast – any wine that has been in new oak barrels, but especially Chardonnay; also mature, unoaked champagne (especially *blanc de blancs*) and Australian Semillon

Tobacco – many reds, but especially claret

Vanilla – wine that's been in new French or American oak, eg Rioja

Wool (wet) – white burgundy

A perspective
on serving

So much dauntingly dogmatic and pompous stuff has been written and preached about the correct way of serving wine, it's a wonder that people don't give up and turn to beer, or at least give up trying to get it right and stock up on tumblers or Paris goblets.

The point is to get things in perspective. Some aspects of serving wine are more important than others. I put temperature at the top of my list. That doesn't mean I carry a wine thermometer or have worked out supposedly ideal and immutable serving temperatures for different wines, but I hope it means that I never serve a red wine lukewarm. Attending to other details, such as glasses, can undoubtedly enhance your enjoyment of wine by bringing out the best in it, but doing the the right thing for the wine should not end up being a stultifying exercise in making everyone else's life a misery, or making everyone else feel inadequate because they don't know the rules. The rules are there to be adapted and broken, as the situation and enjoyment of the wine demand.

The best corkscrews
are those which ease the
cork out vertically – not
at a potentially cork-
breaking angle – and have a
rounded, rather than a
chisel-edged, 'worm' or
screw. The green foil-cutter
(towards the bottom right
and looked at from under-
neath) is a useful, if not
absolutely essential, item.
The brush (on the cork-
screw above) is for dusting
down the capsule of an old,
cellar-encrusted bottle. The
champagne pliers (bottom
right) are for easing out
champagne corks.

(*Above*) **The enormous size and out-turned lip of this glass are designed to show top red burgundy at its best.**

Glass

Like many wine producers, I am a fan of a range of glasses, each one designed for specific grape varieties, types or ages of wine (although I only have a few of the 20 or so different shapes and sizes). I am also very attached to a pair of portable plastic champagne *flûtes* that come in two parts – the stem screwing into the *flûte* – which are perfect for a bumpy ride in a cramped picnic basket or holdall.

You see the point I am making. Fine glasses, expertly designed, do enhance fine wine, but glasses, like wines, may have to be adapted to the occasion. Anything is better than nothing – and, since much of the pleasure of wine is related to the occasion, I have found champagne none the worse for an occasional plastic *flûte* and other wine none the worse for an imperfectly shaped and proportioned glass.

But at home you can afford to be more of a perfectionist, choosing glasses which will show off the wine's colour, smell and flavours. For still wines you should aim to have fine, plain, colourless glass – not chunky, cut, or coloured, which won't allow you to see the wine properly. Wine glasses should also be generously sized to give plenty of room for aeration (I have a pair of glasses for red burgundy that hold a bottle and a half each – as seen to the left – but you will be pleased to hear that these are not necessary unless you are a regular consumer of very elevated Grand Cru burgundy, which sadly I am not). Very roughly, a sixth to a quarter of a bottle should fill a third to half the glass, with slightly smaller glasses traditionally being used for white wine. As for shape, the bowl should be round, and slightly elongated and tapering towards the top, so that when the wine is swirled to release the volatile aromas they are caught in the top of the glass, rather than wafting into the distance. The International Standards Organisation (ISO) glass is an effective and attractive tasting glass, but I find it a little small for drinking wine – although it is certainly good for port.

For champagne, the traditional *flûtes* or slender tulip shapes are ideal: they preserve the bubbles and the delicate, subtle bouquet. The sprawling champagne saucer, or *coupe*, is hopeless as both bubbles and bouquet are lost almost immediately. Sherry's best interests are served by a traditional *copita*, which can also double up as a slightly small port glass (or a malt whisky glass).

(*Below*) **The shape and size of glass can dramatically affect your perceptions of a wine and so it is worth taking time and trouble when choosing. Most of us**

can't run to a different glass for every wine, but it is worth looking at the sizes of these hand-blown glasses by the Austrian firm of **Riedel.** *From left to right:* **for red burgundy (Pinot Noir); young Bordeaux (Cabernet Sauvignon); vintage champagne; white burgundy (Chardonnay); Riesling; vintage port.**

Breathing and decanting (air or hot air?)

A great deal of energy and hot air – complete with variedly inclusive and contradictory results from assorted experiments – has been expended on the subject of whether wine benefits from being allowed to 'breathe' before it is served; and, if so, whether it should be decanted for the purpose or simply left in the bottle with the cork removed. Advocates of breathing (which simply means allowing the wine to come into contact with air) maintain that it helps develop the bouquet and softens the taste – a logical enough mini-maturation process. Those against say that aromas, and consequently bouquet and flavour, are lost, and that all desirable development can take place in the period when the wine is in the glass and the drinker can enjoy every stage of it. There are others who think breathing is wildly overrated as a subject of debate, because it doesn't make much difference to the wine.

Certainly, merely removing the cork from the bottle commits you to drinking it, but promotes very little air contact, so it is hard to see how it can have much effect. That said, with a very old and potentially fragile wine, I draw the cork no more than half an hour or so before serving – time enough to dispel any 'bottle stink' (*see page 16*), but not long enough for bouquet and flavour to fade and die. Equally, if, as is often the case with old wine, I am going to decant it because of the sediment, I do not do so until the last half hour before serving.

With young, vigorous medium- to full-bodied reds, I often pull the cork two or three hours before pouring, simply because that is convenient, but it could be less, it could be more. I usually decant fine reds of medium maturity, 1982 classed growth clarets for example, an hour or 90 minutes before serving. And occasionally, if, after leaving open a bottle of good young red for an hour, I taste it and find it rather tannic – claret, northern Rhône, Barolo, Chianti or California Cabernet, as it might be – I decant the wine to see if aeration will soften the tannins. I can't say that it is invariably effective, but then the mystery and unpredictability of wine is all part of its fascination.

Sediment

Aeration is really only a by-product of decanting. The real purpose of decanting is to remove the sediment (deposited colouring matter and tannin) from the wine so that it doesn't end up in anyone's

(*Above*) **Elegant contemporary decanters based on traditional designs. My favourite is the 'classic' (bottom).**

Wines and grapes mentioned in this chapter are described in more detail in the final part of the book (pages 94–157) and in 'The importance of Grapes' (pages 50–59).

glass. Any good quality red wine of several years' age and even some quite young full-bodied reds that haven't been filtered need to be checked for sediment. But mass market wine is unlikely to produce any. That is about as hard and fast as the rules come nowadays.

Some grape varieties typically throw a heavy deposit (Cabernet Sauvignon and Syrah) and some throw little (Pinot Noir), but the way the wine has been made can have a considerable impact. A wine that has not been filtered, or only lightly so, will produce a sediment. On the whole this means high quality, relatively small-scale, hand-crafted wines, especially in the Old World (top quality Bordeaux is usually lightly filtered, while equivalent burgundies and Rhônes may be entirely unfiltered and the latter, being from the Syrah grape, will start to drop sediment quite young). In California, too, there is a move among some top-notch producers to dispense with the filter to maximise flavour — even on so large a scale as the Robert Mondavi winery (Napa Valley).

How to decant

Helpfully some producers (Chapoutier in the Rhône and Penfolds' in Australia, for example) now point out the likelihood of sediment on back labels. It is, after all, something to be proud rather than ashamed of: it means that none of the wine's precious flavour has been inadvertently filtered out. But, whether or not you know there is sediment, you still need to look carefully to see where it is, because ensuring that all the sediment is gathered in one place is one of the essentials of successful decanting. For this, all you need is a bright light (a spot light, bare bulb, powerful torch,

cycle lamp or even a candle) along with a steady hand for the decanting itself.

Whether you use a decanting basket (one of those baskets with handles that holds a bottle at an angle of about 20 degrees and which pretentious but ignorant restaurants use for serving the wine), or do without, the sediment-manoeuvring stage should start at least 24 hours, and preferably 72, before the wine is to be served. Either put the bottle in a decanting basket or stand it upright. Then, when you are ready to decant, either draw the cork and pour the wine slowly into the decanter without taking the bottle from the basket, or, if the bottle has been standing, tilt it gently and try to pour all in one go.

(Right) **The keys to decanting are getting the sediment in one place in the bottle in advance – and a good light source.**

The advantage of a basket is that the sediment is even less likely to be dislodged when the wine is poured, but the disadvantage is that you cannot see the wine nearly as well as you can if you are holding the bottle directly in front of a light. Whatever you do, watch carefully as you approach the end of the bottle. You may well have to sacrifice an inch, perhaps more, but it is far better to be over cautious than spoil a good bottle with sludge.

Temperatures

Everybody knows that warm white wine is an abomination – but so is warm red and it seems to be far more common nowadays than tepid white. The problem is central heating. 'Room temperature', the traditional axiom for red wine, simply doesn't mean today's centrally-heated room temperatures of about 21°C (70°F). It means 18°C (64°F) at most – and that for full-bodied and tannic red wines, particularly from the New World. Most clarets are best served a degree cooler, Pinot Noirs (including burgundies) a little cooler again, and an increasing number of modern reds, made in a relatively tannin-free, soft, fruity, light style for drinking young – like Beaujolais – are delicious

served at anything from a fairly cool 12°C (54°F) to a moderate 16°C (61°F).

Having said all that, I don't go around dunking a wine thermometer into every glass of wine that comes my way and I seldom even use one at home. The average body, or hand clasping a bottle, seems to me a sufficiently good judge of temperature – perhaps a better one in that it takes into account both atmospheric temperature and ambience. While 17°C (63°F) might be theoretically ideal for claret, the wine is unlikely to be spoiled at 16°C (61°F) or even at 18°C (64°F) – and certainly a wine that is slightly too cool can quickly be warmed by cupping your hands around the glass. If, however, you are lucky enough to be bringing a red wine from a proper cellar temperature of, say, 11–12°C (52–54°F) to 18°C (64°F), you will need to leave it at room temperature for about two and a half hours, or put it in a bucket of 18–20°C (64–68°F) water for about quarter of an hour. If you only have 25 seconds to spare, use a microwave. I don't, but plenty of restaurants do.

If you need to cool a red wine, you can simply put the bottle in the fridge – probably

(*Below*) **Sparkling wines and sweet wines, light-bodied and cheap white wines are best served a little cooler than full-bodied, not very acid whites.**

(*Below*) **Wine warms up quickly at room temperature, so err slightly on the cool side, but don't chill a fine wine such as white burgundy to death.**

(*Right*) **The quickest way to cool wine is to plunge it into a container of iced water. (Similarly, a bucket of tepid water will quickly warm a cellar-temperature red).**

for 20–30 minutes, but this depends, on the temperature of the wine when it goes in, the temperature you want to serve it at, and the temperature of the fridge. You can also make use of more rapid methods – a bucket of ice and water, the deep-freeze, or the back garden in winter, but be wary of bringing these to bear on an old and fragile wine.

White wines should be served between about 6°C (43°F) and 11°C (52°F), but, as with red, err on the low side (chilled wines warm up quickly in the glass). As a guide, but not a gospel, full-bodied, not notably acid whites – especially New World Chardonnays and good burgundy – are the ones to serve at the higher end of the spectrum, along with many rosés. Dry Sémillon, white Bordeaux and Rhine Riesling can be a little cooler, and Sauvignon wines cooler again (7°C/45°F). Champagne and

sweet wines should be served at the lower end (5–8°C/41–46°F), along with light-bodied whites (Muscadet, Vinho Verde and many German and Italian whites), pale rosés and most cheap wines, (the cheapest, including fizz, may be even cooler.)

The quickest way of chilling white wine is to plunge it into a bucket of ice and water. In under 20 minutes, a bottle at 21°C (70°F) will be down to about 10°C (50°F). A freezer will take about 45 minutes to do the same job and you should allow up to two hours in an ordinary fridge.

(*Left*) **A wine thermometer will allow you to be precise about temperature, but remember that there is no single 'correct' temperature for a wine. It may depend on the weather.**

(*Below*) **Pour the wine gently and with the bottle close to the glass – the idea is to disturb the wine as little as possible, especially if it is old.**

(*Above*) **Stoppers for helping preserve part-finished bottles for a few days. Put the bottles in the fridge or somewhere cool.**

Serving order

Naturally, you need to take into account the food being served when deciding which wines you will be serving when, and I go into the intriguing and mouth-watering business of food and wine matching in the next chapter (pages 30–39), but these are the basic guidelines: dry white before red, light before heavy, young before old, dry before sweet. That doesn't mean that you shouldn't drink sherry with soup, simply because it is more alcoholic than the wine that follows, or that you have to continue drinking sweet wines if you have started with foie gras and Sauternes, or that a red wine must always be older than a white that preceded it. They are simply pointers – flexible ones – rather than rules.

Preservation

Once a bottle is opened, the air immediately begins to work on it. At first the effects are likely to be beneficial (*qv* breathing), but exposure to air is, ultimately, the road to vinegar. Devising ways to preserve unfinished bottles of wine was one of the growth industries of the late eighties. Before that, wine drinkers who wanted to save the remains of an unfinished bottle simply had to jam the cork back in, put the wine in the fridge or cellar and just hope for the best.

Unsophisticated as it is, this is still a useful way of doing the job in the short term. You can't expect old wines to survive, but most young whites, rosés and light reds will last a couple of days if the bottle is at least half-full, if it was not relentlessly tipped up and down to be poured and if it was only open for two or three hours. With the same provisos, fuller reds in their prime will often last three or four days. The wines will almost certainly lose a little freshness and taste a little flatter – so it would be a pity to treat a grand or treasured bottle in this way – but they will seldom become unpleasantly oxidised. With red wine you will, of course, have to remember to take the bottle out of the fridge well before you want to drink it (probably a couple of hours, depending on room and fridge temperature). You can put it in a bucket of nearly tepid water, but bear in mind that you have already put the wine through one endurance test and changing the temperature too rapidly could be the straw that breaks the camel's back.

If you know that only half a bottle is going to be consumed, as soon as you open it, decant half the wine into a half-bottle, then recork it and put it in the fridge or cellar. I have had wines keep for weeks like this, but it's not a fail-safe method and it is far better to plan to drink the other half the following day.

Wine conserving gadgets work on two basic principles: removing the air in the bottle to leave a vacuum; and putting an inert gas (usually nitrogen with a little carbon dioxide) that is heavier than air on to the surface of the wine. You don't need to refrigerate wines thus protected (although it makes sense to keep them cool) and the manufacturers would like us to think that they will keep fresh for a week, if not a fortnight. In practice, results seem to me to be erratic.

I don't find the vacuum method sufficiently effective, although the Vacuvin – an inexpensive vacuum pump with reusable stoppers – is in fact the most common preserver and many people swear by it. I sometimes use a Wine Saver (an inexpensive canister of gas that you simply squirt into the neck of the bottle), although some wines stored this way seem quickly to acquire a slightly stale, sweaty smell without actually becoming oxidised. And while experience has shown me that the Vintage Keeper (a far more sophisticated and expensive inert gas device) is clearly the most effective, especially with old wines, I don't use one, largely on the grounds of expense, but also on aesthetic grounds: the large cylinder of gas is attached by tube and valve to the bottle and is a permanent fixture while you are preserving the wine. Imagine it sitting on your dining table.

So what is the solution? It's really very simple: drink, or rather share, any grand bottles in one sitting. And, for fun, try blending the remains of some less grand bottles together – Cabernet with your Chianti perhaps.

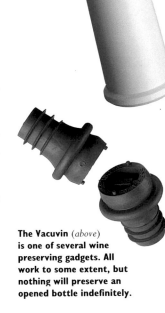

The Vacuvin (*above*) **is one of several wine preserving gadgets. All work to some extent, but nothing will preserve an opened bottle indefinitely.**

(*Left*) **A teaspoon in the neck of a bottle of champagne is said to preserve its fizz in the fridge. If you want to be sure, there are purpose-made, inexpensive stoppers.**

Matching
food and wine

Whenever you find yourself agonising over the matching of wine and food, be reassured that, though there are some foods that need rigorous attention, there are few truly unpalatable combinations.

Chocolate and bone dry Chablis, rare steak and Muscat de Beaumes-de-Venise, mackerel and tannic Barolo all sound horrendous to me (no, not even in the interests of this book could I bring myself to test them), but even so, if anyone has tried them and found them pleasing, that person can't be 'wrong'.

A problem obviously arises if a devotee of, say, the steak and sticky combination decides to serve it to other people. It would be better if he or she had a few self-doubts and played safe, or certainly infinitely safer, with the traditional colour formula — red wine with red meat, dry white wine with fish and white meat, sweet white with puddings. These and other more specific classic marriages have stood the test of time (and sometimes more recently the test of scientific enquiry). So, too, have most of the traditional regional combinations. Drinking the local wine with the food of Bologna, Tuscany, Piedmont, Provence, Burgundy or Alsace is almost always satisfying – although, personally, I draw the line, which many Champenois apparently do not, at drinking dry champagne with puddings.

The difficulty with the natural regional pairings is that gastronomy has become much more complicated in the last couple of decades. Although there has been a welcome recent revival of traditional local dishes – British as well as French, Italian and others – there has also been a great deal of cross-

dressing in cosmopolitan cities around the globe. How do you decide what to drink with Hawaiian Mahi-Mahi garnished with New Zealand Greenlip mussels and kiwi fruit in a blood-orange *beurre blanc*? (I am happy to say that I have not encountered this on a menu, but Tim Hanni, one of the few gurus of food and wine matching, has). The smart answers, I suppose, are don't order that dish, or drink water, but it makes the point, somewhat extremely, that nowadays you need more than the basic age-old maxims – unless you are permanently ensconced in a small, off-the-beaten-track, European wine village, or, equally, in one of London's smart gentlemen's clubs where plain (aka nursery) food is the order of every day and wine lists still seldom stray far from the perceived security of the European classics.

The other point you should reassure yourself on is that while there are some food and wine marriages apparently made in heaven (such as Sauternes with Roquefort) and some foods that are peculiarly treacherous, these are more the exception than the rule. This means, in effect, that most foods can be accompanied happily by several different wine types.

You should be aiming, then, for food and wine that complement each other — in part, simply by

Wines and grapes mentioned in this chapter are described in more detail in the final part of the book (pages 94–157) and in 'The importance of Grapes' (pages 50–59).

their mutual presence – rather than for some magical mutual enhancement. The rather eighties fashion for panels of tasters setting to and palate-testing myriad wines with specific foods and dishes to divine some definitive perfect partnership may produce interesting and sometimes quirky results, but it seldom sets many useful new guidelines, not only because the results from one panel to another are often endearingly contradictory, but because they are usually too specific. They relate to one recipe, one set of ingredients, one chef and one set of tasters or feeders in one set of surroundings. So it's no wonder conclusions vary from one occasion to another.

They are also apt to come up with supposedly definitive pairings that have limitations in practice. I don't deny that dry sherry is surprisingly versatile with food, but most people don't want to go on drinking it beyond the first course – if indeed that far. The 'discovery' that Muscadet's very neutrality makes it a largely non-combative partner doesn't actually mean it makes any thrilling combinations (other than with seafood perhaps). Similarly, goat's cheese and Sancerre or Pouilly-Fumé make a delicious combination when the cheese, with salad, is a starter, but, if it is the cheese after the main course, are you going to want to go back to Sancerre or Pouilly-Fumé, after California Cabernet, Chianti Classico, Barossa Chardonnay, or, if you are eating pudding before cheese, after Sauternes? And drinking Sancerre or Fumé all the way through to the cheese doesn't strike me as much fun either.

Weight for weight

So where do you start? Whether or not you have already decided what colour of wine you want to be drinking, matching the weight, or body, of the wine to the food is usually the key. It should certainly be allowed to take precedence over the colour formula. A delicately poached chicken breast can be rendered almost as lifeless by a heavy, high-alcohol, extravagantly fruity, buttery, oaky Chardonnay as it can by a powerful red Hermitage. Equally, a richly flavoured Coq au Vin would knock a light or dry white for six – a Mosel *Kabinett*, a Vin de Pays des Côtes de Gascogne or a Chablis, for example. In fact a logical answer when cooking something in a significant quantity of wine, whether Coq au Vin or risotto, is to drink the same, or a similar type of wine, but even here you need to be wary of the power of heavily reduced stocks, fumets and sauces – that is intensity of flavour – particularly if using a wine of light to medium body.

Flavour intensity

Intensity of flavour – which may be allied to weight, but not invariably so – can be decisive in either food or wine. Fine German Rieslings can be intensely flavoured but are traditionally light-bodied and low in alcohol; Sauvignon Blanc is another variety with a powerful flavour which, although it is not as light as German Riesling, is seldom really full-bodied. Wines such as these can sometimes be used as a contrast, to cut through food with some richness, or they may complement intensity of flavour – a ripe New Zealand Sauvignon Blanc with the vivid flavour of red peppers in Peperonata, for example.

Acid, salt and sugar

When it comes to the food, take account of its acidity, its saltiness and its sweetness (not least in savoury dishes). A dish with a definite element of acid – a citrus sauce, or a squeeze of lemon – will usually need a wine with acidity to match, otherwise the wine will taste flat. Salty dishes may need a touch of apparent sweetness in the wine: in a red wine this tends to mean obviously ripe fruit, rather than Médoc-like dry austerity, in a white wine it may mean actual sweetness, (Sauternes with Roquefort and port with Stilton are obvious examples). Salty foods,

(Below) **To show off top claret it pays to keep food reasonably simple: this crown roast with a delicate stuffing would be perfect with a Pauillac.**

(Below) **Red meat – in this case venison – in a red wine sauce needs red wine to partner it, but the apricots are a potential pitfall: choose a red with plenty of ripe fruit and body – a California Zinfandel, perhaps.**

especially lightweight ones, may also cry out for acidity: with a white wine this is easy to find; with reds the solution is often to go for the sort of fresh, crisp, low-tannin style that takes well to a light chill (red Loires or Beaujolais, for example).

It is harder to generalise about savoury dishes with some sweetness, simply because the degree of sweetness can vary so much. It may be an integral part of the dish – as in rabbit or pork with prunes – or it may only be an entirely dispensable garnish. I would put redcurrant jelly and mint sauce in the latter category (although I know that their fans would not agree). But with an integral fruit sauce I might veer towards wine with a slight sweetness, such as a Pfalz *Spätlese Halbtrocken*.

Texture

After weight, intensity and specific flavours, there is the texture of some foods to consider. When this is linked to weight, it is straightforward enough – you are unlikely to choose a delicate white wine to sip between chewing hunks of steak – but there are some foods that have a mouth-coating effect that naturally affects your perception of any wine. Certain cheeses are undoubted offenders (*see* Cheese, page 38), but egg and chocolate are potentially worse and are often dismissed outright as inimical to wine. I put them instead into a category of 'would-be food outcasts' – those that need special care – and it is an area that vegetarians should look at and I hope take comfort from, because several of their staples – eggs, vegetables, salad dressings – are often dismissed too readily as unkind to wine.

Would-be outcasts

Soft-yoked egg undoubtedly coats the mouth, effectively blocking the tastebuds and therefore the wine, so I wouldn't waste a great cellar treasure on, for example, baked eggs. That said, eggs' coating quality has not stood in the way of Oeufs en Meurette, the classic starter of poached eggs in a rich red burgundy sauce, which is drunk with red burgundy (I would choose a lesser village wine or a Passe-Touts-Grains, rather than something grand). Eggs in sauces and soufflés seem to me to be without hazards: with mayonnaise and hollandaise, Sauvignon Blanc and young Chardonnay are good; while cheese soufflés, in particular, show off all

sorts of wines rather well. Quail's eggs, with their finer texture, are a treat with champagne or crisp, dry, elegant and not too assertive still whites.

Vinegar doesn't go with wine, but salads with vinaigrette need not be a problem – provided decent vinegar is used (not the fish and chip sort) and used with a good proportion of oil (the quantity depends on the individual oil and vinegar, as well as taste, but start perhaps with five parts oil to one of vinegar). An alternative, a trick favoured in the salad bowls of some top wine producers, is to use vinegar's precursor – wine itself – with less oil (again, proportions depend on oil, wine and personal preference, but three to one would be a start). Another tip is to use walnut or hazelnut oil and serve a Chardonnay, because Chardonnay's nutty character has an affinity with nut oils.

I find mint sauce much more vicious than most vinaigrettes, and I skip it rather than try to accommodate it, but its fans say that it blends seamlessly with a mouthful of lamb and therefore does no damage to wine. If you do find yourself with the lingering flavours of an aggressive mint sauce or vinaigrette – or indeed any other clashing food – a painless sip of water or a chunk of bread will usually dampen them down.

Globe artichokes, spinach, asparagus and even **fennel** have all come in for the wine connoisseur's axe, but only artichokes really deserve it and even they can be knocked into shape. The culprit in artichokes is a substance called cynarin which makes wine taste either sweet or bitter/metallic (depending more on the drinker than the wine), but squeezing lemon quite generously over the artichoke seems to block cynarin and give a chance to young, full Chardonnays, crisp Sauvignons, and fairly basic, peppery, southern French reds (eg Côtes du Rhônes and *vins de pays*).

As spinach tends to be a side dish or an ingredient, rather than a centrepiece (even in vegetarian dishes), it seldom determines the choice of wine, but if you do find that it makes wine taste unpleasantly bitter/metallic it is

(Above left) **Artichokes and wine are natural enemies, but squeezing lemon juice on the artichoke can solve the problem.**

worth trying the lemon juice trick. Alternatively, enrichening spinach with butter, cream or Parmesan and nutmeg usually prevents clashes – so vegetarian dishes based on spinach seldom cause problems.

The distinctive flavour of asparagus is hard on most wines, but a well-concentrated, fruity New Zealand Sauvignon Blanc or a rounded but young and fresh Chardonnay (even burgundy) is usually successful. Lighter whites, which are sometimes recommended, seem to me to get lost, but red Loire wines (Chinon, Bourgueil, Saumur-Champigny) made from Cabernet Franc grapes (which shares a green currant-leaf flavour with Sauvignon) can be a surprising hit. Similar recommendations apply to fennel, which doesn't actually clash with most wines, but can sometimes have a rather bullying presence on the palate.

Oily fish, above all mackerel, both smoked and unsmoked, can do terrible things to wine, so it is probably best to aim for cheap, fairly neutral, bone dry whites like Muscadet, Gros Plant, Touraine Sauvignon, Aligoté (admittedly only cheap by Burgundian standards) or perhaps something slightly softer like a Soave or Beaujolais Blanc. *Fino* sherry is a possibility too.

Hot spicy food, unsurprisingly, kills wine, but a great many Indian and Asian dishes are spicy but not searingly hot – mainly because the main heat culprit, chilli, doesn't feature in them. Spices such as coriander, turmeric, cumin, mustard seed, even ginger, are gentler than chilli, and spicy or notably fruity wines can complement them well. The aromatic spicy wines of Alsace – Gewurztraminer above all, but also Tokay-Pinot Gris and Pinot Blanc – are the obvious choice, and Gewurztraminer can be particularly useful as a match for the rather sweet taste of much Chinese restaurant fare. The concentrated lime flavour of Australian Rieslings and the vibrant gooseberry tones of New Zealand Sauvignons often make a successfully refreshing contrast to spicy and slightly sweet food, and simple, boisterously fruity Australian whites (Chardonnay, Semillon, Chenin Blanc and Colombard) also usually work well, if not subtly. Good dry, but definitely fruity rosés are worth looking out for and, if you want a red wine, try a full, fruity, young Australian Shiraz or Shiraz-Cabernet Sauvignon blend, a good Côtes du Rhône,

a California Zinfandel or a lightly chilled Beaujolais. If you are eating a Szechuan dish or a Vindaloo, stick to beer, water or salt lassi.

Chocolate smothers the tastebuds even more effectively than eggs, but, as with most wine killers, remedial treatment can work. Unrehabilitated neat chocolate and the densest of dark rum truffles are probably best left for coffee, liqueurs or water, but mousses, marquises, puddings and gateaux can be tackled with powerful sweet wines. The richest and darkest may need the strength of flavour and alcohol of old, raisiny fortified wines – Málaga and Australian Liqueur Muscats – but marginally lighter chocolate mousses and puddings often take to Muscat de Beaumes-de-Venise, California and Australian Orange Muscats, Sauternes and old (ie, 20-year-old) tawny port. With positively light frothy mousses, try Sauternes, or Asti or Moscato d'Asti. And if you are still drinking your red wine when it comes to the (chocolate) pudding, make sure it is a lush, ripe, not too tannic California Cabernet or Merlot – sometimes, inexplicably, the combination works.

(*Above*) **Contrasting textures, as well as sweet, spicy and sharp flavours, need to be taken into account with this stir fry. A vividly fruity, crisp Sauvignon or Chardonnay from New Zealand or a fruity dry rosé would make a change from the more obvious choice of spicy Alsace.**

33

Starters

Lumping all the world's starters together may seem cavalier, but they are linked by the fact that at this stage in the meal you are usually aiming at a relatively light and/or a white wine to precede fuller-bodied wines.

With soup you will find that most people don't drink much, but, if you don't want to do without, try sherry (*fino*, *manzanilla* or dry *amontillado* according to the weight of the soup), try matching the principal ingredient (dry rosés can be very good with fish soup), or simply pour a little of the next course's wine.

Pale dry sherries also score well with olives and anchovies and where there are several contrasting elements to deal with – mixed hors d'oeuvres or antipasti, *crudités* with dips, or *salades composées*. With the latter three you could also consider medium weight, moderately fruity or aromatic whites and rosés (eg Austrian whites, Verdicchio, good Pinot Grigio, Hungarian Sauvignon or Chardonnay, Alsace Sylvaner or Pinot Blanc, properly dry Vinho Verde, unoaked white Rioja, Navarra or Provence rosés, *Halbtrocken* German Rieslings). Light- to medium-bodied fruity reds – Beaujolais and other Gamays, young Merlot,

Dolcetto, Montepulciano d'Abruzzo, simple southern French reds – come into their own if meat is involved (eg salami, bacon, chicken livers or duck in antipasti and salads).

Pâtés vary enormously. The most unctuous liver pâtés (above all, that of foie gras) can take unctuous sweet wine – Sauternes – but it makes a heavy start to a meal. I find an aromatic late-harvest Alsace, with its greater zest, a better introduction. Meaty, but less rich pâtés go well with assertive but dry Alsace whites and fruity reds from all over.

Shellfish go with all sorts of dry whites, so choice probably depends a lot on your pocket. If you've splashed out on oysters, you will presumably be in the mood for champagne or top Chablis, but a respectable Muscadet or Sancerre would be fine. It doesn't have to be French of course, but beware anything too assertively fruity or oaky, or short on refreshing acidity. With lobster, too, it is worth going for gold: champagne, great white burgundy or a top Chardonnay from elsewhere, a good white Rhône, dry Bordeaux or Arneis from Piedmont. Prawns can take the same treatment, or more modest wines, and mussels, too, are very accommodating. Crab is trickier, but Chablis is classic and Viognier and German Rieslings with some sweetness (especially *Spätlese*) work well. Scallops also often appreciate a little sweetness – and/or richness. With smoked fish such as salmon and trout,

(*Left*) **Aim to enhance the fresh, crunchy, crystal-clear flavours of the crudités with a wine with similar attributes, such as a tangy fino or manzanilla sherry or a spicy white Alsace.**

champagne, the best dry sparkling wines from elsewhere, aromatic Alsace whites and Riesling *Spätlese* from the Rhine (Mosels tend to be too light) are good.

(*Above*) **Pasta doesn't pose problems, but the sauce may: the acidity of tomato can make wines taste thin – so choose a young, fruity red wine with a bit of bite and body.**

Pasta

Pasta goes with anything – it is the sauce that is of concern. Youngish fruity reds, quite assertive but not necessarily full-bodied, and dry but not astringently so, are the best all-rounders in that they go with meaty and tomato sauces – and tomato, because of its sharpness, can be difficult. The Italians naturally have plenty of answers in Dolcetto, Barbera, real *dry* red Lambrusco, Teroldego Rotaliano, Rosso del Montalcino, young Chianti Classico et al, but most other countries have got something possible – Chilean Merlot, Navarra reds, Côtes du Rhône, *vins de pays*, German Dornfelder, lighter California Zinfandels.

With Carbonara and creamy sauces, go for medium- to full-bodied whites with some flavour – like Arneis or Favorita from Italy, or Chardonnay from anywhere as long as it is not too exuberantly fruity and oaky.

Dry white also goes better than red with Pesto, but it needs to be crisp and firm – an Italian Gavi, a good Pinot Grigio, a Sardinian or Sicilian white, a Rueda from Spain, or, at a pinch, a light Chardonnay or Sauvignon Blanc from Hungary or a Colombard from South Africa.

Risotto is fairly accommodating across the spectrum from off-dry to dry white wines and light reds, but you need to take account of any added ingredients or flavourings and beware of overpowering what should usually be quite a delicate dish.

Fish

Though you certainly shouldn't regard red wines as a problem if you only eat fish, it is worth knowing what is behind the white wine with fish instruction. The main reason is that fish – especially white and shellfish – can make red wines, particularly those with discernible tannin, taste metallic or tinny. The other two reasons are that fish dishes, very broadly, tend to be lighter than meat dishes (and there are more light white wines than light reds), and secondly that fish is often dressed with lemon, an acidity that is easier to match with a white wine. For all these reasons a plainly cooked, fairly delicate white fish (such as sole, plaice, hake or cod), deserves a dry white wine that is not too heavy or too aromatic. That cuts out, for example, Alsace's better wines (but not its simple Pinot Blancs and Sylvaners) and the most

ebulliently fruity New Zealand Sauvignons and Australian Chardonnays, but otherwise leaves a huge choice from Chablis to San Gimignano.

Fish in rich sauces can take richer, fuller wines: white burgundies from the best downwards, other Chardonnays in the Meursault mould (eg California or New Zealand's), Hunter Valley Semillon, Condrieu, Alsace Riesling and Tokay-Pinot Gris, or, if you want to be adventurous, a *demi-sec* Loire wine (Vouvray or Montlouis) from a good vintage.

As far as red wines are concerned, any fish that has been cooked in red wine – as salmon and red mullet often are – calls out to be served with one, but any other fairly full-flavoured or

substantial fish (such as turbot, salmon or tuna) will go with the right kind of red wine or a good dry rosé. Aim for light, low tannin, young reds that you would tend to serve cool: Loire reds (both the Cabernet Franc-based ones such as Chinon and the Pinot Noir-based Sancerre), other young Pinot Noirs, Beaujolais and other Gamays, German Dornfelder, and also simple Italian reds such as Bardolino.

(Left) **Oily fish like mackerel tend to make wine taste thin or metallic. Lemon helps counteract the effect, but, even so, simple wine – sharp, fairly neutral dry white – is best.**

Cahors, Madiran, good Cabernet from anywhere (eg Penedès), and, perhaps surprisingly, the softer, rounder clarets of St-Emilion, Pomerol and Fronsac in preference to top Médocs. Richly-flavoured beef casseroles can take big wines — California Zinfandels and Cabernets, Shiraz, Châteauneuf-du-Pape and northern Rhônes, Brunello, top-notch Tuscan *vini da tavola* and Barolo, Bandol and reds from Provence. Impressive heavyweight wines also suit powerful game such as hare, venison, grouse and casseroled birds, although the depth and complexity of a top Côte de Nuits burgundy can be just as successful, so long as the birds have not been too well hung. Some people swear by the contrasting sweetness of a German *Spätlese* or an Alsace Tokay-Pinot Gris *vendange tardive* with venison, but it is not a combination I am convinced by. Good burgundy is also ideal for young, plainly roasted game birds; so, too, are claret, Rioja and, with pigeon, Bulgarian Cabernet Sauvignon.

Simply roasted lamb or grilled chops are perfect for showing off your best mature clarets from the Médoc and Graves, Gran Reserva Riojas, or Beaujolais Crus. If you are going for a more pungent effect with the lamb, with masses of garlic and rosemary, juniper or even anchovy, choose a younger more vigorous claret or a fruity, fairly full-bodied Cabernet or Merlot from elsewhere (Vin de Pays d'Oc, Buzet, Bergerac, Provence, Penedès, Bulgaria or Chile), a Portuguese red from Bairrada, Dão or

Poultry, meat and game

Clashes of flavour are encouragingly few with meat (although the sweetness of calf's liver and the fatty richness of goose are not without the potential). As far as the red wine with red meat and white wine with white meat rule goes, it only goes so far; it doesn't begin to touch on the weight or intensity of flavour of the sauces, gravies, stuffings and marinades that may dominate or dictate the finished dish.

That said, I don't know of any white wine that goes with beef, whether plainly roasted or grilled, or turned into a rich, pungent stew. And I can't

(Above) **Provided the dressing is not too vinegary, a duck breast salad could be an excuse for quite a fine red – perhaps burgundy – but bear in mind that you shouldn't follow it with a lesser wine.**

recommend a white wine to go with lamb, unless the lamb is leftover cold roast, in which case German Riesling (preferably *Kabinett* or *Spätlese Halbtrocken*) is a surprising success. It somehow cuts through the close-textured density of the cold meat – and works with pork and turkey, too.

Plain roast beef shows off any medium- to full-bodied fine red wine: burgundy, California Pinot Noir, northern Rhône, Chianti Classico Riserva, Barbaresco, Rioja Reserva,

(*Above*) **So long as you don't settle for something too light or too heavy, almost any red wine, from Bulgarian Cabernet Sauvignon to Chilean Merlot, would be a suitable choice with these cutlets.**

the Douro, or a soft, minty Australian Cabernet-Shiraz.

Pork is marvellously easygoing (although apple sauce can be a bit of a killer). Plain roast or chops go with off-dry and dry whites, from neutral to aromatic or spicy, to full-bodied and complex — which means anything from South African Chenin Blanc via Alsace to Premier Cru burgundy. With red wines, all but the heaviest and most drily tannic are possible.

Chicken, turkey, and guinea fowl are the poultry equivalents of pork — extremely adaptable. Roasted plainly they are kind to red, white and rosé, from humble to high quality, but are better with reds if there is powerful, herby, oniony, meaty stuffing to support them. Red wines, such as spicy, peppery southern French reds, are also the obvious answer with red wine based casseroles, while medium- to quite full-bodied whites go with cream sauces.

With duck and goose, you can either go for a white with some sweetness — an

Alsace *vendange tardive*, a German *Spätlese* or a Vouvray *moelleux* — or a classic high quality red from Burgundy or Bordeaux. With Bordeaux, lean towards the softer, riper wines of St-Emilion or Pomerol, or Margaux from the Médoc.

Both liver and kidneys are a good foil for fruity, spicy and quite rustic reds, preferably fairly young — so go for anything from Barbera and Valpolicella to South African Pinotage, Australian Shiraz and Syrah *vins de pays*. The key with pan-fried or grilled calf's liver is to resist the temptation to try to match its sweetness: a supple Pomerol, St-Emilion or

Torgiano is a better option. Sweetbreads need something subtle but mellow — an elegant Volnay or Margaux, or, if in a creamy sauce, a Rhine *Spätlese*.

Sausages vary so much in herb, spice, meat type and fat content that it is difficult to generalise, but full-bodied fruity, spicy reds are usually a strong suit — more or less rustic or grand according to sausage and occasion, so anything from Alentejo to Châteauneuf-du-Pape and beyond.

(*Below*) **Match the richness of the goose and sweetness of the fruits to a late-harvest Alsace, an Austrian or Pfalz Spätlese, or, alternatively, to a great red burgundy, Pomerol or good Australian Shiraz.**

(Left) **White wines – dry and sweet – go better overall with cheeses than do red wines, but that doesn't mean you have to forgo red wine with cheese.**

top Shiraz, Brunello, good Chianti or Barbaresco, tawny or Vintage Character port.

Blue cheeses almost always go better with sweet wines, whether Sauternes, port (Vintage Character and tawny when vintage is out of reach), Recioto della Valpolicella, Bual madeira or even Hungarian Tokay Aszú (four or five *putts* – *see* page 152 for explanation). Goat's cheese really is happier with white wine, whether dry Sauvignon Blanc or something sweet. Brie and Camembert won't do favours for any fine wine, so stick with whatever you are drinking and hope that wine and cheese will at least accommodate, if not complement, each other.

One final point: I have put this section before Puddings, because that is my own preferred order, but if you eat pudding before cheese you will find it easier to continue drinking the sweet pudding wine with the cheese or move on to something sweet and fortified, such as port, as it is hard to go back to dry wines.

Cheese

How we ever came to regard cheese and red wine as natural partners I cannot imagine. Perhaps the success of port and Stilton in this country and Sauternes and Roquefort in France blinded everyone to the fact that cheese and wine, especially dry red wine, often clash – or at least do nothing at all for each other. However much I like red wine and cheese individually and however much I am in the mood for red wine at the cheese course stage, I have to admit that, overall, white wines go better than reds with cheese and that sweet whites have affinities with more cheeses than do dry whites.

All that said, I have not given up dry red wine with cheese and nor need you. You will want to choose both wine and cheese carefully and you may not find yourself serving up many very grand bottles of red wine with cheese, but it can be successful, particularly if it is during a meal that naturally progresses from dry white with the starter to red with both the main course and the cheese to sweet wine with the pudding. (While sweet wine might be better with cheese in theory, where there is pudding as well it can be too much of a good thing.)

On the whole, if you want to serve red wine, you should be looking for fairly mild cheese – which rules out most traditional blue cheeses, mature Cheddars and ripe Camemberts and Bries. You should also aim for fairly hard cheeses, or at least be aware that the mouth-coating texture of soft cheeses, such as Brie and Camembert, is hard work for red wine. The sort of cheeses, then, that do go with red wine – and even quite fine red wine – are mild, young English hard cheeses (young Cheddar, Wensleydale et al) and Cantal, mature Gouda (served regularly with the illustrious clarets in Bordeaux châteaux), Jarlsberg, Gruyère and, providing it is not too strong, Parmesan. With mature Cheddars and other strong hard cheeses (including Parmesan) try strapping red wines such as Hermitage,

Puddings

Apart from the difficulties of chocolate (*qv*), and ice-cream – which really isn't worth trying to match (Asti, Moscato d'Asti or Australian Liqueur Muscat, if you must) – the one 'rule' to observe when matching sweet wines to puddings is to err on the side of sweetness with the wine, otherwise the wine will taste thin and tart. It is easy to be caught out in this way by German *Auslesen* which simply don't have the opulence to stand up to most puddings; *Beerenauslesen* and *Trockenbeerenauslesen* are better, but heavier wines are often easier to match.

Sauternes and its cousins (Monbazillac, Loupiac, Ste-Croix-du-Mont) and botrytised wines from Australia and New Zealand, Muscat de Beaumes-de-Venise and Austrian *Beerenauslese* and *Trockenbeerenauslese* are very obliging with everything from fruit salads, pies and tarts to rich, creamy puddings such as *crème brûlée*, fools, mousses and custards, to more solid ones such as bread-and-butter pudding, cheesecake and other cakes.

The best of the sweet Chenin-based Loires (Coteaux du Layon, Bonnezeaux, Vouvray et al) are also fairly adaptable, although they don't have the easygoing, luscious opulence of Sauternes-type wines and their more prominent acidity needs to be accommodated. They are particularly good at cutting through the richness of cheesecake and also go well with fruits such as strawberries, raspberries, apples, peaches and apricots (and puddings based on them). German *Auslesen* will also go with these fruits if they are not too heavily doused in sugar and cream.

It is also worth bearing in mind Malmsey and Bual madeira, Vin Santo, Moscato di Pantelleria, Spanish Moscatels and Tokay Aszú (five *putts* or Eszencia) for cakes and almond biscuits; and, at the other extreme, fresh, bubbly Asti to complement light, frothy

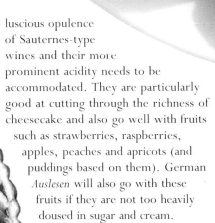

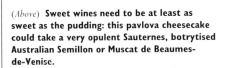

mousses or to contrast completely with the richness of Christmas pudding. Australian Liqueur Muscat is another plum pudding possibility, while all sorts of traditional fortified wines, together with local specialities like Vin Santo, Recioto della Valpolicella and Hungarian Tokay are perfect companions for nuts.

If you really don't like sweet wines and puddings, you could be kind to summer guests by giving them strawberries over which to pour their red wine (straight from glass or bottle). It's done with the best clarets in Bordeaux.

Ways to
store your wine

If it's any consolation, few people have purpose-built, cavernous, subterranean cellars and most wine drinkers have imperfect storage arrangements, but that's not to underestimate the importance of protecting wine from damaging conditions. There is no getting round the fact that good conditions — and by that I don't necessarily mean absolutely perfect ones — are essential if you are keeping wine for any length of time, and the more so the finer the wine and the longer you hope to store it.

Like humans, some wines turn out to be remarkably robust and capable of surviving intact a surprising amount of apparent ill-treatment, but others really are fragile. On the whole, white wines — sweet wines and champagne above all — are more frail than reds, but some reds which have been given the minimum of stabilisation treatment (for example, red burgundies which have not been filtered, in an effort to preserve every scrap of their flavour) are more likely, more quickly, to suffer from adverse conditions. Grape variety also makes a difference — Cabernet Sauvignon and Syrah wines are generally more resilient than Pinot Noirs — but it is far more sensible to try to minimise the risks than cross your fingers and hope that your wines are some of the more long-suffering ones.

Ideal conditions

Temperature

The public enemies of wine are heat, light, lack of humidity and constant movement — but the first two are the ones that cause the most problems. An ideal cellar temperature is 7–13°C (45–55°F), but you can safely store wine within a degree or two of freezing (although obviously it will expand and pop its cork if it actually freezes) or up to 20°C (68°F) — providing you take account of the fact that wine matures much more rapidly at the higher temperatures (and more slowly at lower temperatures) and providing also that you don't allow the temperature to swing from one extreme to another. Constant temperature, or as near to it as possible, is the key; chronic fluctuations are undoubtedly bad for wine.

If a steady temperature coincides with otherwise good conditions, you will probably get away with storage at the average household temperature of 21°C (70°F), albeit with faster-maturing wines as a result, but I certainly wouldn't recommend it, and it is worth bearing in mind that a few hot summer days will catapault many rooms well into the thirties (80°F plus). In the long hot summer of 1990, my kitchen and I sweltered at 32°C (90°F) for days on end and the cupboard-under-the-stairs, once refuge to several wine racks, wasn't much better at 28°C (82°F). Similarly, it is no good priding yourself on maintaining a wine-friendly, cold spare bedroom if it is periodically blasted up to 21°C (70°F) and down again with the arrival and departure of guests. Garages and attics also give a false sense of security by seeming cool: in fact few are sufficiently insulated to prevent dramatic temperature variations.

If this all sounds rather limiting, don't be put off. It is often possible to store wine at an acceptable temperature in an ordinary house or flat, so long as you choose your spot carefully. North-facing walls and nooks and crannies are places to investigate, as are defunct fireplaces and under-stairs cupboards (though not mine). And you may be lucky enough to have a well-insulated garage, coal-hole or loft.

Wherever you choose, keep a resident thermometer under close surveillance and keep an eye out for traces of wine seeping from the cork and out from under the capsule. This is likely to be a sign that the wine has got too hot (and expanded as its temperature has risen).

Light

Sunlight and ultra-violet light are as bad for wine as excessive heat, but are problems usually much easier to overcome. Most wines are partially protected by coloured glass bottles (occasionally coloured cellophane), but you can do your bit by covering wines exposed to light with something such as a blanket. If your storehouse is under the stairs, you won't need to worry.

(*Left*) Cool, dark, dank, dungeon-like underground cellars are the perfect place to store wine. Some of the miles of cellars tunnelled into the hills in the Tokay region have been used since the 13th century.

Humidity

The role of humidity is slightly more controversial, although it is obviously significant that most producers try to keep a relatively high level of humidity in their cellars (in Europe they specialise in quite extraordinarily dank, mouldy, cold ones). Very low

(*Below*) It does nothing for labels, of course, but wine producers are always immensely proud of their mould-encrusted bottles: it shows that their cellars are nicely humid.

(*Left*) Coloured glass, or coloured cellophane, gives wine inside the bottle useful protection against potentially damaging light.

humidity appears to cause oxidation (by allowing water in the wine to evaporate through the cork – because of lower vapour pressure outside the bottle – leaving space for air to move in). That said, most of the notable problems have been with rarefied old wines in the excessively dry atmosphere produced by air-conditioning in the USA. Ideally, relative humidity should probably be between 55 and 70 percent, but above that the only real problem usually is that you begin to lose labels – making choosing a bottle for supper something of a lucky dip ever after.

(*Right*) **These modern versions of the traditional cellar 'bins' are most useful for people who buy bottles by the dozen or half-dozen.**

Wines and grapes mentioned in this chapter are described in more detail in the final part of the book (pages 94–157) and in 'The importance of Grapes' (pages 50–59).

Movement

Wine does not take well to constant movement and vibration, so, if your wine is shaken all day long by high-speed trains or juggernauts outside the door, I would advise you to find somewhere else to mature it. But I have to add the rider that, traditionally, many London wine merchants had their cellars under railway arches – and some still do – apparently with no ill-effect. Normal household movement (even teenagers thundering up and down the stairs all day and night) is unlikely to damage your wine, whatever it does to your nerves.

Car journeys are not kind to wine. So long as they are not too hot and too long (beware those drives back from the south of France and Spain), the

and a spiral staircase at its centre, is sunk into the ground to a depth of between two and three metres (you choose the size). This can be a good option, but, again, it is an expensive one. (I have both the cabinet and spiral cellar-types in my kitchen and have come to the conclusion that I shall never again buy a house without a traditional underground cellar.)

wine should recover, but it is only fair to give it time – a few days – to do so. And certainly, if there is sediment in it, it will really need it.

Keep it horizontal

Bottles should be stored on their sides to keep the wine in contact with the cork and so stop the cork drying out and letting air in. It's as simple as that – and the simplest way of storing wine horizontally is in common-or-garden wine racks. Several firms make these to measure, should you wish to fit out a curiously-shaped cranny. Insulated pigeon-hole type systems (made from polystyrene or something more substantial) can be good, but take up more room and may be much more expensive.

(Above) **The simple wood and metal rack is as functional as it ever was – and nowadays you can have them made to measure.**

(Above right) **Purpose-designed temperature- and humidity-controlled wine cabinets are an efficient, if expensive, option.**

Renting cellar space

If you are buying wine by the case for laying down and you don't have a cellar, the best place to buy it is from a reputable wine merchant who has proper facilities to store it for you (I do that, too). It will cost you, but it will be money well spent. Alternatively there are now a few self-storage systems in the UK (based on a USA practice), where you rent a temperature-controlled vault and come and go with your wine as you please during the day.

Buying a cellar

If you want to splash out, you can actually buy a cellar. Temperature- and humidity-controlled cabinets, rather like fridges, come in various sizes, holding from about 50 to 500 bottles. They are very effective, but space-consuming and expensive. The Spiral Cellar is an ingenious French creation in which a two-metre diameter cylindrical cellar, its walls lined with a honeycomb of concrete wine bins

(Left) **The most ambitious solution to a cellarless house is to install an underground Spiral Cellar, an ingenious French invention.**

The hardest question:
when to drink

The hardest question to answer, but one of the most frequently asked of any wine writer, is 'When will this wine be ready to drink?'. It is difficult for the most straightforward of reasons: there is no single correct answer for any individual wine. Carefully sealed in its bottle, wine continues to change – and although it follows a certain scientific path, no one has been able to devise a formula that predicts precisely the rate and degree of progress of any given wine along the path. I have to say this pleases me immensely, for this aspect of the mystique of wine is surely one that gives a great deal of the thrill and enjoyment.

That mystery still remains is not to suggest we are completely in the dark about what happens behind closed bottles. With past experience of a particular region, vintage or château, or knowledge of the grape variety (or blend), climate and winemaking techniques, it is possible to estimate broadly how the wine will evolve. We know that the most obviously fruity aromas and flavours are gradually replaced by softer, more complex ones (*see* Why and how to taste, page 15) and we know that eventually wine begins to 'dry out' – the fruit fades altogether leaving the acidity to stand out unattractively. We even know that these changes are the result of the small amount of undissolved oxygen in all young wine reacting with the tannins, anthocyanins (pigments), acids and alcohol in the processes of polymerisation (the one which results finally in sediment) and esterification (which gives the more complex aromas). But that's by the by: being familiar with the scientific nitty-gritty of ageing wine is not a direct aid to getting more enjoyment from it and, to date, it has not yielded a magic formula to tell us when a wine is at its peak.

So how do you know when a wine is ready to drink? Perhaps the first point to derive comfort from is that talking about a wine's peak is misleading. It implies that the wine matures to a single perfect peak and then immediately begins to go downhill – miss the day and you've missed the wine at its party best. Fortunately, this just isn't the case. Between the improving and the declining phases there is not a peak but a plateau, during which the wine will continue to change (even if almost imperceptibly), but will be neither improving nor deteriorating. This is the time to drink your wine. But of course you still need to know when the plateau is likely to be reached and how long it will last.

Assuming that storage conditions are favourable (*see* Ways to store your wine, pages 40–43), and bearing in mind that some types of wine age longer than others (*see* below), it is a fair, if very broad, generalisation that the finer the wine the longer it will take to reach its plateau, the longer it will stay there and the slower its eventual descent will be. Conversely, the lesser the wine, the shorter each phase in a consequently shorter lifespan. And put another way, modest wines – that is modestly-priced wines, no matter how grand sounding the château name and illustration on the label and no matter where you bought them – seldom improve with much keeping. They may improve encouragingly in the short-term, losing the angles and edges of youth, but they simply won't have the degree of concentration and the right balance of tannins, acids and so on to allow them to evolve and gain with age.

Wines today are being made with earlier consumption in mind – which means they have riper, softer-tasting tannins and softer-seeming acidity from inception. Even the finest clarets and many Barolos now have these less harsh, more velvety tannins and should therefore reach their peak – or rather their plateau of maturity – sooner. Most classed growth clarets of even the finest vintages will probably be at the start of the plateau after 10 years nowadays, whereas in top vintages of the seventies, sixties and before, they would have needed 15 or more years. Whether the wines will last as long is arguable. The producers say they will (because the rise is shorter but the plateau longer) but we need to wait at least another 10 years before we can judge the results themselves – and by then, tantalisingly, we shall also have a clearer idea which emerging New World areas are consistently capable of producing wines of great ageing potential.

So far, despite the huge expansion of the wine world in the last 20 years, the wines suitable for laying down have not changed dramatically. They are still predominantly the same classic European styles as they always were – claret and Sauternes, northern Rhônes, red and white burgundy, Barolo,

the best Tuscan reds, port, fine German Rieslings, a handful of Spanish reds and Hungarian Tokay. From the New World, wines worth considering include top Australian Shiraz (eg Barossa Valley's, sometimes with Cabernet Sauvignon in the blend), Hunter Valley Semillon, Clare Valley Riesling, California Cabernets from cooler sites such as Howell Mountain and Stag's Leap, and seriously-made Zinfandels.

Vintage charts – guides not gospels

Whatever type of wine you choose, there is one cardinal rule if you are laying it down: you must choose a good vintage (unless you know that a particular property's wine was unusually successful). 'Off' years may be cheaper – indeed, they certainly should be – but they are 'off' because they lack one or both of the essentials for graceful development: concentration and balance. Of course there will always be exceptions (surprisingly impressive wines from slated years, as well as disappointing wines from universally highly rated ones), but, unless you know for sure, it is not worth taking the risk.

Use the vintage charts in the regional chapters of this book and those in other books, in wine magazines and on wine merchants' lists to build up a picture of different vintages (always remembering that the charts are based on leading wines in their class, not modest names). Part of the fun of wine is that opinions vary among the 'experts' – because tastes vary. Different nations, particularly Britain, France and America, have a habit of forming decidedly different opinions of vintages, especially when it comes to saying which is the superior of two or three good to great years – '88, '89 or '90 claret and Sauternes, and '89 or '90 red burgundy, for example. Even within nations there are party lines. Red Bordeaux drinkers in Britain tend to divide into those who like the power and fruit of the more voluptuous, riper claret vintages and those who favour the leaner, more austere years on the grounds that they are more elegant and will ultimately prove to be better balanced. They draw up their vintage charts accordingly. There may be a consensus in the end, but while the wines are still some way from maturity the battle lines are basically drawn stylistically.

Experts also change their opinions and charts when wines evolve differently from the way they anticipated: over recent years there have been several major revisions downwards for '83 red burgundies and several upwards for the '87s. Views on the '85 and '86 white burgundies continue to see-saw.

Personal taste also has an influence on deciding when a wine is at its best. The British generally

Wines and grapes mentioned in this chapter are described in more detail in the final part of the book (pages 94–157) and in 'The importance of Grapes' (pages 50–59).

drink vintages long after French and American wine drinkers have progressed on to more recent ones, but personally I am no great fan of wines that seem to me to be on the edge of decay – just beginning to fade and tire, although undoubtedly complex. I hear the accusations of vinous infanticide, but I would rather drink a wine when it is slightly too young than too old – when it still has plenty of fruit, but probably needs the tannin or acid to soften further. There is no wrong or right about it. It's a matter of taste – and working out your own preference is the fun of the chase.

Nil desperandum – the low-down on what to lay down

It may seem banal to reduce it all down to price, but if in doubt it can be a useful indicator. The cheapest wines, as we've seen already, are not made to improve: whites often need drinking within a year of the vintage and reds within two years (don't forget that the southern hemisphere harvest takes place early in the year, making the wines roughly six months older than European and California wines of the same vintage). Similarly, even slightly more expensive wines have seldom been made to mature, although, as long as they have not been kept in wood too long before bottling (beware Bulgarian reds, for example), they will tend to last longer – keeping their youthful attractiveness and probably softening and filling out slightly, but developing little in the way of complexity. Among whites at this level, Chardonnays and German Rieslings are a better bet for keeping than Sauvignon Blanc, and medium- to full-bodied reds from the fairly tannic grape varieties Cabernet Sauvignon and Syrah may gently improve over a period of three to five years. (Note that most inexpensive clarets are made largely from Merlot which, except in very rare instances, does not have Cabernet's stamina and potential longevity.)

Once you get into higher price brackets, you should be able to find wines worth saving for several years – five, ten, or even more – from styles such as late-harvest Alsace, top white Graves, Rhônes, classed growth clarets and, with great care, burgundy. But don't forget the good vintage rule and only choose producers or properties with a proven track record.

Nil desperandum – in restaurants

A good restaurant wine list is varied, has a choice of half-bottles and wines by the glass, a spread of prices, unfailingly specifies precisely both vintage and producer, has brief tasting notes to explain style and vintage – particularly of less familiar wines – or clued-up, friendly staff to hand all the time, and is logically organised, either by region, style or grape variety. You know it well? Unfortunately there are a great many that fall short of this minimum, but *nil desperandum* – this is my checklist for dealing with inadequate lists and inadequate waiters:

● *Australia and New Zealand's wines are extremely reliable – Chardonnay, Riesling and sparkling wines from both, reds and Semillon from Australia, and Sauvignon Blanc from New Zealand. With white wines go for the youngest available vintage.*

● *Compared with Australasian wines, California's are usually over-priced, but there are some very good Pinot Noirs, excellent Chardonnays and flavoursome Zinfandels.*

● *Dry Alsace whites are usually better value and more adaptable than the Loire's: Pinot Blanc is good with non-meat starters, fish and shellfish, and full-bodied Tokay-Pinot Gris can match richer, spicier food, as well as fish.*

● *Rully, Mercurey, Montagny and Givry are the reliable and affordable end of red and white burgundy – better and not much more expensive than most Mâcons.*

1982–1997: The life spans of four top white wines

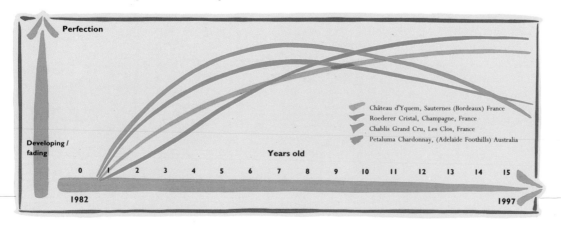

Perfection

Developing / fading

Years old

0   1   2   3   4   5   6   7   8   9   10   11   12   13   14   15

Château d'Yquem, Sauternes (Bordeaux) France
Roederer Cristal, Champagne, France
Chablis Grand Cru, Les Clos, France
Petaluma Chardonnay, (Adelaide Foothills) Australia

1982   1997

(*Left*) **Different wines have different life spans. Most whites evolve more quickly and last less long than reds, but the top sweet wines (like Château d'Yquem) and vintage champagnes (eg Roederer Cristal) are long-lived. New World whites usually have a shorter life span, but South Australia's Petaluma Chardonnay is an exception. It is deliberately made for the long haul.**

● *Excluding '84 and '87, Bordeaux had a great run of vintages from '82 to '90. If you are splashing out, go for the older vintages; if you want a simpler – but supple – claret, choose a straight '89 or '90 Bordeaux or Haut-Médoc. Many classed growth '87s are now pleasingly mature – and reasonably priced. But be more wary of '91 and '92.*

● *Avoid cheap examples of the most common Italian wines (Frascati, Soave, Valpolicella et al), but do take risks with unknowns from Italy, especially if they are not expensive and providing the whites are young. They can be some of the most unusual and rewarding with food.*

● *Red northern Rhônes won't actually be cheap, but they should be a treat. Individual Côtes du Rhône villages such as Valréas, Vacqueyras, Séguret and Cairanne are often good value. Look out also for Lirac and Gigondas.*

● *Red Rioja is usually a safe but uninispiring choice on an uninspired list. Navarra might be better value.*

Alcohol, wine and health

The alcohol content of wine is measured as a percentage of its volume and stated on all labels. Table or light wines (as opposed to heavy or fortified wines such as port and sherry) range from from 5.5 percent (fizzy Italian Moscatos) to 15.5 percent (Recioto della Valpolicella), with a very rough average for quality wines of 11 percent. It's a huge range in terms of your constitution – as well as the wine's – so it is as well to be aware of what you're drinking. (For what it is worth the UK government's suggested maximum consumption is 14 units per week for women and 21 for men – a unit being a small glass of 11 percent-alcohol wine.)

Generally, warmer climates produce higher alcohol, but the picture is complicated by cooler regions often being allowed to chaptalise (increase alcohol by adding sugar at fermentation), and equally, in warmer climates, if you pick the grapes less ripe they will contain less sugar to turn into alcohol and so make lighter, less alcoholic wines. In addition, heavy yields reduce sugar concentration.

There is, then, no substitute for reading the label, but here are some pointers:

● *Champagne and burgundy, despite their cool climate origins, are usually 13 percent (because they are chaptalised), as is, to most drinkers' surprise, Beaujolais – for the same reason. Claret (usually chaptalised) is mostly 12–12.5 percent. Sauternes in a good year is often 14 (and of course very sweet too).*

● *Quite a lot of cheap Australian wines are 11 percent (high yields, early picking), while the more expensive ones are more likely to be 13 percent. In spite of a cooler climate, New Zealand Chardonnays often reach 13.5–14 percent (the grapes being picked late to give time for the high natural acidity to drop). Good California wines are usually 13–13.5 percent.*

● *Sherry ranges from about 16 to 18 percent – the lower figure for finos and manzanillas, the higher one for darker, heavier styles such as oloroso. Most port is about 20 percent.*

● *If you want to keep your alcohol intake in check, most traditional German wines are at the low end of the spectrum (8–9 percent and sometimes less), but be aware that the new drier styles (Trocken and Halbtrocken) are often 10–12 percent.*

Mentioning wine and health is like picking one's way through a minefield, so all I shall say is that there is strong evidence that moderate consumption of wine, especially red, reduces the risk of heart disease and that moderate consumers live longer than total abstainers. But who needs such reasons for consuming something as delicious and life-enhancing as wine anyway?

1982–1997: The life spans of four top red wines

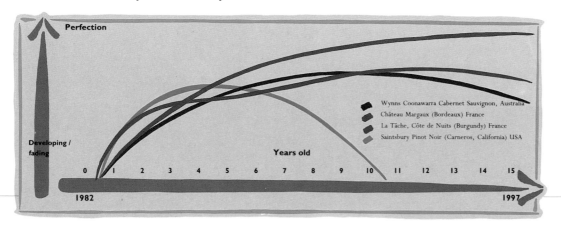

(*Left*) **Generally, the finer the wine, the longer it takes to reach its peak (or plateau) of perfection, and the more gradual its decline. Overall, Old World wines last longer than New World wines and Cabernet Sauvignon-based wines live longer than Pinot Noirs. The graph showing the projected evolution of four top red wines of the 1982 vintage bears this out.**

The making of
first-class wine

2

Wine is simply the fermented juice of the grape, but there are thousands of different varieties of wine grape, each one with its own characteristics. A mere handful are responsible for the main classic wine styles, but when transported to other soils and climates, or when subjected to different winemaking traditions and techniques, they may turn out quite different wines – or they may sometimes produce textbook copies.

The importance of
grapes

Although wine rarely smells and tastes of grapes, the variety of grape, or grapes, in any wine is the principal influence on its style and character. Soil, climate and human intervention play their parts, but grapes are the essential ingredient and prime source of flavour. There are a daunting 4,000 or so varieties in the **Vitis vinifera** *species (this being the species of the vine family almost entirely responsible for wine grapes), but many are very similar to each other and many others are of no significance, either because the wine they produce is poor or very dull, or because they are so temperamental that few growers bother with them.*

I have selected just over 30, dividing them into: classics; other important varieties (a more personal selection of significant and/or distinctively flavoured grapes); others which often appear on wine labels; and varieties that are significant but keep a low profile.

The classics

Classic white grapes

Chardonnay

Chardonnay may be the world's most fashionable grape variety, but it is by no means one of the most planted (that debatable honour goes to an extraordinarily dull variety called Airén spread across Spain, the country with the largest area under vine, but not, incidentally, the largest wine production). Even if, as has been estimated, plantings of Chardonnay doubled between 1988 and 1992 and have continued to increase at that rate, the variety probably still accounts for less than one percent of all *Vitis vinifera*. Clearly, then, Chardonnay is not staging a triffid-like takeover, but that is not to deny its increasing presence and popularity. Growers like

it because it is easy to cultivate – vigorous, resistant and generously productive in most climates and soils (which is why it is appearing in some outlandish-seeming places). Winemakers like it because it is so malleable: it can be fashioned in a whole range of styles, and in Burgundy and Champagne it has shown that it is capable of producing some of the world's greatest wines and most long-lived of whites. Drinkers like it, because, with few exceptions, it gives immediate satisfaction. Full, supple, buttery and fruity, with or without the seductive vanilla-oak flavours of oak barrels, it has no hard edges or aggressive acidity. Whether you are the grower, winemaker or consumer, you seldom have to work at Chardonnay.

Flavours: apple, pear, citrus fruits, melon, pineapple, peach, butter, wax, honey, toffee, butterscotch, vanilla, mixed spice, wet wool (burgundy), minerals and flint (Chablis).

(Left) **Everyone likes Chardonnay: growers because it is easy to cultivate and a generous cropper; winemakers because it can be moulded to order in the winery; and consumers because of its instantly appealing, no-hard-edges style.**

Sauvignon Blanc

This is often the white grape tipped for stardom once consumers tire of Chardonnay, but I am not convinced. Sauvignon just doesn't have the virtues, in the vineyard, cellar or glass, that make Chardonnay such a crowd-pleaser. When conditions are right it produces wine with a strong, but basically one dimensional personality – invigoratingly dry and notably high in acid, with grass and gooseberry flavours. Its very best manifestations come from the vineyards of the French upper Loire and New Zealand and, more erratically, from those of Bordeaux and California.

Flavours: freshly cut grass, gooseberries, flowering currant leaves, cat's pee (not a fault), tinned asparagus or green beans (generally undesirable), occasionally stony or flinty (upper Loire).

Riesling

The true Riesling of German origin (aka Johannisberg, White, Rhine or Renano Riesling) is one of the world's great grapes. In common with Sauvignon Blanc it has both a strong personality – one that is better off without any oak influence – and high acidity, but it is far more adaptable than Sauvignon. It thrives in the cool climates of Europe (Germany and Alsace) and equally in the much warmer climes of Australia, and is susceptible to noble rot (the fungus which attacks certain ripe grapes and dehydrates them so that they give wines of immense richness and sweetness). The result is a spectrum of styles that ranges from dry to intensely sweet and that doesn't need a great weight of alcohol – with as little as 6.5 percent in Germany (although levels can reach 13 percent in Alsace and Australia). In addition, like fine Chardonnay, Riesling has the potential to age for many years. Wherever it is grown, young or old, and whether sweet or dry, Riesling should have a vivid fruitiness and lively balancing acidity.

(Left) **Riesling thrives in cool climates such as Germany's and warm ones such as Australia's, giving a spectrum of wines from light and very sweet to bone dry and quite alcoholic.**

Flavours: crunchy green apples, spiced baked apples, quince, orange, lime (Australia), passionfruit (Australia), honey (sweet wines), minerally notes (especially Mosel), petrol, toast.

Sémillon

Sémillon is the mainstay of white Bordeaux, both dry (especially Graves) and sweet (Sauternes), and it also scales the heights as an unusual dry white in Australia's Hunter Valley. In Bordeaux it is appreciated for its round, lanoliney quality and to a lesser extent, in the young dry wines only, for herbaceous flavours (similar to those of the much sharper Sauvignon Blanc with which it is paired). In the Hunter it is renowned as a long-lived dry white that becomes increasingly honeyed and toasty with age – just as if it had been aged in oak. It is also widely grown in Chile and there is some in South Africa.

Flavours: grass, citrus, lanolin, honey, toast.

Chenin Blanc

A grape of very high acidity and, potentially, great longevity, but also a grape of nastier than average wines when there is insufficient sun to ripen them satisfactorily, unripe Chenin has a cheesy and – sorry – vomit-like flavour. But, in the sort of favourable conditions that don't happen every year in the middle Loire (Coteaux du Layon, Vouvray et al), there are glorious honeyed sweet wines with bracing but harmonious acidity. In lesser years, they are lighter, less concentrated and more likely to be medium-dry or dry, and their high acid is nearly always useful for the dry sparkling wines of Saumur, Vouvray and Montlouis. Elsewhere Chenin Blanc gives simple, soft, crisp, fruity wines (South Africa), and increasingly interesting, serious dry wines (New Zealand).

(Left) **Chenin Blanc needs lots of sun to bring out its intense fruity flavours and soften its rasping acidity. Its greatest manifestations are the botrytised, long-lived sweet wines of the middle Loire in exceptional vintages.**

Flavours: apples, apricots, nuts, honey, marzipan.

Classic red grapes

Cabernet Sauvignon

In terms of status and popularity, Cabernet Sauvignon can be regarded as Chardonnay's red wine counterpart. It is a deep-coloured, thick-skinned grape that produces dark, flavoursome wine, particularly noted for its blackcurrant and cedary, cigar box or lead pencils character. Cabernet Sauvignon wines have the potential (largely because of the tannins which come from the skins) to age a long time and they gain in stature if aged in oak. From the grower's point of view the variety is nearly as accommodating of its environment as Chardonnay, although, if the climate is too warm, the wines will have baked, jammy flavours and will lack structure and focus, and, if denied sufficient sun, will be thin, stalky and herbaceous. The only significant wine producing country that doesn't cultivate Cabernet Sauvignon is Germany (because it is too cold), but Cabernet's heartland is, of course, Bordeaux – claret country – where it is always part of a blend.

(*Above*) **Whether producing some of the greatest wines in the world or simple, fruity, purple vins de pays, the wines of the well-travelled Cabernet Sauvignon vine are among the most easily recognisable reds.**

Flavours: blackcurrant, cedar, cigar boxes, lead pencils, green pepper, mint, dark chocolate, tobacco, olives.

Merlot

Merlot is similar to Cabernet Sauvignon, but it is less tannic and less intensely blackcurranty and gives softer, plumper, juicier, earlier-maturing wines which somehow seem sweeter. The most highly sought-after Merlot-dominated wines are clarets of the Pomerol and St-Emilion regions of Bordeaux. As a varietal wine (unblended with any other variety) it is gaining friends in California (perhaps because California Cabernets have a tendency to be too tannic) and Chile. It produces light, grassy wines in northern Italy, fuller, more claret-like reds in Bulgaria, and is beginning to show interesting results (sometimes blended) in New Zealand's cool climate and South Africa's warmer one.

Flavours: often similar to Cabernet Sauvignon, but sometimes more plums and roses than blackcurrants, more spice and rich fruit-cake, less mint and lead pencils.

Pinot Noir

Chardonnay's red wine compatriot in Burgundy is as ill at ease in the world outside as Chardonnay is comfortable. Pinot Noir is both extremely pernickety about its climate and a much less generous producer than Chardonnay. In Burgundy, achieving sufficient ripeness is always the critical factor (or one of them). It is a variety of relatively low tannin and acidity, medium rather than deep colour and a medium rather than long life span: a shortage of warmth simply yields pale, anaemic, thin wines, with none of the heady red fruits character, the silky textures, the gamey complexity of great red burgundy. In California, Australia and other new wine countries, producers suffer the opposite problem: overripe grapes giving cooked, coarse, jammy flavours. But things are changing and some extremely good Pinot Noirs are now being made in cooler spots, particularly in California, and quality is being helped along everywhere by the use of better clones and a greater variety of them (variety gives complexity).

(*Left*) **In contrast to the easily pleased Cabernet Sauvignon, Pinot Noir is very sensitive to climate and to the way it is handled in the wlnery.**

Flavours: raspberries, strawberries, cherries, cranberries, violets, roses, game, compost, manure.

Syrah

Classic Syrah wines from France's Rhône Valley, epitomised by Hermitage, and from Australia, where Syrah is extensively planted and known as Shiraz, are very dark, full-bodied, powerful, alcoholic wines with great ageing potential. Syrah flourishes in warmer climates than Pinot Noir, and is altogether much more adaptable. In cooler climates it simply produces slightly lighter, more peppery wines, with less intense, ripe berry fruit, less tannin and less meaty richness. From the drinker's point of view, one of the interesting things about Syrah wines is that, despite heavy tannins and undoubted staying power, they often (Hermitage excepted, but Shiraz especially) reach a drinkably mature stage quite soon. The adaptable Shiraz is also used in Australia for sparkling wines — white, rosé and red — and for impressive, sweet, fortified, 'port' styles. Small plantings are starting up in California, to make Rhône-style wines and there is some — called Shiraz — with a burnt rubbery character in South Africa.

Flavours: raspberries, blackberries, blackcurrants, pepper, mixed spice, leather, game, tar.

Other important varieties

Important white grapes

Gewürztraminer

The highly aromatic Gewürztraminer – at its best in Alsace, where it may be dry or sweet, and in the German Pfalz region – is the most distinctive-

(Right) **The characteristically pink Gewürztraminer grapes are the most distinctive-smelling of the wine world.**

smelling of all wine grapes. The wine has an exotic spicy, perfume with a taste of lychees and tends to be full-bodied, sometimes slightly oily textured, quite alcoholic and with lowish acidity.
Flavours: spice (often ginger and cinnamon), Nivea cream, lychees.

Muscat (Moscatel)

If a wine smells of grapes, it is almost certain to be made from one of the Muscat family. It may be dry, as in Alsace; light, sweet and fizzy as in Asti, Moscato d'Asti and Clairette de Die; very sweet as in Moscatel de Valencia (Spain); or very sweet and fortified, as in the heavy, super-sweet, amber-brown Australian liqueur Muscats (aka 'stickies') and the *vins doux naturels* of the Rhône and the south of France (chief among them Muscat de Beaumes-de-Venise, Muscat de Rivesaltes, Muscat de Frontignan and Muscat de Lunel).
Flavours: grapes, oranges, roses (Alsace), bergamot (Alsace), raisins (fortified wines), barley sugar, demerara sugar.

Viognier

A grape important for its rarity. Viognier is responsible for Condrieu, the head-spinningly perfumed, opulent yet dry, full-bodied white wine from a tiny patch of the northern Rhône, and it is grown in very few other places. The problem with it is its unreliability. If the weather doesn't suit, there may be no crop at all and even in a supposedly good year yields are very low (hence Condrieu's prohibitive price), but the good news is that a number of growers further down the Rhône Valley and in Languedoc have been planting Viognier with good early results. It is also catching on in California – there are impressive examples, but at much the same price as Condrieu.
Flavours: may or lime blossom, apricots, peaches, musk.

Why vine age is important

You may have seen the words vieilles vignes *(old vines) on a wine label. This is because the age of the vines, in tandem with other factors such as the number of bunches of grapes produced (yield), has a critical influence on the quality and character of a wine. Vines usually begin to fruit in commercial quantities and are entitled to appellation contrôlée status from their third year, but grape quality and intensity of flavour improves as they age. The exception to this is that some young vines do produce very high quality. Both the world's most sought-after port, 1931 Quinta do Noval Nacional, and the fabled 1961 Château Pétrus were made substantially from the grapes of five- to six-year-old vines, and Chardonnay, especially in New Zealand, often performs well initially, but then goes duller for about four years. The clue to such quality from young vines seems to be restricting yields. In fact the yield of all vines begins to decline eventually (it depends greatly on variety, but often from about 15–20 years old), although quality may continue to improve – hence the grower wishing to draw attention on labels to his old vines.*

So why would any grower advertise the fact that his are jeunes vignes *(young vines)? In fact the growers who occasionally do this are trying to tell you something quite different. They are trying to let you know that, were the vines older (they are probably under three years), they would be entitled to a superior appellation.*

Important red grapes

Cabernet Franc

Cabernet Sauvignon in Bordeaux is almost always blended with this, its softer, less aristocratic first cousin. Cabernet Franc is similar, but produces lighter, less tannic wines with a more pronounced 'green' vegetal character. In the Loire, where it is unblended in Chinon and Bourgueil and mixed with Cabernet Sauvignon in the cheaper Touraine wines, it often has strawberry and chocolate flavours and a smell of potato peelings. It is widespread in northern Italy where it produces light, grassy wines with sweet cassis fruit flavours.

Flavours: green pepper, blackcurrant (berries and leaves), potato peelings, strawberry, chocolate.

(*Left*) **Cabernet Franc rarely has the intensity of colour, flavour or tannin of its famous cousin, partly because its skins are not so thick.**

Gamay

Gamay is the grape used exclusively for Beaujolais and for the lesser red burgundies of the Mâconnais region. A little is also grown around Touraine on the Loire and a few producers dabble with it in California. Its charm is its light, fresh, fruity and uncomplicated style for immediate drinking, although there are some more serious Beaujolais, named after their individual locations: Fleurie, Morgon, Moulin-à-Vent et al, which are fuller and more flavoursome.

Flavours: strawberry, cherry and, in Beaujolais Nouveau, pears and bubblegum.

Nebbiolo (alias Spanna, Inferno or Grumello)

The small, thick-skinned Nebbiolo grape produces some of the darkest, driest, biggest and toughest (both tannic and acid) of red wines. Its stronghold is Piedmont and thereabouts in northern Italy; its two most famous wines are Barolo and Barbaresco.

Flavours: tar, liquorice, violets, roses, prunes, fruit-cake, bitter chocolate.

Grenache

Widely grown in the south of France and, as Garnacha, in Spain, Grenache is also widespread in Australia, where it is mostly used for making cheap, so-called tawny port styles and bag-in-box wines, and it is grown in a small way to produce good Rhône-style wines in California. Grenache is the main constituent of most Châteauneuf-du-Pape and Côtes du Rhônes and is also responsible for the unusual sweet Banyuls. In Spain it partners Tempranillo in Rioja and is much used for rosé (*rosado*). Generally it gives quite alcoholic wines with warm, peppery, fruity flavours, but which have no great staying power unless yields are kept well in check.

Flavours: pepper, raspberry, herbs, in Châteauneuf-du-Pape linseed oil.

(*Left*) **The peppery, alcoholic Grenache grape variety thrives in warm climates and a variety of – sometimes very inhospitable-looking – soils.**

Sangiovese

Sangiovese dominates central Italy, but only aspires to greatness in Tuscany: notably in Chianti, Brunello di Montalcino and Vino Nobile di Montepulciano. At its best in these wines, it is a medium to full, firm, dry, slightly spicy red that ages well. At its most ordinary, it is light and astringent. It is beginning to be planted in California, with some early successes, and could easily become a cult among fashion-conscious drinkers.
Flavours: *bitter cherry, spices, tobacco, herbs.*

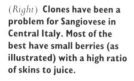

(*Right*) **Clones have been a problem for Sangiovese in Central Italy. Most of the best have small berries (as illustrated) with a high ratio of skins to juice.**

Tempranillo

Tempranillo is grown throughout Spain (under too many pseudonyms to mention here), but is best-known as the mainstay variety of Rioja and Ribera del Duero. Without oak it has quite a fruity, spicy character, but it is far more familiar as a mellow, oaky, vanilla-flavoured red (vanilla being the distinctive flavour imparted by American oak). In fact it is hard to pinpoint the flavours of the Tempranillo grape, which is no doubt why many a distinguished taster has confused mature Rioja with both claret and burgundy.
Flavours: *strawberry, spices, soft buttery toffee.*

Zinfandel

Its origins still a mystery, Zinfandel is California's very own grape variety. While it is much used to make bland 'blush' (rosé) wines, it is also responsible for some wonderful, rich, spicy reds. These are full-blooded wines, packed with ripe berry fruit and supple tannins. Most are ready for drinking within two or three years, but they have staying power and the best will last 10 years.
Flavours: *blackberries, spices, freshly ground black pepper.*

Other grapes often seen

Aligoté

A pleasant but fairly ordinary dry, tangy, full-textured white in Burgundy.

Barbera

Grown across Italy and made in a variety of styles, but most important in Piedmont where it produces red wines that are lighter in style and earlier-maturing than Barolo and have a sour cherry flavour and pronounced astringency.

Colombard

Colombard grapes produce inexpensive, light, soft, fruity white wines in southwest France, especially Vin de Pays des Côtes de Gascogne, and base wine for the local brandies, armagnac and cognac. Also popular in California, South Africa and Australia.

Hybrids, and Seyval Blanc (the odd grape out)

Hybrid is a dirty word in most wine circles. Hybrid vines are crosses of Vitis vinifera and other, lesser quality types of vine, such as Vitis labrusca, which give wines with a strange taste, usually referred to as 'foxy'. They have invariably been crossed in an effort to produce a vine that can stand up to a particularly difficult climate – the east coast USA and Canada, for example. Although they are not accepted for the production of so-called 'quality wine' in the EC, they can occasionally produce very respectable results. Seyval Blanc is the most notable, although its advocates in England and Wales say that it is not a hybrid, but an interspecific cross. I won't go into the genetics and semantics, but suffice to say that Seyval Blanc is not only largely weather-proof and disease-resistant in Britain, but it also produces some of our best wines – typically crisp, aromatic and fruity, but with an attractive extra weight and smoothness.

One advantage increasingly being touted by the supporters of Seyval (and its kin) is that because it is so resistant to disease it needs very little treating in the vineyards – and no one can deny that that is good for the environment.

Clones

Clones, one of the great buzz words of the seventies, are vines that have been specially selected and laboratory bred from one parent vine, chosen, say, for its resistance to disease, high yields, good grape colour, earlier ripening fruit or whatever – the aim being to fill the vineyards with healthy, reliable vine plants, rather than weak, disease-prone ones. Nowadays there is greater emphasis on having a variety of clones in a vineyard, to give a larger range of potential flavours in a wine, instead of trying to find one super-strain. Followers of 'biodynamie' (see page 87) do not approve of clonally selected vines.

Marsanne

A component of white Hermitage (from France's Rhône Valley). On its own, capable of strong, herby, lime marmalade flavoured wines in the Rhône and Australia. With oak, has ageing potential.

Müller-Thurgau

A Riesling-Silvaner cross planted all over Germany and largely responsible for Liebfraumilch; the most common variety in England, too, where it gives more characterful whites with crisp, privet hedge aromas and also a (not necessarily unpleasant) cat's pee pungency.

Pinot Blanc

At its most characterful as grown in Alsace, like a light, unoaked Chardonnay – fresh and leafy, with appley, buttery fruit.

Pinot Gris (alias Pinot Grigio, Tokay or Ruländer)

Light, crisp and rather neutral as Pinot Grigio in Italy and as Ruländer in Germany; and makes fat, talc-perfumed, honeyed white wines – both dry and sweet – in Alsace.

Scheurebe

A more interesting Riesling-Silvaner German crossing, with a grapefruit character and which makes good sweet wines and dry white wines. Also present in the UK.

Sylvaner

One of the less distinguished and least distinctive of Alsace white grapes, but not unattractive; also grown in Germany (called Silvaner) – to best effect in Franken.

Low profile grapes

Carignan

Much planted in France's Rhône, Provence and Languedoc where it is mainly used to pad out such red wines as Corbières, Minervois and Fitou.

Melon de Bourgogne

The neutral white grape that produces Muscadet; only the growers of Muscadet now bother with it – after all, there are plenty of other neutral white grapes to choose from elsewhere.

Palomino

Sherry is the white Palomino's single, but important, claim to fame.

Trebbiano (or Ugni Blanc)

One of Europe's dullest but most planted varieties – used in white *vins de pays* such as Côtes de Gascogne, and in Italy for the likes of Soave, Frascati and Orvieto; also provides neutral wines distilled into cognac and armagnac.

(Left) **If yields are kept low, Trebbiano can produce pleasant wine, but it is at its best when blended with something more characterful**

The main classic wine styles,
and alternatives

If the wine world has moved faster than ever before in the last two decades, this is the chapter that demonstrates it above all. A generation ago you could divide wines into two broad categories: the great, almost exclusively French, classics; and the myriad localised regional styles. There was a degree of cross-fertilisation, and cuttings and winemakers did sometimes travel, but it was all very limited; wine styles, whether classic or obscure, belonged to their regions. But that began to change at the end of the liberating sixties, first in California and then, throughout the seventies and eighties, in other countries and continents.

A completely new and rapidly expanding category of wines now exists: wines made anywhere in the world in the image of the great classics – Cabernets that seek to emulate clarets, Chardonnays that model themselves on white burgundy, sparkling wines that want to be mistaken for champagne.

The key to the change was grape varieties. The pioneers of these new wines had their own climate, their own soils; all they needed, they decided, was the same grape varieties. If they wanted to make a white burgundy type, they planted Chardonnay. If they wanted an ersatz claret, they put in Cabernet Sauvignon. And in doing all this they actually simplified rather than complicated the wine world they were expanding by giving us 'varietals' — wines made from, and named after, single grape varieties.

Obvious as such a strategy may seem now we are familiar with seeing grape varieties on labels, 25 years ago it was a novel approach. Traditional European wines were, and still are, named after their place of birth – whether a vast area like Bordeaux, or one of its small, high quality subregions such as St-Julien. (True, Alsace is an exception as its wines are named primarily after their grape varieties, but even here the recent trend has been towards greater locational identification, with the recognition in the eighties of 50 small top-quality sites or *crus*.) The result was that previous generations of wine drinkers seldom knew or cared which grape variety a wine was made from, just so long as it was made from grapes not banana skins.

But the new producers had not been brought up in this traditional atmosphere, born of hundreds of years of experience, where the primacy of *terroir* (*see* pages 82–83) was unquestioned and, indeed, enshrined in the rules of each *appellation contrôlée* or *vin de pays*. (So much so that it is *terroir*, not the grower, that dictates the grape varieties of a given wine and it is actually illegal to grow, say, Cabernet Sauvignon in Champagne, Merlot in Burgundy or Chardonnay in Bordeaux). As the new producers saw it, so long as the climate was comfortably warm, which of course it was in places like California's Napa Valley, they did not need to worry about its precise details and they certainly did not pay much attention to soil character. If they had the grapes, then the winemaker in his spanking new high-tech winery could do the rest.

The choice of grape variety in these new countries is still the choice of the grower, but the pen-

dulum has swung in the last decade. Without actually learning to revere dirt, producers have begun to respect it a little more. They still do not give much for its mineral and (hot topic in France now) its microbial content, but they do lay great store by soil temperature, drainage and water-holding capacities. They also spend a great deal of time seeking out the perfect, cool 'microclimate'.

The descriptions of the classic styles and the new alternatives that follow are inevitably broad brush-stroke portraits. In so vast a continent as Australia, where Cabernet Sauvignon is the second most planted red grape, there could never be one single, narrowly defined style; there isn't one California style either – any more than there is just one for Bordeaux itself. In other countries, that have been starved of investment and contact with new ideas, the wine industries are at an intermediate, partially modernised stage. Here, too, it can be hard to get the style in focus. All that said, there are some identifiable broad national and regional characteristics.

Wines and grapes mentioned in this chapter are described in more detail in the final part of the book (pages 94–157) and in 'The importance of Grapes' (pages 50–59).

(*Below*) **The influence of the great classic wine styles of Europe – above all France – is felt in hot-seats of wine learning and hotbeds of wine production in countries and continents in both hemispheres.**

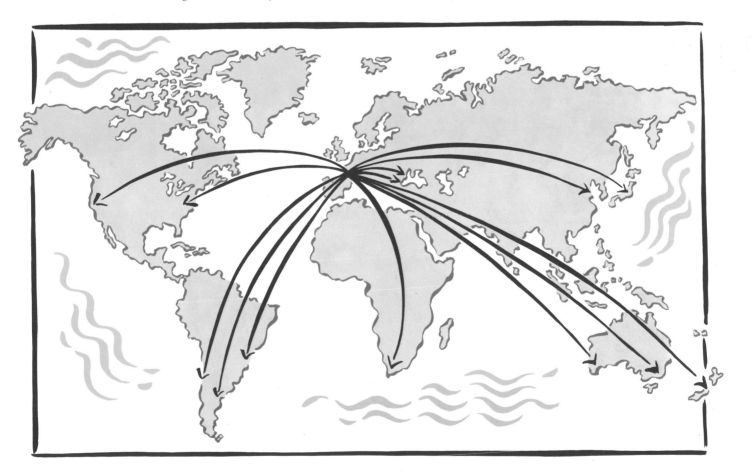

(*From left to right*) **The classic, high-shouldered red Bordeaux bottle used for Cabernet Sauvignon, Merlots and blends such as Cabernet-Shiraz all around the world; the sloping-shouldered burgundy bottle used for most of the world's Pinot Noirs (but not Alsace's); two versions of the sloping shouldered bottle, here used for white burgundy and Pouilly-Fumé; the tall slim green bottle used for German Mosel (a taller, slimmer version is used in Alsace and a brown version is used for Rhine wines); the heavy glass bottle, designed to withstand the pressure within, used for champagne and other bottle-fermented sparkling wines; the high-shouldered Bordeaux bottle in colourless glass for Sauternes; a typical fino sherry bottle; the heavy, dark – almost black – glass of a vintage port bottle; and the sloping shouldered bottle as used throughout the Rhône.**

Red Bordeaux

Small wonder that red Bordeaux – claret to the British – should have been the first and most copied of the classics. Bordeaux is the world's largest fine wine region, and, quite simply, the best wines taste sublime – even if you do sometimes have to wait 10, occasionally 15 or more years for them to reach their peak of maturity. Of course, with such a large region there are considerable variations in taste, but in many ways this is more a question of different levels of quality (the higher the quality, the greater the concentration of flavours, the more new oak barrels used and the greater the complexity) than it is of diversity of style. There is really only one stylistic divide in this respect and that concerns grape varieties.

Claret is popularly thought of as a Cabernet Sauvignon wine – and it is certainly the grape variety almost all the new overseas producers planted when they were setting out to make their copies, because it is the major variety in all the illustrious names of the Haut-Médoc (on the left bank of the Gironde estuary) and the red wines of Graves to the south. But red Bordeaux is never a varietal, it is always a blended wine (from Cabernet Sauvignon, Merlot, Cabernet Franc and sometimes some Malbec and Petit Verdot) and Cabernet Sauvignon does not dominate overall. That distinction goes to Merlot, the predominant variety of the right bank appellations such as St-Emilion and Pomerol and of almost all the lesser clarets, from plain Bordeaux to the likes of Côtes de Blaye and Côtes de Castillon.

Cabernet Sauvignon and Merlot are similar in taste and are beautifully complementary – as the Bordelais discovered a century ago on replanting their vineyards after the devastating phylloxera plague – and blended together have a characteristic and identifiable taste. As well as the keynotes of blackcurrant, cedar and pencil, look for the typically deep colour which changes from purple to brick red with age (for more on colour *see* Why and how to taste, pages 10–21); expect to find the taste of new oak and tannin in the better young wines; and don't be surprised to find green pepper, dark chocolate, tobacco, mint, minerals, olives and cloves. In older wines the complex flavours might include suggestions of autumnal undergrowth (even mushrooms), dried fruit and fruit-cake.

Broadly speaking, the alternatives to claret come from warmer, drier climates and, because they are usually made from only one grape variety, are simpler wines. They may have greater power, equal or more obvious fruit, and enough tannin and acid to guarantee a lifespan of five or more years, but a varietal Cabernet or Merlot, seldom scales the heights of complexity, elegance or longevity of a great Bordeaux – which is why aspiring producers in the new wine world, especially in California, are increasingly adding a little Merlot and even a spot of Cabernet Franc to their Cabernet Sauvignon.

(*Below*) **The pretty town of St-Emilion presides over the appellation of the same name on Bordeaux's right bank. Here, where Merlot dominates the vineyards, the wines are slightly softer, broader and more spicy than those of the Médoc across the river.**

USA

Nearly 20 years ago a California Cabernet Sauvignon from Stag's Leap Wine Cellars in the Napa Valley beat four of Bordeaux's five First Growths (top château wines) in a competition in Paris. There have been similar sensations since and the French riposte is invariably that the California style – all power and upfront fruit – simply overwhelms the more refined, slower to mature French style, and would equally overpower most food and the palate of any drinker who tried a second glass. There is a certain truth in this: California Cabernets and Merlots, despite being toned down since those early days, tend to be big, ripe, oaky and more tannic than any other country's. But the very best – which include some of those now using the classic Bordeaux blend, and the high profile joint Bordeaux-California ventures such as Opus One (Château Mouton-Rothschild and Robert Mondavi) – do rank with fine claret. (As well as names like Opus and Dominus, look for the marketing name 'Meritage' used by some winemakers to indicate the traditional Bordeaux combination of grapes.)

There is no fail-safe way of distinguishing a California Cabernet from, say, an Australian one, but if the power, weight and particularly tannin of the wine are especially striking, I'd plump for California. And if there is a whiff of eucalyptus, too, that can be another clue to California origins.

The Washington State style of both Cabernet Sauvignon and Merlot is lighter and crisper than California's and therefore more like Bordeaux. It differs in having a distinctly herbaceous character,

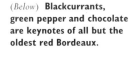

(*Below*) **Blackcurrants, green pepper and chocolate are keynotes of all but the oldest red Bordeaux.**

often with a hint of cloves, and is attractive so long as it is tempered by vibrant blackcurrant fruit.

Australia

There are few Australian Merlots, but a whole array of Cabernet Sauvignons and Cabernet-Shiraz blends. You might expect Shiraz (the same grape as Syrah of France's Rhône Valley) to give quite a different style of wine, but in fact it marries very well with Cabernet, enhancing the spice and chocolate elements and often giving a blackberry note to the fruit. The Australian style of Cabernet is ripe, full and fruity, and often has a delicious supple mint flavour (especially in Coonawarra Cabernets). It is softer and less dry-seeming than Bordeaux and less tannic than most California Cabernets.

New Zealand

The cool, wet climate naturally yields a lean, light style and brings out the herbaceous, grassy, stalky characteristics of Cabernet Sauvignon, but some fleshier wines, usually blends with Merlot, are now appearing from the warmer North Island. These suggest that New Zealand's Bordeaux blends, while remaining limited, are going to be increasingly perfectly formed in the classic claret mould.

South America

The best Chilean Cabernets and Merlots are medium bodied and well structured, but with more piercingly vivid blackcurrant flavours than claret. There is great potential, but yields are often too high (*see* page 138) and winemaking technology

(and therefore average quality) lags behind California's and Australia's.

It is hard to pinpoint an Argentine style, because the wine industry is more backward than Chile's, but Argentine Cabernet is not usually marked by the Chilean brilliance of fruit. Instead it tends to have a mellower, more spicy character (echoes of St-Emilion) and this is even more evident in the pure Malbec wines – Malbec being one of the least used of red Bordeaux grapes.

South Africa

The wine industry in South Africa is still emerging from years of international isolation and an inflexible wine regime. A handful of Cabernets, Merlots and blends prove that this is an environment capable of producing impressive claret-like reds, but there are still some rather hot-rubbery ones and some that are fruit-lacking and astringent.

Eastern Europe

Bulgarian Cabernet Sauvignons are medium to full bodied with very approachable, rounded fruit and the classic cedar and tobacco character of claret. Large oak casks give the wines a spicy wood character.

Romania has a surprising amount of Cabernet planted and the quality of those I have tasted has been good, very much in the Bulgarian style.

Moldova is the genie in the bottle. Some very fine claret-like wines from the sixties and seventies have emerged from the Purkar winery in recent years – and some young modern Cabernets are now being made by an Australian team in other wineries. Definitely a region to watch.

France

Until comparatively recently, the only French alternatives to claret were those from the satellite appellations of Bordeaux and the further reaches of the Southwest, and from the Loire. The former included the grassy, blackcurranty reds from Bergerac and Côtes de Duras, the slightly firmer, more claret-like Côtes de Buzet, and a couple of altogether tougher wines – the Malbec-based Cahors and the Tannat-based Madiran – neither of which resemble Bordeaux very closely.

The Loire reds were the light- to medium-weight Cabernet Franc wines of Chinon, Bourgueil and Saumur-Champigny, with their vegetal, green pepper or potato peelings character and, in good vintages, raspberry fruit and gentle chocolatey tones – but they were only ever loosely related to

(Above) **More sunshine, blending Cabernet with other grape varieties, such as Sangiovese, and ageing in different kinds of oak can give gently spicy or, in the case of Provence, aromatic herby wines.**

red Bordeaux. All these still exist as alternatives, but there are now a multitude of enjoyable, if not particularly complex, full, fruity Cabernets and Merlots from the Mediterranean south: intense, aromatic, herby Cabernets from Provence; full, ripe Vins de Pays d'Oc varietals, sometimes enriched by oak ageing; and many other *vins de pays* from the formerly scorned Midi. In style they tend to fall somewhere between the restraint of Bordeaux and the exuberance and ripeness of Australian Cabernet.

Italy

Northeast Italian Cabernet (often Cabernet Franc, although labels don't say so) is mostly light and undistinguished and bears little relation to red Bordeaux, but there are some superb Cabernets and Cabernet Sauvignon-Sangiovese blends from Tuscany (the so-called super-Tuscans which are due to be raised shortly to DOC from their humble *vini da tavola* classification). With the concentration and youthful austerity of fine claret, they usually combine slightly more weight and fullness and a smoky spice character.

Spain

Spanish Cabernet first hit the headlines in 1979 when a wine from Penedès, Torres' 1970 Mas La Plana, was voted best red by a 60-strong international (but French dominated) blind-tasting jury in Paris. This classic, rich, quite tannic Cabernet has spawned several good followers in the Penedès region, as well as the slightly lighter, elegant wines of the Raimat estate in Costers del Segre, but most Spanish winemakers are more interested in making a Rioja-like wine than a claret-like one (nothing wrong in that, of course).

Portugal

Portugal wisely concentrates on its own fascinating grape varieties, but red Bairrada often has a cedary quality reminiscent of claret, and Barca Velha, Portugal's unofficial 'first growth' is, indeed, like a mature classed growth Bordeaux (despite being made from port grapes). There is also Quinta da Bacalhôa, a one-off, dense, oaky cassis-packed Cabernet-Merlot blend made near Lisbon.

Other one-offs

Château Musar is a wild, spicy, concentrated Lebanese wine that tastes like a cross between claret and Rhône wine – in so far as it tastes like anything else at all. Yarden is a ripe, mouthfilling, but crisp Cabernet from Israel: more powerful, more New World than Bordeaux.

Red burgundy

If claret is by far the most widely mimicked of red wines, burgundy is the one that has most challenged – and frustrated – those who have tried to replicate it elsewhere. The extremely fussy Pinot Noir has belligerently thwarted most attempts to make it settle abroad. As it is the only red grape variety of mainstream burgundy (that is the Côte d'Or with all its famous and famously tiny villages and vineyards), its behaviour has very effectively limited the development of convincing red burgundy-style wines. And, while Cabernet Sauvignon is capable of developing attractive regional characteristics, depending on climate or *terroir*, no new region has yet shown that it can give some desirable different dimension to Pinot Noir.

This is great news for Burgundians, but not for all the rest of us who would love to be able to experience more of, and more cheaply, those ethereal scents and silky textures: that signature combination of elegance and gorgeous pure fruit flavours (raspberries, strawberries, cherries, cranberries…) with, as the wine matures, burgundy's unique *goût de terroir*, the strange decaying, composty, gamey or farmyardy richness which may come from the limestone soil, wild yeasts, the grapes themselves, bacteria – or all four.

The two principal difficulties with growing Pinot Noir are its sensitivity to climate and its predilection to mutate. Pinot Noir is so prone to mutate that many of the early overseas growers originally planted disease-resistant, high-yielding, but poor quality clones; and they tended to plant just one, instantly reducing their chances of achieving complex wines. Having sorted out climatic

and clonal requirements and been harvested at exactly the optimum moment, Pinot Noir needs to be handled in the winery with particular care – that is to say as little as possible.

All that said, the end of the eighties saw breakthroughs in several parts of the world, so much so that many of the younger generation of Burgundian producers have responded to the challenge by striving to improve the quality of their own wines. The result is rising standards of Pinot Noir in both the Old World and the New.

USA

The discovery of some ideally cool, sea breeze-chilled pockets in California – especially Carneros, the valleys of Santa Barbara County, and the Russian River Valley in Sonoma County – has transformed the quality and style of the state's Pinot Noirs. Their number will always be limited, but the best young wines are beautifully aromatic, have a great purity and freshness of fruit and, with punctilious oak ageing, develop some complexity. This is not (yet?) the decaying, farmyardy complexity of great mature burgundy, but not all California's Pinot Noir producers consider this a cause for regret.

In the mid-eighties, before California Pinot Noir had found its feet, cool-climate Oregon in the Pacific

(*Below*) **The pure fruit flavours of cranberries, raspberries and cherries are signature notes of great red burgundy.**

Northwest was being touted as the promised land. It could yet turn out to be, but the wine industry is still very young, especially to be tackling so fickle a subject as Pinot Noir. At present the Oregon style is strong on refined, classic fruit aromas and flavours, but lighter on breadth and excitement.

Australia

Pinot Noir has a far longer history here than in California, but as a source of alternatives to burgundy, Australia lags behind. As in the USA, the seeking out of cooler climates in the eighties has brought what success there is, particularly in the Yarra Valley, Mornington Peninsula and Geelong (three regions around Melbourne), but even here the wines, which are expensive by Australian standards, tend to have the delicious fruit of young burgundy, but not its breadth and velvety depth. Tasmania clearly has potential, but has yet to realise it, while most Western Australian attempts at Pinot leave me wondering whether it is ever going to be really at home here.

New Zealand

The cool climate and southerly latitude make highly promising Pinot Noir territory on the South Island. The industry is still in its infancy, but there have been encouraging starts – wines with flavour and finesse – in Martinborough, Waipara in Canterbury, and Central Otago.

South Africa

Until recently there was only one good South African Pinot Noir, Hamilton Russell (from the southerly Walker Bay region), which, though fairly light, is distinctly burgundian, with typically silky-sweet burgundian fruit. But the availability since 1987 of better clones should soon begin to yield some serious competition.

France

Côte Chalonnaise wine is hardly an alternative to burgundy, it is burgundy, but from the rather underestimated region south of the Côte d'Or where the villages of Givry, Mercurey and Rully produce good value wine with plenty of fruit, but less concentration than the classic style. They are much closer in spirit (as well as geographically) to the Côte d'Or than the Pinot Noirs of Sancerre and Alsace: red Sancerre (and its less fashionable neighbour Menetou-Salon) and Alsace are altogether paler, lighter and thinner than burgundy. Beaujolais is also technically part of Burgundy, but its wines, made from the Gamay grape and by an idiosyncratic production process ('carbonic maceration', *see* page 89), are quite different – with the exception of Moulin-à-Vent, the most powerful of Beaujolais wines and one that, from a good vintage, can become increasingly burgundian after five or so years.

Others

Germany will never be a profound red wine producing country, but a small band of new wave producers is showing that Pinot Noir (there called Spätburgunder), especially when lightly oaked, need not be pale and vapid.

In Spain, Torres in Penedès and Raimat in Costers del Segre are the only two producers to be successful with Pinot Noir (albeit giving it a distinctly Spanish spicy-oak character), but few have tried.

(*Above*) **The village of Vosne-Romanée in the heart of Burgundy's Côte de Nuits is famous for its Grand Cru vineyards – Romanée-Conti, La Tâche and Richebourg among them – which produce the most splendidly aromatic, rich and velvety of red burgundies.**

White burgundy

Great white burgundy doesn't come in just one style. It doesn't even come in just two – the wine of every village has its characteristic nuances – but it is possible all the same to differentiate between two distinct styles: those of Chablis and the Côte d'Or. The Chablis area, Burgundy's cold, frost-susceptible northern outpost, produces a wine that is minerally, steely, streamlined and bone dry. It shares little with mainstream white burgundy from further south other than a hard-to-define savoury, almost vegetal complexity which both acquire with age. Chablis is the style of white burgundy that has almost totally eluded the rest of the world (the reason seems to be Chablis' rare soil type). In contrast, the Côte d'Or style – epitomised by the rich, fat, buttery, walnuts-and-cinnamon Meursault wines and the similarly full-bodied, but slightly tauter, firmer, fleetingly smoky character of Puligny-Montrachet – has proved to be much more promiscuous (even if the quality of its very greatest examples has yet to be matched).

The reason is Chardonnay. Chardonnay, from which almost all white burgundies and certainly all the great ones are made, despite being appreciated for the full-bodied, flavoursome wines it mostly produces, doesn't actually have much personality.

(Below) **The richness of the great white burgundies is expressed in aromas of walnuts and hazelnuts, toast and butter.**

That is its virtue. It can be moulded pretty much to order, which means winemakers in the New World can, if they wish, play down their non-burgundian

(*Left*) **Looking down on to the mist-filled valleys of Burgundy: the best vineyards are on the slopes rather than the valley floor. This is Vézelay, south of Chablis, the home of the drier, steelier, more minerally style of white burgundy.**

tropical fruit flavours and enhance the buttery, nutty, toasted ones that mark the burgundian end of the spectrum.

Chardonnay's malleability means that in many cases regional styles may be even more blurred than for other varieties: a style can so easily be less a reflection of a particular *terroir* and more an indication of the producer's financial resources and intended market. To get the creamy, nutty flavours of fine burgundy, for example, the winemaker needs to mature the wine on its flavour-giving lees in a proportion of, if not all, new French oak barrels that cost approximately £300 ($460) each; he must also ferment it in the same barrels rather than in huge, easy-to-monitor-and-maintain stainless steel tanks. There are shortcuts, but these tend to give simple, flattering tastes in the short-term but not the depth, texture, complexity and longevity of great burgundy. For these there is no way round time, effort and expense.

USA

The keynotes of the California Chardonnay style are very similar to the Cabernet ones – ripe fruit, power, oak. But the better Chardonnays – coming from newer, cooler regions south of San Francisco, as well as the traditional high quality areas of Napa Valley, Sonoma and Carneros – are not the alcoholic overweights they were 10 to 15 years ago. (Nor are they the lean, ascetic aberrations that appeared in the mid-eighties when the pendulum swung, mercifully briefly, too far the other way). Their fruit flavours, even from the cooler vineyards, are always likely to be riper, slightly more exotic than burgundy's; the buttery, vanilla oak taste is nearly always more prominent (whereas in fine burgundy oak is used more to give structure and ageing potential than specific flavours); the acidity is lower; and California Chardonnay is made to be drunk within a few years. But that doesn't stop the best wines from developing some complexity. The less good are over-filtered, squeaky-clean, with fruit, oak and nothing else (all other flavours having been stripped out by over zealous use of new technology in the winery) and cheap California Chardonnay usually has a slight sweetness that palls very quickly.

Of the other states producing Chardonnay, New York – Long Island with its mild, maritime climate even more than the Finger Lakes – is showing the greatest promise: already there are some wines with a nutty, yet elegant richness that more than fleetingly resembles that of Puligny-Montrachet.

Washington State is still finding its feet in a style somewhere between that of California and the rather austere, sharp character of neighbouring Oregon. And Texas, surprisingly, is one to watch, though Chardonnay is still in its infancy.

Australia

Australia doesn't produce Chablis-like Chardonnays, or light, aromatic, flowery ones like those of Italy's Alto Adige, but most other permutations can be found. The warm areas, such as Barossa Valley and above all Hunter Valley, produce the fattest – packed with ripe pineapple fruit and a butterscotch richness. Cooler areas, such as Padthaway, Yarra Valley, Margaret River (in Western Australia) and Tasmania are capable of much more European style Chardonnays – concentrated and racy, with well-defined citrus aspects. But the Australian wine industry is the one most geared to producing whatever style of wine is required by the buyer, so these are by no means hard and fast styles.

Blends of Semillon and Chardonnay may, with their waxy, citrus taste, remind you of Australian Chardonnay, but they are unlikely to remind you of burgundy. Curiously, though, Hunter Valley Semillon develops, without any oak ageing, a rich, toasted, honeyed character in maturity that is more than a little burgundian.

New Zealand

In five years New Zealand has shot to the forefront of the world Chardonnay stage. The cool climate, particularly of the Gisborne area, can ripen Chardonnay to perfection, giving fruit flavours of great clarity and concentration, but not the tropical fruit salad character of hot countries. When high natural acidity and alcohol are complemented by full, buttery richness and toasty oak, results can be impressively Meursault-like.

South America

The average Chilean Chardonnay is not on a par with those of California, Australia or New Zealand and is even more unlikely to be mistaken for burgundy. At present, they are generally cheaper productions, with pleasantly ripe fruit, medium body and a certain amount of oak to give immediate flavour rather than structure and complexity – but they are improving with every vintage.

South Africa

Chardonnay only really began to take off in the second half of the eighties with the availabiliy of

(*Above and below*) **New World Chardonnays are usually much more boldly fruity than white burgundy.**

better clones, so it is early days. The evolving character looks destined to be less ebulliently fruity, more European-style than California or Australian, but many producers still need to be less heavy-handed with the oak.

France

As with red burgundy, the lesser known southern areas of Burgundy itself are a good starting point in the search for alternatives – the Mâconnais for lightish, creamy, appley Chardonnays and Côte Chalonnaise villages for slightly fuller-bodied ones. Chardonnay de l'Ardèche from further south, as made by Burgundian Louis Latour, is also convincingly burgundian in a creamy, savoury way. Other French Chardonnays tend to fall into one of two main categories: crisp, fruity, flowery and unoaked (Haut-Poitou, Vin de Pays du Jardin de la France and Savoie), a style which bears little resemblance to any burgundy, apart perhaps from having the crispness of Chablis; and the ripe, fruity, often oaky *vins de pays* of the south (particularly Vin de Pays d'Oc) which have a lot of the New World in them, but also something of Burgundy too.

Italy

There are two sharply contrasting styles of Chardonnay: the well-established, but entirely indigenous, light, crisp, aromatic, fruity wines of the far north (Alto Adige and Friuli) for drinking within two to three years; and the big, rich, oaky wines made (as *vini da tavola*) by famous names in the red wine areas of Chianti, Brunello di Montalcino, Barolo and Barbaresco. They are designed, on Meursault lines, to compete with the world's best and are mostly very impressive, if occasionally a little too oaky and very expensive.

Spain

Chardonnay has not penetrated much of Spain, although the handful in Penedès are mostly good and one, Milmanda, which has real burgundian complexity, is world class. The Raimat estate in Costers del Segre turns out buttery, fruity, oaked and unoaked versions which are more New World in feel than French.

Others

Bulgaria, Hungary, Portugal, Canada, Israel, China, even chilly Germany's Pfalz region et al have all produced creditable Chardonnay – and, no doubt, yet more will join this most fashionable of bandwagons. Styles are still evolving, but, because unknown, they sometimes offer very good value.

Sancerre and Pouilly-Fumé

Sauvignon Blanc, the only grape of the Loire wines Sancerre and Pouilly-Fumé, is both assertive and uncompromising. In at least 95 percent of cases, these, its classic manifestations, are wines to enjoy when young – when intensely aromatic, even pungent, mouth-wateringly crisp and bone dry, with the smells and flavours of newly cut grass, gooseberries, currant leaves (sometimes the black-currants themselves) and often a flinty, stony or slightly smoky quality. But Sauvignon is pernickety about its climate. If, as happens periodically in the Loire, it sees too little sun, and particularly if this is exacerbated by the vines being allowed to over-produce, it will be mouth-puckeringly tart and thin. On the other hand, if it sees too much warm sun, as it tends to in California and Australia, or it is allowed to develop too much foliage, it will develop a clumsy herbaceous character with unattractive flavours of tinned asparagus and green beans, rather than the racy, fresh, pithy herbaceousness. It is fussy, too, about its soils, performing best in limestone and

(*Below*) **Textbook Sancerre and Pouilly-Fumé have the unmistakeable Sauvignon aromas of freshly cut grass and gooseberries and a slightly smoky, flinty character.**

(*Above*) **Sauvignon Blanc is much less easy to please than Chardonnay, but it is at home in the cool of Château de Nozet in Pouilly-Fumé.**

flint soils (as in the Upper Loire) and least well in rich, fertile soils (like many of those in California).

Sauvignon is no more flexible in the winery, although having few options at least makes the winemaker's life simple – provided he is skilled at handling those few options. On its own (that is without Sémillon, its traditional partner in white Bordeaux) it seldom takes to oak, although Californians who are fond of their own oaked Fumé style would disagree. The successes with oak tend to be where the wine has been fermented, as well as matured, in barrels and these are the only wines with the potential to develop with age.

New Zealand
France and New Zealand are the two countries that produce outstanding Sauvignon Blanc in any quantity, but New Zealand, which only began producing it commercially in the eighties, is the more consistent, because of its climate. The New Zealand style, epitomised by the Marlborough region, is almost explosively intense and vibrant, vividly grassy, with crunchy gooseberry flavours and tangy acidity (and no oak) – Loire-like, except that it does not have the minerally pungency.

USA
There is a handful of fine California Sauvignons (or Fumé Blancs), where the fruit flavours are concentrated, steely and crisp and oak has lent structure and depth, but most of the rest lack charm, varietal character and acidity – and are not helped by a sweetness of residual sugar. Partly this is a matter of taste: Americans like Fumés like this – ie, quite unlike Sancerre and Pouilly-Fumé; European palates do not.

Livelier, more classic Sauvignons come from Washington State, where conditions are ideal in the river valleys east of the Cascades, and, surprising though it may seem, from Texas, where vineyards are situated high up to benefit from cool nights.

Australia
Sauvignon Blanc is one of the few varieties that Australia's varied vineyards and talented winemakers seem unable to handle. Good examples of pure Sauvignon (as opposed to Semillon-Sauvignon blends in an altogether different style) are rare and there do not seem to be any up-and-coming regions.

South America
In the last few years Chile has begun to produce some new-style Sauvignons with a typically fresh, grassy character. They don't have much concentration, or the bite of a Sancerre or Pouilly-Fumé, but they are useful cheaper alternatives to New Zealand Sauvignon and are improving year by year.

South Africa
The South African style of Sauvignon – simple, grassy and fresh – is akin to Chile's. Prices are similar too.

France
Fashionable Sancerre and Pouilly-Fumé have three small, unfashionable near-neighbours and followers – Menetou-Salon, Quincy and Reuilly. Menetou-Salon comes closest in style and quality, but happily at prices some way below. Sauvignon de Touraine from further down the Loire is less concentrated with a more one dimensional grassy character – but reasonable prices – and Haut-Poitou's Sauvignon, from just south of the Loire is usually more impressive with its zesty fruit and acidity.

Sauvignon in Bordeaux tends to be aggressively grassy, even stalky, and most is wisely blended with Sémillon, but Bergerac and Côtes de Duras on the Dordogne to the east produce some attractive gooseberry-flavoured Sauvignons. Sauvignon de St-Bris is an oddball from northern Burgundy which tends to be heavier in style than Sancerre or Pouilly-Fumé but with some of their pungency. Growers in the *vin de pays* regions of the south are also beginning to dabble with Sauvignon: results with this tricky grape are inevitably mixed, but worth trying.

Italy
There are quite a few pockets of Sauvignon scattered in Italy, but not much in the way of coherent styles (it is often blended with other varieties and/or oak-aged in the Bordeaux manner). The principal exception is the wines of Collio in Friuli, which have much much more character and concentration than those of Alto Adige, and have the penetrating intensity of Sancerre and Pouilly-Fumé, but with slightly sweeter fruit. The new Tuscan wine, Poggio alla Gazze, hasn't yet achieved the steely French intensity, but is already very impressive.

Spain
Crisp, medium-bodied, herby whites from Rueda may contain Sauvignon Blanc and are the nearest Spain gets to the mouth-watering French style – except, that is, for Fransola, a mostly Sauvignon blend from the ever-innovative Torres in Penedès.

Others
Bright, fruity, clean-cut, but not particularly assertive Sauvignons are now coming out of Hungary and Moldova.

German Riesling

So unfashionable is Riesling wine that British wine merchants often now encourage Australian producers to abandon the traditional tall slim Riesling bottle in favour of a burgundy or Bordeaux shape. Some producers go a stage further and drop the name Riesling altogether in favour of an amorphous 'Dry White'. Either way the strategy works: it sells more bottles. But, sadly, I can't believe it does anything to help restore the reputation of the classic German Riesling styles, which sank steadily in the seventies and eighties as the name was increasingly abused.

Ironically, it was most abused on its home territory – by the rising tide of ever blander and more dilute, semi-sweet Liebfraumilch, Bereich Nierstein, Bernkastel et al. These wines were increasingly made from less fine grape varieties, such as Müller-Thurgau, and unfortunately, consumers erroneously associated them with Riesling. Elsewhere it suffered from imposters – most importantly in Europe from Welschriesling (variously called Laski Rizling, Olasz Rizling or Riesling Italico), but also in California, from Gray Riesling (or Pinot Gris) and Emerald Riesling, in Australia from Semillon, and in New Zealand from 'Riesling-Sylvaner' (Müller-Thurgau).

(*Above*) **Steep slopes in the chilly northern climate of Germany's Rheingau region are ideal for picking up the best of the sun.**

(*Below*) **German Riesling flavours range from crisp, green apple in the Mosel to sweet peaches and apricots in the warmer Pfalz.**

In fact German Rieslings span the spectrum of bone dry to extremely sweet, but the classic styles are the medium-dry to medium-sweet *Kabinett*, *Spätlese* and *Auslese* (for more on the official classification of German wines *see* Germany, page 110–11). Even among these, the fruit flavours range from the crispest and crunchiest of apples with a twist of lemon (Mosel), to the riper, slightly spicy flavours of the Pfalz and the honeyed apricots and peaches of the sweet wines. With age Riesling develops a distinctive petrol (or kerosene) character and soft honeyed notes, but for those who don't care for the petrol notes, one of the great joys of the variety is that, despite its longevity, Riesling is also scintillating in its youth.

Australia

Riesling and Australia have gone hand in hand since German settlers in the Barossa Valley arrived with cuttings. Today it is a high quality and commercially important variety in many regions, but the best wines come from Clare Valley and from Eden Valley (in the Adelaide Hills). These are inevitably bigger and more alcoholic than German Rieslings, but their flavours are not dissimilar. The distinctive Australian character is a mouth-watering lime flavour, often with a touch of passion-fruit or guava. With age, the best wines develop a honey-and-toast, occasionally a petrol character, but the petrol character is less sought by Australians.

New Zealand

While most winemakers have been concentrating on Sauvignon and Chardonnay, those who have put some effort into Riesling have shown that New Zealand's cool maritime climate makes it well worth while. The style is more Germanic than any other – crisp, fragrant and fruity, but less steely or minerally. There are some good late-harvest (sweet) wines too.

USA

Riesling is not a widely successful grape in the USA. The vast majority of California Rieslings are off-dry, fairly bland, commerical wines, although there are a few that are stunning, opulent and sweet. Washington State and Oregon are climatically more suited and Washington in particular produces some good wines, in all styles from dry to lusciously sweet. But perhaps the best American Rieslings – certainly the most Germanic – are those from the Finger Lakes in New York State.

France

Alsace, at one time annexed to Germany, is the only region of France to grow this German grape variety and the wines are altogether bigger, drier and more alcoholic in style than their German counterparts. At their best (from limited yields) they have marvellous, slightly spicy apple flavours and distinct minerally notes which need time to show through an initial austerity, but the cheaper versions all too often have a rather unripe, stalky, apple-pips-and-skins character. In good vintages, some grapes will be picked late in the autumn (when they have become extra-ripe) to make *vendange tardive* and *sélection des grains nobles* styles. These are rich, ripe and concentrated, although in the case of *vendange tardive* not necessarily very sweet, and they are also bigger and more alcoholic than their late-picked and botrytised counterparts from Germany.

Austria

Rieslings from Austria are one of the wine world's great secrets, perhaps because the Austrians drink them all themselves. If you do get the opportunity, expect to taste top quality, gloriously fruity, aromatic wines that lie between Alsace and Germany in style and weight.

Italy

There is not much true Riesling in Italy (most is the inferior, unrelated Italico Riesling) and what there is is usually rather neutral.

(Left) **In Australia, particularly in Clare Valley, Riesling emerges with a delicious lime flavour.**

Champagne

(*Above*) **The Aube, the southernmost of Champagne's subdivisions, concentrates on the red grapes Pinot Meunier and Pinot Noir.**

Champagne producers are still convinced – or at least they say they are – that to make an equivalent sparkling wine it is not enough merely to plant the same grape varieties (Chardonnay, Pinot Noir and Pinot Meunier) in a comparable cold climate (assuming such exists) and to reproduce the champagne method (the *méthode champenoise* – or *méthode traditionelle* when used outside Champagne – in which a second fermentation and maturation on the flavour-giving lees take place in bottle). In terms of style the new sparkling wines tend to be more overtly fruity with softer acidity and less structure than champagne, which makes them ready to drink sooner, but also shorter-lived. The trend is certainly towards greater elegance, but the majority still just lose out to champagne when it comes to complexity, underlying intensity (as opposed to upfront flavour) and length of flavour. And there are three particular facets of champagne's character that prove hard to reproduce, or at least match: the subtle but rich, biscuity, bready, yeasty flavours that it develops from ageing on its lees (undergoing the process called yeast autolysis); the toasted, nutty character that comes not from oak but simply from maturing Chardonnay; and the gorgeous raspberry fruit of good Pinot Noir-based champagnes.

Other sparkling wines do not match up to champagne, the Champenois maintain, because they do not come from the same type of chalk soil. And it is perfectly true that there is very little chalk or limestone in New World vineyards. But growers counter that it is not the chemical properties of the chalk and limestone that are significant but their physical properties – they drain well, but also retain moisture at depth without becoming waterlogged –

and these physical properties are certainly not the exclusive preserve of French chalk/limestone soils.

Whatever the truth of claim and counter claim, from the point of view of sheer finesse and complexity, the finest champagnes still undoubtedly have the edge over the best of all the rest – and no doubt they should when they cost consumers so much more. But, equally undeniably, the best Australian, New Zealand and California sparkling wines (most of which, ironically, are made by, or in conjunction with, champagne houses) are superior to the worst champagnes selling at much the same price. Moreover, although the quality of the poorest champagnes should now be starting to improve as a

(*Below*) **The rich, biscuity, hazelnuts character of champagne is the aspect that is hardest to reproduce – elegantly – elsewhere.**

result of more rigorous production laws introduced in 1992, the standards of New World sparkling wines are improving with every vintage as wine-makers master the processes, as grape quality rises with increasingly mature vines and as stocks are built up of the older 'reserve' wines that are so fundamental to champagne.

USA

In California there are now nine champagne houses making sparkling wine, either on their own or in partnership with local firms, and the results range from quite good to very good indeed when leaner fruit flavours are matched by some creamy depth. While cooler areas like Anderson Valley and Carneros are gaining ground, there are impressive results from the warmer Napa Valley. There are also particularly good wines emerging from some of the Californian producers without Champagne connections – although, just to confuse matters, these are often labelled 'Champagne' in the USA where (unlike Europe) there is no protection of the name.

All eyes have also been on the cooler state of Oregon recently, where the champagne house Laurent-Perrier has invested, but it is going to be the end of the century before any of its new fizz is actually released.

Australia

Alongside masses of admirably cheap, cheerfully clean, soft and fruity sparkling wines which don't have much in common with champagne, Australia has an increasing number of high-class Chardonnay and Pinot Noir blends from cooler areas such as the Adelaide Hills, southern Victoria and even wind-swept Tasmania. These usually have slightly more fruit flavour (apple, citrus, melon) and a little less creamy depth than champagne, but the Champenois cannot afford to feel complacent. (As in California, when in Australia watch out for bogus use of the name champagne.)

New Zealand

With sparkling wines, as with still white wines, New Zealand has made the world sit up. It is early yet but the quality is already excellent and, in at least one case (made by expatriate Champenois Daniel le Brun in the Marlborough region), the result has come closer to champagne than any other sparkling wine. The Champenois must watch out.

France

The closest French approximation to champagne is Crémant de Bourgogne, but it is not all that close.

Although made from the same grapes it is a coarser wine – buttery, but also cabbagey.

Blanquette de Limoux from the south has improved in recent years, but it is hard to confuse its appley, slightly earthy flavour with champagne's. Similarly, Saumur and Vouvray from the Loire, made from the Chenin Blanc grape, have a different style. They tend to be quite acid, and in mediocre years rather stalky, but in good vintages Vouvray in particular can have a lovely sweet fruit and toasted nut character. Crémant d'Alsace has a more flowery fruity style than champagne, as does Savoie sparkling wine at its best.

Spain

Spain turns out a sea of *cava* (sparkling wine) and producers have been trying hard to improve quality, but the basic problem is the undistinguished local grapes they use. Only the enjoyable Chardonnays of the firms of Codorníu and Raimat bear some slight resemblance to champagne.

Italy

Italy, too, produces vast quantities of sparkling wines, many using the *metodo classico* (*méthode traditionelle*), but most are not very champagne-like. The exceptions, mostly from Franciacorta in the north, range in style from much crisper and leaner than champagne to much richer and fatter (and occasionally impressively toasty).

UK

English and Welsh wine producers have recently identified sparkling wine as an area suited to their cool maritime climate. It is early days yet for most of them, but some crisp, dry, elegantly fruity wines are being made — albeit at a price.

India

The Omar Khayyam brand of sparkling wine is proof that you can do anything if you are determined enough. The vineyards are high in the hills southeast of Bombay and the Indian owner has brought in Champagne expertise. Quality has been a bit erratic in the eight years since the first bottles were released, but when good you could mistake it for champagne.

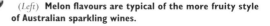
(Left) **Melon flavours are typical of the more fruity style of Australian sparkling wines.**

Sauternes

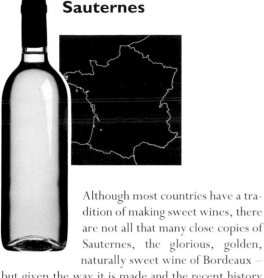

Although most countries have a tradition of making sweet wines, there are not all that many close copies of Sauternes, the glorious, golden, naturally sweet wine of Bordeaux — but given the way it is made and the recent history of Sauternes, perhaps that isn't surprising. Great Sauternes, with its luscious taste of honey and *crème brûlée* offset by flavours of apricot, peach and pineapple, and its lanolin texture, is the product of Sémillon and Sauvignon Blanc grapes which have been horribly shrivelled and dehydrated by a fungus (*Botrytis cinerea* or 'noble rot') that only appears in particular warm, humid autumn weather conditions. Some years it doesn't arrive at all, in which case, if you are lucky, you will be able to make a very good sweet wine, but not one with the extraordinary honeyed opulence, unctuousness and longevity of a classic vintage. In addition, because of the dehydration of the grapes, you need at least

twice as many to produce each bottle of wine as you do to make red or dry white Bordeaux of comparable quality.

As for history, Sauternes was in the doldrums for decades until the eighties. Unfashionable, unloved and neglected, prices had dropped until it was scarcely economic to produce a fine wine, which meant that producers didn't try and standards were often very low. No wonder there were few pioneers of the Sauternes style elsewhere. The turnabout came in 1983 with a long overdue outstanding vintage (rapidly followed by very good

(*Above*) **Morning mist and afternoon sun are the ingredients Sauternes properties such as Château Guiraud hope for in the autumn to induce 'noble rot'.**

(*Below*) **Honey, apricots and pineapple – some of the flavours that give great Sauternes its lusciousness and intensity.**

ones in 1986, 1988, 1989 and 1990). Wine drinkers suddenly realised what they had been missing. Sauternes became fashionable, expensive and sought after and was tentatively followed by a few more winemakers elsewhere.

USA

In California, as in Australia, most botrytis-affected wines are made from Riesling, but even these, because of their more powerful style, are sometimes as Sauternes-like as they are Germanic. There are also some excellent Sémillon-Sauvignon botrytis wines being made in the classic way – although it is more usual to induce botrytis artificially either in the vineyards or after picking. The clue to most sweet wines is the description 'late harvest'.

Australia and New Zealand

Despite the amount of Semillon grown and made into dry white wine, Sauternes-style botrytised Semillon is rare in Australasia. The first such wine was a 1982 made by De Bortoli in the mass-market wine producing region of Murrumbidgee in New South Wales. It caused a sensation, but even so there has been no rush to follow. There are, though, more botrytised Rieslings. Labelled 'Beerenauslese', 'Trockenbeeren-auslese' or 'Late Harvest', these are made in a Germanic style: sweet, concentrated and fragrantly fruity – and lower in alcohol and with much less fat than Sauternes.

France

Cérons, Premières Côtes de Bordeaux, Ste-Croix-du-Mont, Loupiac and Cadillac are Bordeaux appellations quite close to Sauternes that are capable of producing wines in the same manner, but in a lighter style. Sadly standards are not generally high but, where producers try, the results are often more attractive, modestly priced alternatives. Much the same can be said for Monbazillac in the Bergerac region to the east, although here, if anything, the situation is even more disappointing because Monbazillac was once a wine counted in the same breath as Sauternes.

(*Left*) **Orange and orange marmalade are among the flavours that make sweet Hungarian Tokays so distinctive.**

Moving north, botrytis sometimes affects Chenin Blanc grapes in the Loire Valley, giving to wines such as Coteaux du Layon, Bonnezeaux, Quarts de Chaume, Vouvray and Montlouis a wonderful depth of honeyed fruit (apricot, apple, nectarine...) and a flavour of almond marzipan, always underpinned by the high acidity of the Chenin grape. They never have the opulence and fat of Sauternes, but they have such intensity they can last an extraordinarily long time. Vouvray and Montlouis can also be dry, or medium-dry wines (as well as sparkling) so look for the word *moelleux* (sweet) or some indication of a special *cuvée*, or selection.

In Alsace, when noble rot strikes, producers make *sélection des grains nobles* wines. From Gewurztraminer grapes (highly individual, aromatic and spicy, sharing with Sémillon an oily character), the wines can have a surprisingly similar weight and texture to Sauternes.

Germany

It doesn't make sense to leave out Germany's superb *Beerenauslese* and *Trockenbeerenauslese* wines – made from nobly rotten Riesling grapes in fine vintages – but they are quite different in style from Sauternes. Intensely sweet, fragrant and honeyed, they have great ageing potential because of their higher acidity, but are much less fat and alcoholic than Sauternes.

Hungary

Hungary's historic sweet wines, Tokay (or Tokaji) Aszú and Eszencia, are like no other wines, but they deserve a place here all the same. Fabled for their curative and life-giving properties – as well as their own, apparently indefinite, lifespan – they are made from botrytised grapes, idiosyncratically processed, then matured in a sherry-like manner. The result is a cornucopia of Christmas pudding, orange marmalade, baked apple and toffee flavours, against a sherry-like oxidised background – odd but delicious.

Austria

Austria's dessert wines, mostly from Burgenland, are more similar to the German style than to Sauternes, but to some extent they are a half-way, or perhaps a quarter-way house. The best – which are at last just beginning to be seen outside Austria – have an extraordinary concentration and harmony of fruit and botrytis aromas and flavours.

Sherry and Port
– the two great fortified wines

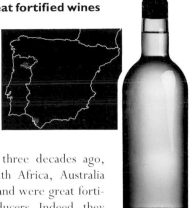

Only two or three decades ago, the USA, South Africa, Australia and New Zealand were great fortified wine producers. Indeed, they made and drank little else, but when the age of table wine dawned in these countries, fortified wines began to decline in popularity, and consequently production. There are increasingly few of them and increasingly few exported. The classics themselves, on which these wines were based – sherry above all – have also been having a hard time of it with today's consumers. We should beware of letting these great pre- and postprandials fall from the late 20th century repertoire.

Sherry, from the Jerez region of Spain, was once the classic aperitif in Britain, but it started to go out of favour around 1980 and consumption has been in free-fall ever since – a shame because the pale, dry *fino* and *manzanilla* styles really are perfect appetite whetters – and also surprisingly versatile with food (*see* Matching Food and Wine, pages 30–39).

The trouble is that the dryness of most sherry seems austere to palates brought up on the typically ripe, soft, fruity wines of today. So sherry nowadays is a taste that often has to be acquired – just as wine itself – but once acquired ever hooked. The problem is compounded by the fact that a great deal of sherry exported to Britain isn't true to type. It is deliberately sweetened to make it more saleable, with the result that most people (believing that *amontillado* is medium sherry and *oloroso* is sweet) never experience the real things: *fino* and *manzanilla* that are mouth-wateringly crisp and dry, with the yeasty tang of the quintessential *flor* yeast and in the case of *manzanilla* a sea-salty freshness; *amontillado* that is equally bone dry, but darker in colour, fuller bodied and with a nutty character; and *oloroso* – still dry, but richer, fuller, warmer and nuttier, without the yeasty tang (*see* Spain, page 128).

Of the imitations, Australian sherry styles come closest in quality and character to their role models, with some particularly good 'Finos'; South Africa still has a substantial fortified wine industry producing reasonably good sherry types, although never achieving the finesse of the best (Australia and South Africa produce sherry styles by inoculating the newly fermented and fortified wines with *flor* yeast); and USA sherry styles are no longer significant – perhaps because they were so seldom any good.

In Europe, Cyprus continues to turn out rather coarse copies, while Britain continues to make low grade, cheap British sherry from reconstituted grape concentrate rather than from fresh grapes (but from the end of 1995 it

(Below) **The chalky albariza soil of Jerez that suits the Palomino grape so well.**

will no longer be allowed to call itself sherry). Montilla from Spain is another cheap alternative, broadly similar to sherry, but unfortified and lacking the depth of flavour.

When sherry was the classic aperitif, port was the classic wine taken late-on in a meal with stilton, and sipped for long after it. Made from indigenous grape varieties grown high up the Douro Valley in Portugal, but traditionally aged in the port shippers' Lodges at the river's mouth at Porto, port is sweet, red, heavy and alcoholic – almost everything that modern table wine isn't.

Despite the single strong image, there are actually several styles of port (including medium or dry white port drunk as an aperitif), but the main divide is between bottle-aged port, epitomised by vintage port, and wood-aged tawny port. In character they are very different. Vintage port, made only in the best years and seldom ready to be drunk before it is at least 10, sometimes 20 years old, is very deep coloured, intensely fruity (often reminiscent of blackcurrants, plums and dried figs), rich, very sweet, often chocolatey and, when young, extremely and undrinkably tannic. Vintage port should not taste of wood. By contrast, the aptly named tawny is much paler and browner (indeed tawny) and has a mellow, nutty, slightly woody, dried fruit character, derived from contact with air during its long maturation in porous wooden casks. Unlike vintage port, it should be served lightly chilled and can even make a good aperitif.

In theory, both vintage and tawny are copied in the new wine producing continents. In practice, the tawny styles heavily predominate, but they tend to be a compromise between the two. In South Africa even more than Australia, tawny styles tend to be much fuller, fruitier and more powerful than gen-

(*Above*) **Harvesting the terraced or steeply inclined port vineyards of the Douro Valley is back-breaking and sun-burning work.**

uine tawny port. The most successful vintage styles are made in tiny quantities in Australia and are usually based on the Shiraz (Syrah) grape, which gives a more aromatic and usually sweeter wine.

In Europe, sweet red fortified wines are made in the south of France in Rivesaltes and Banyuls. Lower in alcohol than port, they are made from the Grenache grape and aged in wood to give a lighter, spicier, woodier style than tawny's.

Italy's answer to port is its idiosyncratic sweet Recioto della Valpolicella. This is not a fortified wine, but is more alcoholic than normal table wine because the harvested grapes are left to dry (dehydrate and become more concentrated) before fermentation. If the wine stops fermentation before all the sugar has been converted into alcohol, the result is intense, sweet wine, with complex, bitter cherry fruit and rich, herby, sometimes gamey flavours. (If the wine ferments to dryness the result is Recioto della Valpolicella Amarone.)

(*Below*) **The fuller styles of sherry – amontillado and oloroso – share with tawny port a nutty character; vintage port is intensely rich and fruity with the flavours of blackcurrants and plums as well as dried fruits.**

Hermitage and Côte Rôtie

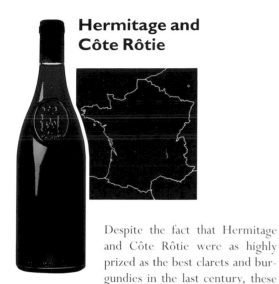

(*Above*) **The steep Hermitage hill on the east bank of the Rhône is difficult to work, but worth the trouble because of its favourable exposure to the sun and granitic soil.**

Despite the fact that Hermitage and Côte Rôtie were as highly prized as the best clarets and burgundies in the last century, these great red Syrah wines from the northern Rhône, with their immense colour, body, flavour and longevity, have not been much emulated. Their popularity is rising again now, but for a long time the tide seemed to be against wines with such massive colour, body and tannin – against wine, particularly Hermitage, the more massive and famous of the two, which took time to show its enticing berry aromas and rich gamey complexity through a mask of often tarry, leathery tannins. Even Australia, with far more of the Syrah grape (under the name Shiraz) than France and its greatest wine called Grange Hermitage (although the Hermitage part has been dropped in Europe), doesn't really produce many Hermitage likenesses. Indeed Grange's creator in the fifties was inspired by claret – he had never been to the Rhône Valley. Most Shirazes, with a spicy berry flavour and often a typically Australian mint character (although this is more obvious in the blend with Cabernet), are softer, suppler, shorter-lived than the Rhône Syrahs. Even the impressive, weighty, age-worthy exceptions, which are mostly small productions of very old Barossa vines, are approachable much younger.

California has its cultish Rhône Rangers – the not very serious name given to wines made from the Rhône grape varieties (Syrah, Grenache, Viognier, etc) and their undeniably serious winemakers. Some of the Syrahs are outstanding – often in the slightly more perfumed, more elegant Côte Rôtie mould than the hulking Hermitage one, but they are made in tiny quantities at inevitably high prices.

Syrah *vins de pays* from the south of France are a new and growing breed. They don't have the weight, depth, complexity or tannin of northern Rhônes, but they often have the typical Syrah berry fruit, peppery spice, succulence and a mouth-filling texture.

Others

The wines above are by no means the only classic and traditional styles that have a strong identity, but they are the ones that have become international, as producers in distant countries have tried to emulate them. For widely recognised, but less travelled styles, go back to the Grapes chapter (pages 50–59) and refer to:

Gamay (for Beaujolais)
Nebbiolo (for Barolo)
Sangiovese (for Chianti)
Tempranillo (for Rioja)
Gewurztraminer (for Alsace Gewurztraminer)
Muscat (for Beaumes-de-Venise and Australian liqueur Muscats)
Sémillon and Sauvignon Blanc (for dry white Bordeaux)
Melon de Bourgogne (for Muscadet)

Then find further details in the regional chapters.

(*Below*) **The Syrah grape gives the wines of the northern Rhône tantalising berry aromas and great power.**

The vineyards:
where and why

Grapes are certainly the principal influence on the style and quality of a wine, but they are only the starting point — and as growers in the new wine world have discovered in the last quarter of a century they are not necessarily the best place to begin.

In contrast to France, where any wine aspiring to a status above basic plonk (*vin de table*) has to be made from grape varieties specifically authorised for the relevant region or appellation, the general *modus operandi* of the new pioneer producers was to acquire a plot of land in sunny California, Australia or wherever and choose their grape variety, or varieties, according to whim and/or sales aspirations. After all, vines grow in any temperate climate and flourish with plenty of warmth, water and space, so why worry about the type of soil, topography or nuances of climate — all those factors (and more) that the French combine under the name *terroir* and believe in with near religious fervour?

Why? Because flourishing vines are not necessarily the key to great or even good wine. They tend instead to produce large quantities of dilute, flavourless grapes which naturally produce dilute, flavourless wine — the vinous equivalent of large woolly-textured Mediterranean apples. Whether, as Western European tradition has it, vines really need to 'struggle' to yield grapes with the quality potential to make great wine is debatable, but there is no doubt that, with few exceptions (Coonawarra being one), for wines with any pretentions to quality and style, they need to be planted in soils where they can put down deep and wide root sys-

tems. And they don't do that if everything is presented on a plate (irrigation, fertilisers, superabundant sun and so on) at more or less surface level. They simply go into overdrive producing excessive foliage and bland grapes.

(*Above*) **Spraying water on the vines is, perhaps surprisingly, an effective way of warding off frost damage in Chablis.**

(*Below*) **Astonishingly, these stones at Domaine de la Solitude are not only characteristic of Châteauneuf-du-Pape, but they have advantages: above all, they re-radiate heat at night.**

Soil

Looking at the ideal conditions for vine cultivation – so far as such an ideal exists – it is no coincidence that the long-established European vineyards are on land where very little else thrives. Vines do, it seems, like poor soil – but there is more to it than that. Whether or not growers in the past identified the relevant factors, European experience over centuries has shown that the best soils are those that encourage root penetration, are well-drained and yet at the same time are capable of holding water without becoming water-logged. Limestone, as found in Burgundy and Champagne, but, tellingly, very little in the New World, fits this prescription perfectly; so do other rocky and gravelly soils such as those in the finest claret vineyards of the Haut-Médoc in Bordeaux. Stony soils (sometimes incredibly stony, as in Châteauneuf-du-Pape) are in fact the best all-rounders across a range of climates, for they have the advantage of being easily warmed and the capacity, through their stones, to re-radiate the heat at night, they are not too fertile and they do not readily erode. Moreover, stony soils are mostly found towards the bottom of hills and slopes, a position which often also has distinct climatic advantages such as good air drainage and exposure to the sun.

Whether in addition to a soil's physical properties, its chemical composition (mineral and microbial) influences the taste of the wine it produces is a moot point. Basically the French believe it does; the New World will have none – or not much – of it. While there is no scientific evidence to support the French view, there is no arguing that certain soils are associated with particular grape varieties and, more to the point, with particular wine styles and tastes. Plenty of experienced tasters find a slaty taste in many Mosels, an earthy taste in red Graves and a gun-flinty, steely character in Chablis, all of which they attribute to the soil.

Climate

Although to the French, with their notion of *terroir*, the influences of climate and soil are inextricably bound, the role of climate is actually more clear-cut. Put very simply, growers in the Old World are often near the limits of successful vine cultivation and so they live with the annual prospect of too little sunshine and too much rain to produce a perfectly ripe and flavoursome crop. They also get much greater variation in quality and style from vintage to vintage. Those in much of the New World live with the prospect of too much warmth and (though they may well irrigate – to the horror of Europeans) too little rain to produce grapes with subtlety and balanced fruit, acid, alcohol and tannin. They do, however, get more consistent results.

The outcome of all this is that, to date, the world's greatest wines have come from the hotter years in the best European vineyards, for Europe, it appears, has greater quality potential, but, ironically, less likelihood of it being realised.

But growers in the New World are not taking this lying down. Increasingly, in California, Australia and South Africa, the emphasis is on microclimate, the localised climate within a climate reflecting the lie of the land – the pocket sheltered from the prevailing wind, the slopes catching cool sea breezes, fogs, an extra hour of sun or cooler night-time temperatures. Not surprisingly, the 'perfect' microclimates being sought out are essentially closer in spirit to the cooler climatic conditions of their European role models (even though, in Australia in particular, irrigation is always going to be essential). The results, already, are some great wines – both subtle and complex – but, as in Europe, there is less certainty of them being produced every year.

(*Below*) **Cooling fog, drawn in off the Pacific, is a familiar – and welcome – sight on hot days in the Napa Valley.**

Choices in the vineyard:
tending vines

Having appropriate grape varieties in suitable soil under a favourable climate does not, alas, guarantee you good wine – and it is not only that you need a good winemaker. Well before the winery and cellar stage, you need to have cared for your vines properly – trellised, trained, pruned, treated for disease and inclement weather and picked them to their best advantage.

The value of careful husbandry was one of the great lessons that producers in the New World began to learn in the late eighties. Until then, they had put almost all their efforts into what happened in the winery, believing that science and technology were sufficient to ensure good wine. What they found of course was that they ensured sound, technically correct wine, but, as any cook could have told them, the end result could only ever be as good as its ingredients. Today the pendulum has swung firmly towards the vineyards.

Pruning and training

Looking at the neat rows of trellis-trained vines in many a modern vineyard, it is perhaps hard to visualise how, left alone, most vines would become rambling masses of branches, shoots and leaves climbing up any available trees. The more luxuriant they became, the more the grape bunches would be shaded from essential sunlight and the more erratic

(*Below*) **Some New World producers have begun to question the value of hard winter pruning, but in the Old World, as here in Champagne, it is a key stage in the vineyard year.**

their growth would become. This is the traditional view that explains the overwhelming norm of hard pruning, whether by hand or machine, during a vine's winter dormant period.

But in recent years this tradition (like so many others) has been challenged in the New World, particularly in Australia, where some growers have abandoned the expensive practice of winter pruning altogether (they do a minimal amount of summer pruning) and have apparently found that, contrary to previous evidence, unpruned vines show considerable self-discipline: they not only keep their vegetation growth in check, but they produce bunches on the outside of the canopy where there is maximum exposure to sun. Supporters of such 'minimal pruning' say that, although yields increase, so does quality. The majority of producers have yet to be convinced and it is certain that pruning will remain a primary quality controller for the time being.

Another hot topic, related but less controversial, is 'canopy management' – the canopy being the potentially sunlight-blocking foliage. The aim of this practice is simply to allow leaves and fruit the best possible exposure by using a combination of techniques including new trellising systems, shoot thinning, summer pruning and leaf removal.

Yield

All the above practices affect the grape yield (output) and the yield affects wine quality – high yields adversely so – which is why the French *appellation contrôlée* system (*see* France, page 96), and the many other appellation systems based on it, specify maximum yields and ban irrigation. But the equation isn't as simple as that. While there is no denying that there comes a level of output above which quality deteriorates (basically all the flavours are diluted), there are all sorts of variables to consider.

Grape variety is the obvious one: the quality of Pinot Noir grapes begins to suffer at lower yields than Chardonnay, for example. Place is another: a harsh climate will naturally produce lower yields than a more moderate one. The density of planting is yet another and particularly tricky one: yields are often measured in volume per hectare, but the number of vines planted per hectare varies enormously – being much lower, for example in the New World, where mechanical harvesters are widely used (and need room to move up and down the rows) than in regions such as Burgundy where mechanisation is very limited. Generally speaking, wide spacing is thought to be less good for quality because the vines' roots tend to spread lazily hori-

The modern plagues

There are two modern vine plagues. One of them, eutypiose, is new, but the other, phylloxera, is a great 19th century wine catastrophe revisited. Phylloxera arrived in Europe on vine cuttings from America around 1860 and within two decades had wiped out most of the vineyards of France and much of the rest of vine-growing Europe and California. This time though, its area of destruction is limited largely to California because it is here that vines have the type of roots the tiny louse Phylloxera vastatrix lives and feeds on. Most other wine regions' vines have, following the 19th century devastation, been grafted on to a type of American rootstock that phylloxera doesn't like; or, as in Chile, there are natural barriers (mountain, sea, desert) to phylloxera penetration. Unfortunately, California growers were recommended a rootstock that has turned out not to be resistant to phylloxera. The result is 'a billion dollar nightmare', as the American Wine Spectator put it, with wholesale replanting during this decade. The crumb of comfort is that it is a chance to replant with better vines and according to the latest research.

Eutypiose, or, more graphically, 'dying arm disease' or the Aids of the wine world, is a fungus that appeared in France in the early eighties, first on the Ugni Blanc vines of Cognac, but now increasingly in other areas and on all sorts of grape varieties. Cabernet Sauvignon and Sauvignon Blanc are among the most susceptible, but none is immune. It has such a long incubation period (five to ten years) that research into prevention and cure is slow. So far, there is no cure, only some preventative measures.

(*Below*) **Traditional 'pergola' training with local granite supports in Galicia, northern Spain – a far cry from the New World's 'canopy management'.**

zontally rather than down through layers of soil containing different nutrients. Finally, there is the unarguable, but seemingly irreconcilable, fact that in Bordeaux and Champagne since 1982 the best vintages have been some of the largest.

There is no neat formula. In the end it has to be the responsibility not of the law but of the individual to produce the yield he or she deems appropriate to the quality of wine intended (not everyone, after all, is aiming for the stars). This might be done by a combination of pruning (winter, spring and summer), 'green-pruning' (removal of excess bunches in summer) and by considered use of fertilisers and other treatments. Which brings me neatly to another contentious area: products applied in the vineyards.

Going 'green'

In fact this is not nearly as controversial as it would have been even five years ago, as the 1992 International Symposium of Masters of Wine amply demonstrated: what was billed as the grand debate on 'Nurture versus Nature' ended up as the grand consensus. From growers through to academics, buyers and sellers, the mood was overwhelmingly green, and the gist was avoid chemical fertilisers, apply organic ones judiciously, reduce to a minimum vineyard sprays against fungi, viruses and pests and, as far as possible, use only the 'natural' ones, such as copper sulphate and natural predators. Yields will be lower, but that can be considered a positive effect. In many cases the same additive-free thinking extends to the processes in the winery, although there is a marked reluctance all round to jump headlong into the organic camp with its inflexible rules and its residual sandals-and-socks image.

Ripening and picking

You might think that deciding when to pick would be the easiest of decisions – you harvest, surely, as soon as the grapes are ripe. Well, yes and no. The grape is quite a complex fruit and deciding when it is at the optimum point of ripeness for the intended style of wine can be nail-biting (even without worrying about such threats as impending storms). Leave it a fraction late and acidity will begin to drop, resulting in increasingly flabby, short-lived wines – whites in particular. Pick a little too early and the sweetness of the fruit will be muted and probably dominated by acid, giving a tart taste (especially to white wines), and/or tannin, which

(*Above*) **Biodynamie, practised here at Coulée de Serrant in the Loire, means rigorously traditional cultivation methods.**

gives to red wines a harsh, dry, perhaps bitter taste and feel.

The difficulty is exacerbated by the fact that physiological and chemical ripeness can get out of sync. In Bordeaux in 1989 – theoretically an excellent vintage – some Merlot grapes were found to be ripe in every respect except for their tannins. When growers waited for the tannins to ripen, acid levels began to drop menacingly.

Overall, though, the art and science of harvesting at the best possible time has improved in the last decade or so, largely because of advances in winemaking. To take but one example, since winemaking is the subject of the following chapter, red grapes in Bordeaux are now generally picked later and riper than they were before control of fermentation temperatures was widely exercised, because, with such control, the higher sugar levels in the grapes need not cause fermentation to overheat and

From organic to biodynamic

Only a few years ago, 'Biodynamie', organic vine growing taken a stage further into the realms of the cosmos, as inspired by Rudolph Steiner, still looked distinctly cranky. But the first few years of the nineties have seen some of France's top growers in Burgundy and the Rhône taking an interest, and some have taken the plunge – parts of the famous Domaine Leflaive in Puligny-Montrachet are already half-way along the seven-year road to conversion. (Seven years is the length of time demanded by the rules of Biodynamie for the soil to clear itself of residual weed-killers, chemical fertilisers and synthetic crop sprays.) But Biodynamie is much more than soil management and crop cultivation using only natural and homeopathic treatments of animal and plant origin (manure, dandelions, camomile, nettles and so on) and avoiding clonally bred vines. Its most important function, to quote one its most impassioned disciples, Nicolas Joly of Coulée de Serrant in the Loire, is to 'support the life of the soil by reinforcing its links with the solar system and its cosmic background' – ie, what is actually happening in the sky. In practice this means working the vineyards and the wine according to the moon and stars. Cranky? French growers have been doing this to some extent for generations, bottling wine in the spring in accordance with the phase of the moon, for example.

stop early. Riper grapes mean sweeter, richer fruit flavours and riper, more attractive tannins.

The other critical decision, although hardly a last minute one, is whether to pick by hand or by machine. In some regions, Champagne and Jerez for example, mechanical harvesters are banned, and in others, such as Bordeaux and Burgundy, they are allowed but are little used – at least by the top properties. Hand-picking is gentler and more discriminating, say its advocates, but in the New World, where mechanical harvesters (and pruners) prevail, their supporters say the most sophisticated modern machines are sufficiently gentle and have the added advantages of being much faster than humans and available without complaint at all hours – not least in the dead of night.

(*Right*) **Mechanical harvesters are unusual in Burgundy, where landholdings are often tiny: rows of pickers bent double are a far more common sight.**

The
winemaker's role

In some ways winemaking is the easy bit. If nature and nurture have provided ripe, healthy grapes, there really is no excuse for poor wine, as the process by which grape sugars are converted into alcohol and carbon dioxide during fermentation is as simple and natural as it has always been. Indeed, wine will make itself, provided the weather is reasonably warm and that natural yeasts, which appear as the bloom on the grape skin, have not been killed off by chemical sprays in the vineyards. That presumably was how it all started.

It would be daft, though, to imply that winemakers were in any way redundant. Wine left to make itself would in most cases soon be bacterially spoiled – on its way to vinegar – because once it has finished fermenting it needs to be protected from oxygen. But, as the pendulum has swung more towards the role of the grower in the vineyard in determining quality, so it has swung away from the wine-maker as interventionist wizard, a role which reached its apogee in some of the high-tech wineries of California and Australia in the seventies and eighties.

Wines and grapes mentioned in this chapter are described in more detail in the final part of the book (pages 94–157) and in 'The importance of Grapes' (pages 50–59).

Making red wine

Crushing

Once picked, the aim is to get all grapes to the winery as quickly and as smoothly as possible – ideally, although this is usually more important for white grapes, transported in stacks of small plastic crates, rather than in one heavy mass in the back of a huge truck where the bunches at the bottom will get squashed by those above. At the winery the vast majority of red grapes are put through a 'crusher' to break the skins and gently release the juices ready for fermentation, and, depending on the grape variety and region, to remove all or some of the bitter, tannic stems (some are often left on in Burgundy, but they are almost always removed in Bordeaux).

The exceptions to the crushing rule are red grapes for sparkling wines – these are fermented using the Beaujolais method of whole berry fermentation (which gives light, fruity, aromatic, low tannin wine) – and the best red grapes of the Douro, those destined for long-lived vintage port. Many port producers, having tried mechanical alternatives, have come back to old-fashioned treading – by warm and gentle human feet – although some find that feet are even more effective if the grapes have been given a swift preliminary pre-crush by machine.

Fermentation

After crushing, the 'must', the pulp of skins and juice, is fed into large fermentation vats which vary from traditional open-topped wood vessels to glass-lined cement and fibreglass (neither usually associated with the highest quality wines) and to giant, stainless steel, closed tanks. A small amount of sulphur dioxide, as protection against oxidation and an antiseptic, may be added (or may have been added at the crusher stage), but this is more especially needed for white wines. In cooler climates, such as the main French wine regions, sugar may be added to both reds and whites (in a process called 'chaptalisation') to bring the potential alcohol up to a reasonable level. And in many regions, particularly warm New World ones, acid may be added, although, again, this balance adjustment is more usually applied to white wines.

To get fermentation started immediately a winemaker has several options. In cool climates, he might heat the must, and he might use yeast activators and/or, particularly in the New World, cultured yeasts. These are much more reliable than

Red wine: the vital stages

1 TREADING OR CRUSHING THE GRAPES Treading, the traditional method, for vintage port is not just a quaint custom put on for the benefit of visitors, but the best way of breaking the grapes to extract the colour and tannin from the skins.

2 FERMENTATION Either in closed vats or open-topped vessels. Temperatures may be carefully controlled or they may not. Whichever approach, this is the stage where yeasts convert grape sugar into alcohol and therefore juice into wine.

3 SUBMERGING THE SKINS During fermentation a 'cap' of skins rises to the top of the bubbling mass and has to be pushed down regularly, either mechanically or by prodding with a pole, to ensure colour leaches out of the skins into the liquid.

4 PRESSING Red wine grapes are crushed before fermentation but pressing is carried out afterwards. The left-over pulpy grape mass is put through a press to yield tannic 'press wine' – which may or may not be blended in to improve the final wine.

5 MATURATION Few red wines are actually fermented in barrels, but most of the better ones – especially those intended to improve with age – are at least partially aged in new oak barrels to give them depth and complexity.

6 RACKING As they mature, red wines drop a sediment – they are removed from this in a process called racking, in which the wine is moved gently from one barrel to another clean one... the final transfer is to the bottling line.

wild strains, but the argument against them is that, in dispensing with the indigenous yeasts in favour of laboratory-cultured ones, you lose some of the regional individuality of wine. (This is particularly the case with the malleable Chardonnay grape, for which there are some very popular – in the New World – Burgundy-type cultured yeasts giving extra rich, buttery flavours.)

When fermentation is underway, stopping the temperature from rising too high is crucial. Over-hot musts produce coarse, stewed-tasting wines and, if the temperature gets completely out of control, the yeasts will be killed off before they have finished converting sugar into alcohol. Most reds are therefore fermented somewhere between 21 and 28°C (70–82°F). The other essential during red wine fermentation is to keep the skins submerged, so that their colour (the flesh of most red wine grapes is as colourless as that of white grapes), tannin and flavours are leached out into the liquid. Carbon dioxide given off by the yeasts constantly pushes the skins to the top, so they need to be regularly punched down again with a pole or kept submerged mechanically.

Fermentation may take only a few days, but if so, the results will be light reds for early consumption. More serious reds are more likely to take two, if not three or four, weeks. Either way, the wine will then be drawn off the skins (although this may be done part way through fermentation to make a less tannic wine) and the skins will be pressed. The winemaker may then add some, or all, of this sturdy, tannic 'press wine' to give the original wine more body, or he may leave the decision until spring.

Malolactic

The final stage of fermentation for all reds (but only some whites) is the 'malolactic fermentation', the conversion of astringent malic acid into softer lactic acid. Nowadays this is usually induced (by adding appropriate bacteria) straight after the alcoholic fermentation, but some traditional and non-interventionist winemakers allow it to happen of its own accord when temperatures begin to rise in the spring.

In theory the wine is now ready to drink. In practice most red wines need time to soften, but those intended for immediate drinking – fresh, fruity, Beaujolais-type wines – will be fined and filtered to remove sediment and any other foreign bodies prior to bottling.

Oak

Most of the world's serious red wines are matured in small new oak barrels (of 225 litres or so capacity) for between four and 24 months to develop that elusive attribute – complexity. And preferably the oak is French, because France, with everything else going for it, also manages to have the finest oak, from forests such as Allier, Nevers and Limousin. Oak gives flavour (especially vanillin) and tannin, and, being porous, allows limited, but significant, beneficial interaction between wine and air.

The age of the barrel is fundamental: the newer the barrel, the more it gives to the wine, so after three or four years it has little left to impart. Another important variable is its charring, or 'toast': the higher the toast the more intense the flavour.

Compared with French oak, American tends to give a less subtle, more pungent sawdust-and-spice taste, as does Slovenian. Baltic oak, in contrast, is so tightly-grained it gives little in the way of flavour. Other woods, such as chestnut in Italy, tend to be rather assertive. More common, notably in Australia's lower middle range wines (and illegally in Spain and the south of France), is the cheap oak-chip treatment. Oak chips are put into huge tanks of wine (usually in net bags) to give a quick oak fix. It doesn't make for subtlety, but gives a simple toasty-oak flavour to wines for early drinking.

Final stages

During wood ageing, the winemaker still has a few crucial tasks. Most barrels need to be topped up periodically to compensate for evaporation and the wine must be 'racked'. This is the drawing off of wine from one barrel to a clean one, leaving behind the sediment that has been deposited (the number of rackings depending on the duration in barrel and the type of wine). Some wines also need to be blended. This may be because they are made from more than one grape variety (claret, for example), or because the winemaker has so far kept wine from different vineyards separate. Before bottling, the wine will be fined to remove impurities, either traditionally with egg white or with a commerical clarifying agent such as bentonite. Most wines will also be filtered, to further ensure their stability, although there is a trend among top producers, especially in Burgundy, the Rhône and California, to dispense with filtration on the grounds that it strips wines of character.

Tannin

There is much debate in the wine world about whether today's great red wines from the classic regions – claret, burgundy, Rhône, Barolo – will last as long as their predecessors, and the ripeness, or softness, of the tannins is at the heart of the debate. Tannin, the dry, slightly bitter, mouth-coating substance that makes cold tea so unpleasant, is essential for wine, especially red, that is going to be aged (whites rely more on acidity), but winemakers since the eighties have been aiming for less aggressively tannic wines – wines, simply, that are suppler and ready for drinking sooner. They achieve this by picking the grapes later, so that the tannins in the skins, stalks and pips are all riper; by removing the stalks, which contain tannins that are more bitter than those in the skins; and by crushing gently, so that the pips, which contain the harshest tannins of all, are not split. And, if maturing the wine in wood, which is another source of tannin, they make sure that they buy good barrels, made from well-seasoned, properly toasted oak, and they are careful not to leave the wine in them for too long. But none of this answers the fundamental question as to whether contemporary classics will last as long as their predecessors. The winemakers say they will, because tannins are present, although different, but they would say that, wouldn't they? Only time will tell.

Making white wine

White winemaking is essentially the red wine process without the grape skins. The grapes (which may be white, red or both), are crushed, destemmed and pressed before they are fermented, although a few winemakers practise 'skin contact', a period of a few hours' pre-pressing when the juice is left on the skins to draw additional aromas and flavours from them. Before fermentation the juice may be clarified, either by allowing natural cold settling, by filtration or by centrifuge, but the latter two methods are harsh, taking away more than just the residue of skins, pips and stalks.

Both the duration and the temperature of fermentation vary considerably, but are directly related. Modern, light-bodied and aromatic whites are often fermented very slowly for up to four weeks in stainless steel tanks at temperatures as low as 10°C (50°F) – to retain all the freshness of the grape. Most will then be racked, filtered, cold stabilised (so that if subjected to cold later in their lives they do not turn cloudy in the bottle) and bottled within three to six months of the harvest. Traditional European and full-bodied whites tend to be fermented more quickly at higher temperatures – up to 20°C (68°F), or even 25°C (77°F) – in barrel, to give bigger, richer flavours. Whether whites undergo malolactic fermentation is the winemaker's choice. Most burgundy and champagne does, and it adds to their complexity, but in warmer climates where acidity is naturally lower it is usually prevented (with extra sulphur dioxide, or filtration).

Some wines will then be aged in new oak; some will get a quick, cheap dose of oak chips; and the finest full-bodied whites, especially Chardonnays and Sauternes, will have already been fermented in new oak barrels because this gives even greater depth and complexity (light and aromatic styles are seldom oak-fermented). In addition, the lees (dead yeast residues) may be left in the barrel to be stirred up regularly over several months to give creamier tastes and textures. Oak-matured whites are then usually racked, filtered (although not invariably) and bottled at between four and 20 months.

Rosé wine

Making rosé, is more or less a half-way house between white and red wine. In a very few instances, the law allows winemakers to make rosé simply by blending finished white and red – eg pink champagne – but the colour of most still rosés comes directly from the skins of red grapes. This may be before fermentation, either by crushing the grapes and leaving them to macerate for up to 36 hours, or by very gently pressing whole bunches to release delicately tinted juice, or from a brief fermentation with the skins. Whichever the method, after fermentation rosé is handled very much in the manner of white wines.

White wine: the vital stages

I ARRIVAL AT THE WINERY Perfect grapes, especially white grapes, can be spoiled by delays and heavy handling between vineyard and winery, so speed is of the essence: harvesting, transport and crushing must take place quickly and carefully.

2 PRESSING After crushing – or even sometimes nowadays without crushing – white grapes are pressed to release all their juice. It is important to press before fermentation so contact between juice and the skins, pips and stalks is minimised.

3 FERMENTATION The face of the ultra-modern wine industry: stainless steel vats are good for white wine fermentation as they enable efficient temperature control and therefore control over yeast activity and the style of the finished wine.

4 FILTERING THE WINE Carried out before fermentation, to clarify juice, and/or now, afterwards, to make sure the wine is clear and stable. Some say it strips wine of flavour, but those in favour say the best filters (below) are quite gentle enough.

5 WHY FILTER? Before and after – two glasses of the same Chardonnay: the one on the left is unfiltered, that on the right has been passed through the vacuum filter seen left.

6 MATURATION Full-bodied white wines are then frequently aged in new oak barrels to give richness of flavour and texture. (The best wines may also have been fermented in the barrels.) Bottling may either be from vat or from barrel.

Sparkling wine

If yeast and sugar are added to finished wine, fermentation will start all over again, and if the carbon dioxide given off has no means of escape it will be trapped as bubbles in the liquid – thus sparkling wine. But there is sparkling wine and sparkling wine. The quality and style of the base wine are critical: the finest, notably those for champagne, are very pure, but thin, acid and fairly neutral – the result of scarcely ripe grapes, hand picked and pressed very gently in whole bunches. The nature of the container in which the second fermentation occurs is no less important. The best results – the most complex and subtle – are achieved when it takes place in the original bottle and the wine is then left there for some time (a minimum of 15 months in Champagne) with its lees: the dead yeasts gradually break down giving the typical creamy, bready, brioche char-

acter of fine champagne. This is the traditional method and there is no matching it, but it is an expensive and time-consuming process – the removal of the sludgy yeast sediment, before the wine can be topped up with a dose of grape spirit and sugar (*liqueur d'expédition*) ready for release and sale, being not the least part.

An easier way of dealing with the sediment – one often used in the New World – is to transfer the now sparkling wine to another bottle, leaving the spent lees behind, but it never produces quite such finesse and such long-lived bubbles (a give-away to this method is a label which states 'fermented in the bottle' as opposed to '… in this bottle'). Less good again, but cheaper, is the *cuve close* or tank method where the second fermentation takes place in a vast tank. Finally, for the lowest grade of fizz, there is carbonation, where carbon dioxide is simply and very cheaply pumped into still wine.

Sweet wine

Excluding fortified wines, the vast majority of sweet wines are white, and their sweetness is natural grape sugar – from unusually sweet, ripe grapes – that has not been converted into alcohol, or, as for some German wines, has been enhanced by the addition of sweet grape concentrate (*Süssreserve*). At high sugar levels yeasts find it hard to work and may give up at 8–9 percent alcohol (as in great German wines) or may struggle on until they are killed at 15–16 percent. More commonly winemakers halt the fermentation themselves (with sulphur dioxide, refrigeration, racking or centrifuging) at the point when they feel sugar, alcohol and, no less important, acid levels are all in harmony.

The grapes for sweet wines, picked late in the autumn, are essentially dehydrated (to a greater or lesser extent), hence the high levels of sugar and acidity. They may actually be shrivelled – 'raisined' – on the vine, as happens in Jurançon in southwest France in the best years; they may be spread out and dried (raisined) on mats, or hung up to dry, as with Italy's *passito* and *recioto* wines; or, most significant of all, they may be shrivelled on the vine by a grey mould called noble rot (*Botrytis cinerea*). In certain warm, humid weather conditions this ugly but benificent mould appears in Sauternes, Germany, the Loire, Alsace, Tokay and Austria and is responsible for all the greatest sweet wines. In less favourable conditions, in the New World, noble rot may be sprayed onto grapes in the vineyards or even the winery.

Another way of producing immensely concentrated sweet wines is to freeze the water out. In Germany grapes are left on the vines – occasionally into the New Year – to make *Eiswein*. In newer, warmer wine regions, 'ice wine' is artificially made by freezing the harvested grapes – a similar technique has been applied in Sauternes when the grapes have been swelled – and diluted – by rain before or during picking.

(*Left*) **Remuage, or riddling, is the critical process of gradually turning and upending the maturing bottles of champagne, so that the sediment slides down into the neck of the bottle.**

Fortified wine

Wines that have been fortified (usually with grape spirit) are also often sweet, because the fortifying alcohol is added to the fermenting wine before all the sugar has been converted. Port is the classic example; others include Muscat de Beaumes-de-Venise and other southern French *vins doux naturels*, Australian liqueur Muscats, Bual and Malmsey madeiras. But the spirit can also be added at the end of fermentation to produce a dry fortified wine, for example sherry (the sweet styles being sweetened later, as also with Verdelho madeira).

Much of the character and quality of the major fortified wines – port, sherry and madeira – comes from their long years spent peacefully maturing in bottle or wood, further details of which are outlined in the Styles chapter (pages 79–80) and the Spain and Portugal chapters (page 128 and pages 132–33).

Organic winemaking

Organic winemaking, the natural corollary to organic vine growing, gathered momentum, aided by intermittent wine scandals, throughout the eighties, and finally, in January 1993, the EC got its act together and gave (typically fuzzy) definition and legal status to organic, biologique or ecologico wine. To give the Brussels bureaucrats their due, getting a consensus on what precisely constitutes organically produced wine is not easy – witness the numerous voluntary organic associations in Europe which still cannot agree on common standards, even though they now have to abide by the EC ones. The theory, of course, is that, as in organic vineyards, only 'natural' rather than synthetic chemical products should be used for winemaking. The antioxidant and antiseptic sulphur dioxide, in as low doses as possible, usually counts as one of these, and egg whites, for example, are universally recommended for fining, but other products are less clear-cut. Even so, there is a trend towards reducing the chemical input in vineyards and wineries and it is one with which few people would argue.

(*Left*) **Luscious sweet wines are produced in Italy from grapes which have been laid out to dry – to 'raisin' – in airy rooms on straw mats.**

Where the best
wines are made

3 The world wine map has changed almost beyond recognition in the last quarter of a century. Countries, and even whole continents, have opened up to produce exciting, high quality wines. In the Old World – slow to respond to the challenge from the New at first – run-down vineyards are now being revitalised, new regions and wines have been developed and wines which never used to travel beyond their local bars and restaurants are now sold in cities thousands of miles away.

France

Italy produces more wine than France, Australia produces it more reliably, Bulgaria produces it more cheaply – and yet, for centuries, France has been regarded as the source *par excellence* of high quality. Even today, with the best producers of the New World challenging France at every turn, the challenge is still essentially on French terms. If France didn't exist, the wines of almost every other country in the world would be vastly different.

It is the distinctly unpromising climates of France's greatest wine regions that, paradoxically, are critical to quality, because, although wine can be made anywhere warm enough to ripen grapes, fine wine is made at the margins, where it is only just warm enough and, in poor years, not warm enough at all; Champagne, Burgundy, the Loire and even Bordeaux specialise in this kind of knife-edge climate.

France's other secret is its soils. They are varied enough to suit just about any grape variety of almost any quality — which means that, although the country's reputation inevitably rests on its finest wines, it also produces everyday wine to satisfy the smallest pocket. And nowadays, with improved winemaking skills finding their way into the back-

woods, *appellation contrôlée* wine no longer has a monopoly on quality and excitement.

Appellation contrôlée (or AC) wines are at the top of the pyramid, but it is important to realise that AC status does not actually guarantee quality. By regulating grape varieties, yields, minimum levels of alcohol and maturation periods, what it guarantees is origin and style, but, as a general rule, the more tightly specified the region the better the wine is likely to be. Between AC and *vin de pays* is *vin délimité de qualité supérieure*: a small group with similar, but less strict, rules, and a tendency to be promoted to AC.

Vins de pays (literally, 'wines of the countryside'), of which there are well over 100, also come

(Right) **With its new 'varietal' vins de pays, Languedoc has been dubbed the 'New World' of Europe, but it is also a region where tradition dies hard – and the traditional wines from old vines and low yields can be sensational.**

from specified areas and grape varieties, but these can be very wide-ranging indeed. The catch-all regional *vins de pays* are: du Jardin de la France (covering the Loire), du Comté Tolosan (Midi-Pyrenees), des Collines Rhodaniennes (Rhône-Alpes) and, by far the most important, Vin de Pays d'Oc (Languedoc-Roussillon), producing close to a 10th of the world's wine in a colossal range of styles. Within these four are many much smaller *vins de pays* with much more tightly defined local styles.

Alsace

Unlike most areas of France, the warm, dry, sunny region of Alsace in the northeast identifies its aromatic white wines (and limited output of reds) primarily by grape variety – even the small percentage of production which comes from the 50 individual vineyards now designated Grand Cru. Grand Cru wines, which may only be made from the region's four best white varieties (Riesling, Tokay-

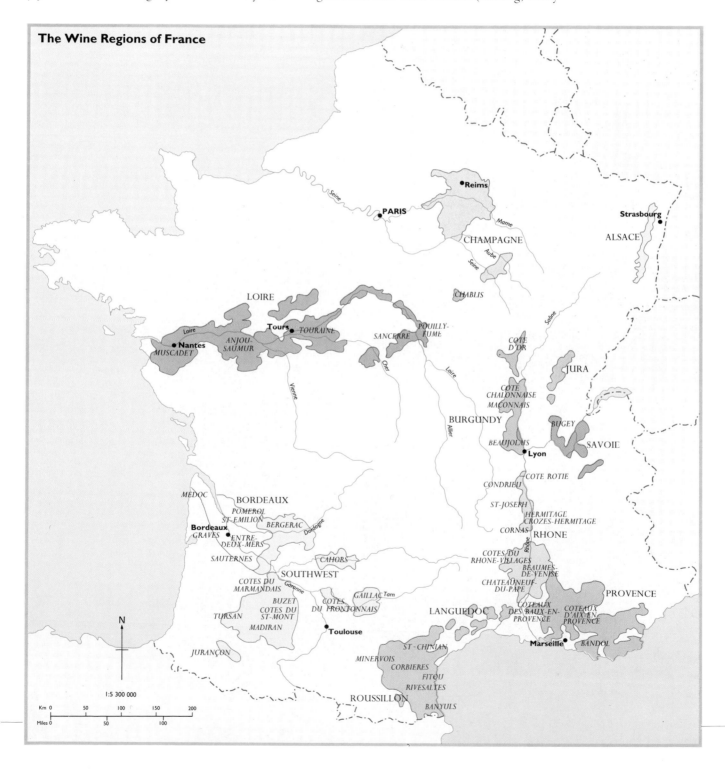

The Wine Regions of France

Pinot Gris, Gewurztraminer and Muscat), have greater depth and ageing ability.

Accounting for a larger proportion of the bottles on our shelves are producers' own 'prestige' labels, given various Réserve or Cuvée names. While these indicate a quality higher than the individual producer's average, there is no structure for comparing one producer's Cuvée with another's Réserve.

The other indicators to look for on labels are *vendange tardive* or *sélection des grains nobles*. These are high quality, concentrated wines made from sugar-rich late-picked grapes in good vintages. *Vendange tardive* wines are semi-sweet to sweet depending on the year. *Sélection des grains nobles*, made only from the four top grape varieties, are sweeter and richer because they are made from botrytis-affected grapes.

The wines

Crémant d'Alsace

The *méthode traditionnelle* sparkling wine of Alsace (made by the same method as champagne) can be good value. It is usually made from Pinot Blanc, sometimes with Riesling, and best drunk young.

Edelzwicker

Often now sold simply as Alsace, Edelzwicker is the inexpensive, often attractive everyday white blended from Sylvaner, Pinot Blanc and Chasselas.

Gewurztraminer

Grown nowhere else in France, Gewurztraminer gives full-bodied, exotically scented wines, often with a slight oiliness. The best late-picked wines are drunk locally with foie gras.

Muscat

Little-grown but delicious. Young Muscat wine, with its dry, rose-petal freshness is an excellent aperitif.

Pinot Blanc

Perfumed but lighter and less spicy than Tokay-Pinot Gris, Pinot Blanc (aka Clevner or Klevner) is usually straightforward, with refreshing, scented, appley fruit flavours.

Pinot Noir

Alsace's only red grape is seldom more than a shadow of its burgundian self, but in ripe years it can be well coloured with good flavour. Served young and cool, it makes a very good summer red.

Riesling

In Alsace, the classic Riesling of Germany gives wines of greater body and ripeness, whether dry or late-picked. Grands Crus and producers' special labels can be austere early-on but often live for years; lighter versions are best young.

Sylvaner

Simple, appley dry wine, mostly used for blending.

Tokay-Pinot Gris

This is how Pinot Gris is known in Alsace, but the Tokay part is soon to be dropped. It makes fat, spicy, sometimes honeyed and nutty wines, including superb sweet ones.

Alsace vintages

1992	8	★
1991	6	★
1990	9	★
1989	9	★
1988	8	★
1987	6	▲
1986	7	▲
1985	9	▲

Key

0–10 quality rating
(10 = top wine)

▲   must drink

★   can drink, but no hurry

▼   must keep

(*See also* **When to drink**, pages 44–47)

Bordeaux

Bordeaux in southwest France is the world's largest fine wine region and red Bordeaux – or claret – has always dominated the international wine market. The top 60 or 70 wines, most of them ranked in the famous 1855 Classification, may take 10, 15, sometimes 20 years to mature and then remain at their peak for many more. But there is far more to Bordeaux than illustrious names (and phenomenal prices). This large region is home to over 13,000 wineries (châteaux both great and humble, and cooperatives) and no fewer than 54 appellations, rising from the catch-alls Bordeaux and Bordeaux Supérieur (the latter has slightly stricter production rules and half a degree more alcohol) to the individual communes, such as Pauillac and Pomerol, which boast the great names and the highest price tags. There are also white wines, dry and sweet, some *crémant* (sparkling), and even some rosé and *clairet* (light red, from which the English 'claret' derives).

Classifications, rankings and categories

Wines have been classified and ranked in various parts of the Bordeaux region since the last century and there are now several classifications (*see* Graves, St-Emilion and Sauternes), but first and foremost is still the 1855 Classification of the Médoc. This ranked the top 59 châteaux as *crus classés*, 'classed growths', in five ascending tiers from Cinquièmes Crus (Fifth Growths) to Premiers Crus (First Growths), simply according to the prices they fetched. The First Growths were châteaux Lafite, Latour, Haut-Brion (actually in the Graves) and Margaux. Mouton-Rothschild had to wait another 118 years to join their ranks and its promotion is the only change there has ever been to the classification. No one doubts, however, that, were it revised now, there would be more changes: the internationally loved Lynch-Bages, for example, would certainly be raised from Fifth Growth – probably to Second.

A handful of the 200 Médoc properties that call themselves *crus bourgeois* would also almost certainly find themselves, by virtue of their fine vineyards and no-expense-spared winemaking methods, elevated to *cru classé*, but the majority are properties of lower aspirations. They aim for wines above average in quality with the potential in good vintages to improve with a few years in the cellar. Crus Grands Bourgeois and Crus Grands Bourgeois Exceptionnels are superior subdivisions of the category, but unfortunately for the consumer they may not be identified as such on labels.

Below the *crus bourgeois* come the myriad unclassified properties. Dubbed *petits châteaux*, these are everyday clarets that can usually be drunk within a year or 18 months of the vintage and seldom benefit from much more than three or four years' keeping.

There are also brands (the most famous of which is Mouton-Cadet). The Bordeaux merchants and cooperatives that make most of these are aiming for consistent taste and quality year in year out, so the

READING BORDEAUX LABELS

Generally speaking, French labels are reasonably succinct and logical.
From top to bottom: **Château La Dominique** is the name of the property (sketched); the label then tells us (twice) that its appellation (AC) is St-Emilion and its official classification within this AC is Grand Cru Classé; the vintage is 1986 (ie it was made from grapes of the 1986 harvest); the owner and grower of the grapes (propriétaire récoltant) is C Fayat; the wine was bottled on the estate (mis en bouteille au château); the alcohol content is a typical (of Bordeaux) 12.5%; it is a standard bottle size (75cl); and the label even tells us which country we are talking about.

(*Left*) **Not every part of France is wine growing country: the sand of Les Landes is not ideal for wines, although in some parts of the world, such as the Sables du Golfe du Lion in the south of France, sand planted with vines has the advantage of being phylloxera-free.**

(See page 98 for key to symbols)

Bordeaux vintages (red)

Médoc & Graves

Year		
1992	6	▼
1991	5	▼
1990	9	▼
1989	9	▼
1988	8	▼
1987	6	▲
1986	8	▼
1985	9	★
1984	4	▲
1983	8	★
1982	9	★
1981	7	▲

St-Emilion & Pomerol

Year		
1992	5	▼
1991	4	▼
1990	9	▼
1989	9	▼
1988	8	▼
1987	6	▲
1986	7	★
1985	9	★
1984	3	▲
1983	8	★
1982	8	★
1981	7	▲

wines are often blends from anywhere in the Bordeaux region and may be non-vintage (without a vintage date) because they are a blend of years. Generic wines – those simply called Médoc, St-Emilion, etc – are more specific regional blends, and occasionally they may come from a named property.

The so-called Second Labels are in a different league. These are the wines from major châteaux which have been rejected as not quite good enough to go under the main château label and bottled separately under a different, but often recognisably linked, name (eg Carruades de Lafite, Les Forts de Latour) and sold more cheaply. So long as you are wary of poor vintages, these can offer an earlier-maturing taste of the château style at a considerably lower price.

Grapes

Virtually all red Bordeaux is a blend of grape varieties: predominantly Cabernet Sauvignon (the most famous) and Merlot (the most widespread and the chief variety in simpler, early-drinking clarets), together with Cabernet Franc and sometimes some Petit Verdot and Malbec. The whites, both the sweet and the dry, are based on Sémillon and Sauvignon Blanc, sometimes with a little of the aromatic Muscadelle.

Wines and regions

Graves

To the south of the Médoc and the city of Bordeaux, the slightly warmer climate and distinctive gravel soils of the Graves region produce Bordeaux' best dry whites, and clarets with a spicy/tobacco, even earthy characteristic. All the classed growths (the Graves was classified in the 1950s) are in the northern third, which now has its own AC – Pessac-Léognan – but there is good value to be found under the Graves appellation. There is also a little-used AC for sweet whites: Graves Supérieures.

Médoc

The vineyards of the Médoc run in a long, narrow strip along the left bank of the Gironde, north of the city of Bordeaux and out towards the coast. The Bas-Médoc, nearer the sea, is the area of lesser quality, while the thinner, more gravelly soils of the Haut-Médoc to the south are home to some of Bordeaux's finest red wine châteaux, including of course the *crus classés*. These lie in the six communes that have their own appellations: Margaux, St-Julien, St-Estèphe, Pauillac, Moulis and Listrac.

Pomerol

Pomerol is a tiny region of tiny estates with outsize reputations commanding outsize prices: its famous Château Pétrus makes one of the world's most expensive wines. The appellation lies on the right bank of the Dordogne where the cold, water-retaining clay soils suit Merlot better than Cabernet Sauvignon. The high Merlot content gives wines that are fleshier and more voluptuous than the typical Médoc claret, but no less concentrated or long-lived. The wines of the Lalande de Pomerol appellation just to the north are less expensive, though not cheap. (There is no white Pomerol.)

St-Emilion and satellites

This compact appellation south of Pomerol makes Merlot-based red wines that are generally softer and earlier-maturing than those of the Médoc, and often have a notably spicy quality. The best wines are classified as Premier Grand Cru Classé, followed by Grand Cru Classé, and this is the only Bordeaux classification to be regularly revised. There are also five 'satellite' villages which may add the name of St-Emilion to their own – St-Georges, Montagne, Puisseguin, Lussac and Parsac.

Sauternes and satellites

Great Sauternes, made from botrytis-affected Sémillon and Sauvignon Blanc grapes in the south of the Bordeaux region, is one of the world's most opulent sweet white wines which, from a good vintage, will last for two decades or more; in years of little or no botrytis it is lighter and shorter-lived. There are 25 classified châteaux, with just one Premier Grand Cru (the fabled Château d'Yquem), and the rest divided fairly evenly between Premiers Crus and Deuxièmes Crus. Sauternes is made in five villages, but one, Barsac has its own AC which means the wine can, confusingly, be labelled either Barsac or Sauternes. Among the satellites, Cérons makes the least interesting wines, while Loupiac and Ste-Croix-du-Mont on the other side of the Garonne produce some attractive, lighter-bodied, much cheaper alternatives to Sauternes.

Other regions

Entre-Deux-Mers (between the rivers Dordogne and Garonne) is the largest and one of the prettiest regions in Bordeaux. The AC is for dry whites only and, while the best are clean and crisp, they are basically modest, inexpensive wines. Reds from the region, sold as Bordeaux or Bordeaux Supérieur (very occasionally, somewhat confusingly, as Graves de Vayres), are similarly basic, simple clarets for drinking young. The adjoining Premières Côtes de Bordeaux, which runs along the east bank of the Garonne, has more potential and is beginning to fulfil it: reds, both oaked and unoaked, are worth seeking out, as are the dry whites (though only entitled to Bordeaux Blanc or Bordeaux Supérieur ACs), and the sweet whites under the AC Cadillac. The Côtes de Castillon and Côtes des Francs in the east are near St-Emilion both geographically and in style, while Fronsac and Canon-Fronsac, just to the west of Pomerol, produce mostly Merlot-based reds, often of good quality. The larger regions of Bourg and Blaye, to the north, also make reliable red wines, with some white in Blaye – the best wines of Blaye are sold under the name Premières Côtes de Blaye.

Bordeaux vintages (white)		
Sauternes		
1992	4	▼
1991	3	★
1990	9	▼
1989	9	▼
1988	8	▼
1987	4	▲
1986	8	★
1985	6	▲
1984	5	▲
1983	9	★
1982	5	▲
Dry whites		
1993	8	▼
1992	6	★
1991	4	▲
1990	9	★
1989	9	★
1988	8	★
1987	6	▲
1986	7	▲
1985	6	▲
1984	3	▲
1983	8	▲

(*Left*) **St-Emilion, to the north of the Dordogne river, is quite different in feel and in its wines from the Médoc: properties are much smaller; the soils have more clay and sand; and Merlot predominates over Cabernet.**

Burgundy

Compared with the appellations of Burgundy, even Bordeaux's 'tiny' Pomerol looks big. Burgundy, running down eastern France from Chablis to Lyon, is about one-fifth the size of Bordeaux, and its classifications, its whole structure and mentality are different. Despite its much smaller area, it has far more appellations than Bordeaux, with parcels of a few hectares (which would fit into a Bordeaux château's vineyards many times over) having their own AC status, each divided among many growers. There are no châteaux in the Bordeaux sense – just growers and *négociants* (merchants who buy wine or grapes, blend, mature, bottle and sell the result under their own label). The latter used to be more important, but interest in, and regard for, the more individual wines of growers has increased. Merchants, as a consequence, have made efforts to get away from their strong 'house styles' and let the characteristics of the different vineyards and villages show through.

Classifications

At the top of the tree are the 30 or so Grands Crus, which are individual vineyards with their own appellations (Le Montrachet and Bâtard-Montrachet, for example). The next best, Premiers Crus, are also individual vineyards, but they attach the name of their village to their own name (eg Puligny-Montrachet-Les Pucelles). Below this level wines are sold under their village names (eg Puligny-Montrachet), or as basic Bourgogne.

Grapes

Burgundy not only differs from Bordeaux in its grape varieties, but in the way it uses them: burgundy is almost never a blended wine. The great reds are made from Pinot Noir, the great whites from Chardonnay, Beaujolais and much red Mâcon is made from Gamay grapes, and the incidentals are Sauvignon Blanc for VDQS Sauvignon de St-Bris and Aligoté for Bourgogne Aligoté. Passe-Tout-Grains, a blend of Gamay and Pinot Noir grapes, is the insignificant exception.

Wines and regions

Beaujolais

The southernmost area of Burgundy produces the familiar, juicy, fruity red wines of Beaujolais. The two simplest are Nouveau, released a few weeks after the harvest each November, and basic Beaujolais (often the same wine released later). Beaujolais-Villages from 39 better villages should be slightly fuller and last a couple of years, and Beaujolais from the 10 top villages, the Crus, should be meatier and capable of at least three years' age. The Crus are Brouilly, Chénas, Chiroubles, Côte de Brouilly, Fleurie, Juliénas, Morgon, Moulin-à-Vent (the biggest and longest-lived), Régnié and St-Amour. Whites are sold as Beaujolais Blanc or St-Véran.

Burgundy vintages (white)		
1992	7	▼
1991	5	★
1990	8	★
1989	9	★
1988	8	★
1987	6	▲
1986	9	★
1985	8	★
1984	5	▲
1983	7	▲

Burgundy vintages (red)		
Côte d'Or		
1992	7	▼
1991	6	★
1990	9	▼
1989	8	★
1988	9	★
1987	7	▲
1986	7	★
1985	9	★
1984	4	▲
1983	6	▲

Beaujolais Crus		
1992	6	▲
1991	9	★
1990	7	▲
1989	9	▲
1988	7	▲

(See page 98 for key to symbols)

(*Left*) **Corton, the Grand Cru of Aloxe-Corton in the Côte de Beaune produces both red and white burgundies of great power and richness.**

Chablis

More famous than Beaujolais, Chablis is the crisp, dry white from limestone soil in the north of the region. Traditionally it has a characteristic whiff of gun-flint, though nowadays much is aged in new oak *barriques* and is fatter and more nutty. There are seven Grands Crus and 17 Premiers Crus; Petit Chablis comes from lesser sites and is generally inferior to plain Chablis.

Côte Chalonnaise

The four villages at the southern tip of the Côte d'Or – Mercurey, Givry (both producing nearly all red wine), Rully (red and white) and Montagny (all white) – are all ACs in their own right, but are also entitled to the AC of Bourgogne Côte Chalonnaise. Both reds and whites can be impressive 'mini Côte d'Or' wines at a fraction of the price. The village of Bouzeron has its own AC for Aligoté, in recognition of its superior conditions for growing this slighty tart, but drily flavoursome grape variety.

Côte d'Or

The Côte d'Or, a string of hills running north-south and divided into the Côte de Nuits in the north and the Côte de Beaune in the south, is the heart of Burgundy; the fabled names – Vougeot, Vosne-Romanée, Volnay, Beaune, Pommard et al – roll off the hills. The Côte de Nuits produces mostly red wines – bigger, more substantial ones than the Côte de Beaune which makes whites such as the famed Meursault and Montrachet as well as reds. Wines from the Côte de Beaune-Villages, Côte de Nuits-Villages and Hautes-Côtes are well worth looking at in good vintages, but the nearest thing to a bargain that Burgundy has to offer is probably a basic generic Bourgogne from a good grower.

Crémant de Bourgogne

Burgundy's *méthode traditionelle* Chardonnay and Pinot Noir sparkling wine can be a useful half-price champagne-substitute – but don't try to age it.

Mâconnais

Generally reliable, but seldom really exciting (and no longer very cheap) reds and whites come from this area in the south of Burgundy. Mâcon Supérieur has an extra degree of alcohol; Mâcon-Villages is an AC for whites only. Both reds and whites may attach the name of one of 43 superior villages, such as Lugny or Viré, if appropriate. St-Véran, Pouilly-Fuissé and Pouilly-Vinzelles are ACs for white wines.

(*Above*) **From the gentle inclines of the Grand Cru Grands Echézeaux in the Côte de Nuits come some of the most elegant yet long-lived of red burgundies.**

(*Left*) **If the sun shines in the autumn as the leaves are beginning to turn, Champagne's gently rolling vineyards look beautiful, but once winter sets in in this northerly region, it can get very cold.**

Champagne

Champagne comes from just one place, a region about 90 miles northeast of Paris with Reims and Epernay at its heart. The chalky soil and chilly climate combine to give ideal conditions for ripening Chardonnay, Pinot Noir and Pinot Meunier just sufficiently to make the sort of acidic still white or rosé base wine to turn into fine sparkling wine.

Styles and quality

In fact the climate is so marginal that most champagne is non-vintage: instead of being the product of a single year which might well taste thin and sharp, it has some older champagne blended in to give it roundness. In good years, however, vintage champagne is made: this is kept longer before it is released (at least three years compared with 15 months) and will have more depth and the potential to age for several years, even a decade or more. Most, but not all, so-called prestige *cuvées*, the sort of top quality champagnes that sell under a fancy name at a very fancy price (Dom Pérignon for example), are vintage.

Blanc de blancs is made from white grapes (Chardonnay) only and is an elegant and increasingly fashionable style. The much less common *blanc de noirs* is white champagne made from black grapes only and is usually quite full bodied. Pink champagne can be made with a large proportion of Chardonnay or none at all, so it can be quite a delicate style, or a full, fruity one if mostly Pinot. *Brut*, the style we see mostly in Britain, is very dry; Extra Dry, confusingly, is slightly less so. A champagne which is advertised as 'recently disgorged' (*récemment dégorgé*) has been aged for an extra-long time and has only recently been taken off its lees (*see* page 92); as ageing is one of the keys to champagne quality, recently disgorged wines (which will be expensive) have more depth and complexity and, because they have spent time on their lees, more freshness. (Bollinger has cleverly registered the initials RD as one of its own trademarks, leaving everyone else to cope with the unwieldy full-length.)

Grand Cru and Premier Cru on labels are not the guarantee of quality that one might expect: Grand Cru means that the grapes used are the region's most expensive, coming only from the 17 finest villages; Premier Cru is applied to the next best 40 villages and the grapes from them are therefore the next most expensive. But good grapes alone do not make good champagne and the Grand and Premier Cru classifications do not impose production rules. The two terms are most often seen on small-scale champagnes made by growers (rather than by houses such as Moët & Chandon, which buy in most of their grapes or still wine from several sources, or by cooperatives), and the quality of these ranges from superb to dire. Fortunately they are usually relatively cheap, so there is more incentive to take a risk. The tiny letters RM, for *récoltant manipulant*, on the label indicate one of these growers.

If you don't want to take a risk, UK supermarket own-labels are usually reasonably reliable, if never thrilling, cooperative produce. The brands of the large houses (the famous names) are more expensive, but they should be of consistent high quality, each with its own house style. Mostly they are, but a minority spoil the show.

Champagne vintages		
1992	6	▼
1991	7	▼
1990	10	▼
1989	9	▼
1988	8	★
1987	5	▲
1986	7	▲
1985	8	★
1984	2	▲
1983	8	★
1982	9	★

(See page 98 for key to symbols)

Loire

We tend to think of the Loire as white wine country, but in fact an enormous variety is made: as well as whites in all permutations of sweetness and dryness, there are rosés, reds and sparkling wines too. The one thing that links them all, apart from the meandering Loire river, is that the fairly northerly location means that they are generally light-bodied – the very sweet wines being the exception.

Muscadet

This light dry white from the Loire's cool Atlantic coast, is the antithesis of bold, full flavoured New World wines, but Muscadet has its place, so long as it is well made and reasonably priced (neither of which it always is). The best area is Muscadet de Sèvre-et-Maine which fortunately accounts for most of production, but what gives Muscadet character and freshness is the 'sur lie' method – leaving the wine on its lees (see page 91) until it is bottled. This term appears on labels, but bear in mind that it is abused by big merchant companies – estate-bottled wines are the safest bet. Gros Plant, Muscadet's VDQS sibling, is even lighter, drier and sharper and generally tastes better on its home ground – preferably with oysters.

Anjou-Saumur

Upstream from Muscadet in Anjou-Saumur the main white grape is Chenin Blanc. The best wines are the nervy, minerally, dry Savennières, and the sweet, nobly-rotten (and immensely long-lived) Coteaux du Layons. The latter include the distinguished *crus* of Bonnezeaux and Quarts de Chaume.

The principal red grapes, Cabernet Franc and Cabernet Sauvignon, make the Anjou and Saumur reds and rosés. The best is the soft, raspberry-perfumed, slightly earthy, red Saumur-Champigny; the most familiar is the usually unexciting, sweetish Rosé d'Anjou, a blend of Cabernets and other varieties.

Touraine

Fresh, raspberry-scented Cabernet Franc is the star of this eastern half of the central Loire. Chinon, Bourgueil and St-Nicolas-de-Bourgueil, are the best reds – best drunk young and cool except when from the ripest vintages when they can improve for up to five years. Touraine's other great wines are Vouvray and Montlouis which are made from Chenin Blanc grapes and may be dry (*sec*), semi-sweet (*demi-sec*) or immensely sweet (*moelleux*), depending on the vintage (and not always saying which on the label); and they may also be sparkling.

Sancerre, Pouilly-Fumé and the Upper Loire

Way upstream, deep in France, the Loire grapes change to Sauvignon Blanc in the renowned Pouilly-Fumé and Sancerre ACs and their cheaper, but sometimes good satellites Menetou-Salon, Quincy and Reuilly. VDQS Sauvignons of Haut-Poitou (an area of good-value Gamay and Chardonnay too) are lighter, but often delicious. Red and rosé Sancerre,

Loire vintages		
Coteaux du Layon		
1992	6	★
1991	4	▲
1990	10	★
1989	9	★
1988	8	★
1987	4	▲
1986	8	★
Sancerre		
1992	7	▲
1991	6	▲
1990	8	▲
1989	8	▲
1988	8	▲
Red wines		
1992	6	★
1991	5	▲
1990	9	★
1989	9	★
1988	8	★
1987	5	▲

(*Left*) **Wending its way for the best part of 600 miles from the middle of France to the sea in Brittany, the Loire is home to an array of different wines: Saumur is famous for its sparkling wines, but the reds can be delicious.**

(*Above*) **Châteauneuf-du-Pape has not only given the world a famous red wine – its wine regulations, drawn up in 1923 by Baron Le Roy of Château Fortia (above), formed the basis of France's entire appellation contrôlée system in 1936.**

made from Pinot Noir, can be stunning in ripe vintages, but is always expensive. Red Menetou-Salon is a worthy substitute.

Sparkling wines

Méthode traditionelle sparkling wine is made all along the Loire (but not in Muscadet). It can be good and crisp, and is made mainly from Chenin Blanc. The most general AC is Crémant de Loire, but Saumur is the one most often seen. Vouvray and Montlouis can be attractively soft, fruity and nutty.

Other ACs

The Loire abounds in self-explanatory ACs such as Gamay de Touraine (as good as and cheaper than much Beaujolais), Cabernet d'Anjou, Cabernet de Saumur (among the best rosés). There are also less known wines: Cheverny (red and white), and Cour-Cheverny (white only) – both worth investigating.

Rhône

The Rhône, rather like the Loire, yields a host of different types of wine – red, white and rosé, still and sparkling, dry and sweet – but, whereas the Loire's bias is towards light and white, in the much warmer, more southerly Rhône region big, magisterial, long-lived reds dominate. Viticulturally, the Rhône starts south of Lyon and runs south to Avignon, but in doing so it divides into two distinct areas. In the hilly, rocky north, where vineyards perch on terraces chiselled out of near-vertical granite, just one grape is grown for red wines: Syrah. In the south, where the river and the land broadens, so, too, does the range of vines: Syrah is joined by Grenache (the most widely planted), Carignan, Cinsaut, Mourvèdre and several others. And to the white grapes of the north – Marsanne, Roussanne and Viognier – the south adds Grenache Blanc, Ugni Blanc, Clairette and Muscat.

Northern Rhône

The dark, muscular, tannic reds of the northern Rhône often need five or even 10 years to soften and develop their fascinatingly complex flavours – their extraordinary combination of gamey, leathery or tarry richness, fragrance and ripe berry fruit. The two stars are Côte Rôtie, the most perfumed, and Hermitage, the most magestic. Crozes-Hermitage is the much improved, lighter, earlier-drinking cousin of Hermitage. St-Joseph is similarly less long-lived, but it has a seductive, smooth, blackberry flavour which can be enjoyed from youth to about six years; Cornas is bigger, blacker and more tarry, but give a good producer's wine 10 years and it will develop and rival the more expensive Hermitage.

Traditional white Hermitage lives for decades, its austere, herby, almost medicinal character mellowing to nutty, straw flavours; the modern style – fruity and perfumed – can be drunk young, as can the whites of St-Joseph and Crozes-Hermitage. The rare and costly Condrieu, made from Viognier, has an extraordinarily heady bouquet and voluptuous, silky, yet dry palate.

Southern Rhône

A large appellation producing large yields mean variable quality for Châteauneuf-du-Pape: the red wine (the bulk of the region's output) is invariably warm, spicy, ripe and alcoholic, but only the best estates achieve the intensity and balance needed to make a wine that lasts six or more years. In contrast, the smaller nearby appellations of Gigondas,

Vacqueyras and Lirac produce richly fruity, robust, spicy red wines, that are not only cheaper, but also more reliable.

Progress in the general appellations of Côtes du Rhône and Côtes du Rhône-Villages (the latter covering the 16 best villages) in the last few years means that there is a much greater chance now of finding a peppery, plummy Côtes du Rhône or a slightly fuller Villages wine. The lightish, fruity reds of Coteaux du Tricastin, and the often fuller ones of Côtes du Ventoux are also wines worth looking out for.

With the exception of a few expensive Châteauneufs, the whites of the south used to be flabby and alcoholic: standards have risen and wines are much fresher, but it is hard to get excited about them unless choice is limited.

Rosé, sparkling and sweet wines

The best rosés include those of Tavel which are full-bodied, powerful and spicy, while those of Lirac are slightly lighter; both can be very good, so long as they are drunk young.

The Rhône's most delicious sparkling wine is the idiosyncratic Clairette de Die, a fragrant, grapey, gently fizzy, Muscat-based wine that is refreshingly low in alcohol. Crémant de Die Brut is much less interesting, and I can't work up much enthusiasm for the rather unrefined St-Péray either.

Beaumes-de-Venise is one of the red wine villages in the Côtes du Rhône, but it is famed for its golden, grapey, barley sugar-sweet, fortified Muscat which has its own AC.

Rhône vintages (red)		
north		
1992	6	▼
1991	7	▼
1990	9	▼
1989	8	▼
1988	9	★
1987	6	▲
1986	6	★
1985	9	★
1984	5	▲
1983	9	★
south		
1992	6	★
1991	5	▲
1990	9	★
1989	9	★
1988	8	★
1987	4	▲
1986	6	▲
1985	8	★
1984	5	▲
1983	8	▲

(See page 98 for key to symbols)

The Southwest

The southwest covers a large, disparate area sandwiched between Bordeaux, the Massif Central and the Pyrenees where wines divide into two distinct traditions: the Bordeaux look-alikes – red, dry white and sweet – based on the Bordeaux grape varieties; and the often little-known but potentially more exciting wines made from unusual local grapes such as Manseng (both Petit and Gros), Fer-Servadou, Tannat and Négrette.

Bergerac, basically a continuation of St-Emilion on the Dordogne, is the Bordeaux side of the coin. It produces large quantities of wines, the majority of which are for early drinking and very reliable, but there are a few estates making some that are more serious and oak-aged. Other names to look for include Côtes de Buzet, Côtes du Marmandais and Pécharmant for reds, Montravel for dry whites, and Côtes de Duras and Côtes de St-Mont for both. Monbazillac is a sweet wine enclave of Bergerac; quality is erratic – a pity as the best is very good.

Cahors from the Lot Valley to the south of the Dordogne, shows the Southwest's wilder side. These days it is not the tannic, black wine of legend, but the Auxerrois grape (alias Malbec) still makes it a chunkier, more austere wine than claret or Bergerac. It usually takes three or four years for its slightly spicy, buttery, blackberry fruit to shine and the best last several years. The Tannat-based Madiran is another traditonally big, tough wine that has benefited from producers' efforts to bring out fruit flavours without losing essential personality.

Other characterful local wines include Gaillac, Béarn and Côtes du Frontonnais among the reds,
Gaillac also among the whites, and Jurançon, a distinctive, vibrant white that ranges from dry to very sweet and can be excellent in all forms. But of all the Southwest wines it is a simple *vin de pays*, Vin de Pays des Côtes de Gascogne that is the success story of recent years. The base wine of the Armagnac region, it has made its name as the source of cheap and cheerfully fruity, light, grassy, dry French white.

The South

The south of France has come to be regarded as the 'new California' because of its willingness to experiment, and the astonishing transformation in quality that has resulted. Languedoc-Roussillon, the region running from the Spanish border to Nîmes, which even 10 years ago was still producing little but the poorest of plonk (which made its mark nowhere except in the EC wine lake), has become one of the most progressive in the world.

The red grapes that are widespread in this region, the Carignan and Cinsaut, tend to be graceless and fruitless, but nurturing old vines, reducing yields and adding modern winemaking can do wonders, especially when better varieties like Mourvèdre, Cabernet Sauvignon and Syrah are blended in. The ACs of Corbières, Minervois and Fitou all make some exciting reds now – gutsy, herby, spicy, and full of fruit, and the best (especially oak-aged Corbières) can be cellared. Standards have also risen in the general ACs, Coteaux du Languedoc, Côtes du Roussillon and Côtes du Roussillon-Villages; good Coteaux du

READING FRENCH WINE LABELS

From top to bottom: **The vintage is 1992; the name of the property is Domaine de Lissac; no grape variety is specified, but Blanc Fumé suggests, by its association with Pouilly-Fumé, a Sauvignon Blanc-based dry white wine; its French wine law classification is vin de pays and it is a Vin de Pays d'Oc; it has been bottled not at the property but somewhere else, which usually implies a cooperative or négociant (in this case, HDR are the letters of 'flying winemaker' Hugh Ryman who uses several cooperatives).**

(Left) **In Roussillon, close to the Mediterranean coast and the Spanish border, gnarled old Grenache vines produce the distinctive Banyuls wines, France's answer to port.**

Languedoc is like Corbières, while the Roussillon wines tend to be a little lighter and juicier.

The other triumph for Languedoc-Roussillon is its *vins de pays* which now provide some of the best value wines – reds, whites and rosés – in France. These range from small-scale wines from dynamic estates in the numerous small *vins de pays* (Coteaux de Murviel to name but one), to modern oaked and unoaked varietals – especially Chardonnay, Sauvignon Blanc, Cabernet Sauvignon, Merlot and Syrah – in the all-embracing Vin de Pays d'Oc. These latter, often coming from hitherto down-at-heel cooperatives, compete head on with wines from Australia and the rest of the New World – and it is no coincidence that many of the winemakers here are Australian or Australian-trained.

The situation with Provence was different. Quality was seldom bad, but it was mostly of a mediocrity that didn't justify the prices based on proximity to fashionable Mediterranean resorts. The wines will never be cheap, but the rosés are now fresher and fruitier, and there are some impressive reds. Bandol's are especially good – deep, spicy, herb and berry-flavoured with the potential to age a decade (Bandol rosés are attractive, too, but expensive). In ascending order of quality, the ACs of Côtes de Provence, Coteaux d'Aix-en-Provence and Coteaux des Baux-en-Provence are increasingly making herby, blackcurranty reds (often benefiting from some added Cabernet) and nicely-structured, almost creamy rosés; the whites are generally clean, but unexciting. Both Costières de Nîmes – sturdy, spicy reds and gentle fruity rosés – and Côtes du Lubéron – simple, fresh reds, whites and rosés – are useful cheaper alternatives.

Sparkling and fortified wines

Crémant de Limoux proves that, given the acidity of the Mauzac grape and the *méthode traditionelle*, the hot south can even make very creditable sparkling wine. The South is also the home of *vins doux naturels* – sweet wines made from semi-fermented grape juice fortified with brandy. These can either be made from Muscat (as in Beaumes-de-Venise) and made to be drunk young and fresh, like Muscat de Frontignan, Muscat de Rivesaltes and Muscat de Lunel, or they can be based on Grenache and barrel-aged to develop the distinctive, oxidised, woody *rancio* character – for example Banyuls, Maury and Rivesaltes.

Savoie and Jura

The crisp, racy, intense white wines from eastern France's Alpine Savoie region almost all find their way to the local ski resorts, but are well worth trying. They are mostly made from the Roussette grape, but Jacquère and Chardonnay are also good. Look out for Roussette de Savoie, the more general Vin de Savoie, Apremont, Seyssel (especially the sparkling) and Bugey.

The main varieties of the Jura region are the easygoing, ever popular Chardonnay (used for good still and sparkling wines) and the strange, nutty, resiny white Savagnin; for reds they are Pinot Noir and the oddball Trousseau; and the main appellations are Côtes du Jura and Arbois. But the speciality of the region is the intense, dry, sherry-like Vin Jaune, made from Savagnin and matured under a film of *flor* yeast for at least six years in barrel.

(*Left*) **The Alpine vineyards of the Savoie region near Grenoble and Lake Geneva produce zesty, fragrant, dry white wines.**

Germany

German wine is like no other. Although the grape varieties are not unique to the country, the wines have a particular blend of fragility and strength, of delicacy and concentration, that marks them out from the Cabernet Sauvignon and Chardonnay bandwaggon rolling across the rest of the wine world.

German wine is ruled by its climate. That might seem an obvious statement, but nowhere else (except Austria, which uses a similar system) is the wine law based on the simple premise that a ripe grape makes better wine than an unripe one. There are of course territorial designations. As the law stands at present, the country is divided into 13 regions, and these are subdivided into *Bereiche*, which are subdivided into *Grosslagen*, or large sites (but these are currently being phased out), which are in turn split into *Einzellagen*, or single sites (in other words, single vineyards, which may also be described as *Gutsabfüllung* if their wines are estate-bottled, rather than from a cooperative). Thus the label will give the geographical origin of a wine, often in minute detail — but the ripeness of the grapes remains the crux of the matter.

At the bottom of the scale, usually only accounting for about two percent of output, is *Tafelwein*. This is very basic table wine, invariably chaptalised (*see* page 89) and blended. *Landwein*, a step above, is supposed to be the equivalent of French *vin de pays*, but it has never attracted the same attention or generated the same interest and production is negligible. The bulk of German wine usually — although it depends on the vintage — comes into the next category, *Qualitätswein bestimmter Anbaugebiete*, or QbA; this is 'quality wine' from one of the 13 regions.

So far so simple. But to rise above this (usually fairly basic) level, a wine must come not from a superior patch of land, but must be made from properly ripe, or even overripe grapes. This, in a land whose most northerly vineyards may have trouble ripening at all in a cool summer, is considered to be the key.

Qualitätswein mit Prädikat (QmP) is the term given to any wine ranking higher than QbA and production is usually less, although in 1990, for example, QmP accounted for 60 percent of the harvest. QmP means quality wine with special attributes, and it falls into six categories, none of which may be chaptalised.

Kabinett is the lightest; above it comes *Spätlese*, which means 'late-picked'. *Auslese* is made from specially selected bunches of grapes; *Beerenauslese* is made from individually selected berries, often affected by noble rot. *Trockenbeerenauslese* is made from selected berries that have been shrivelled on the vine by noble rot and therefore make intensely sweet wine. *Eiswein*, made from grapes frozen solid on the vine during Germany's icy winters, is also very sweet — and rare. *Beerenauslese* is sweet too; so is *Auslese*, though less so, and *Spätlese* can be anything from dry to semi-sweet.

Dry German wines (the label will bear the word 'Trocken') are a fashion among quality-conscious producers. If the wines have the ripeness to balance their acidity, they can match food well, but mostly

(Below) The Rheingau in the heart of Germany has a reputation for long-lived Rieslings — and for aristocratic estates. Schloss Vollrads, owned by Graf Matuschka-Greiffenclau, is said to be the oldest family-owned wine business in the world.

The Wine Regions of Germany

they are too tart for non-German palates. A compromise style is half-dry (or *Halbtrocken*). *Spätlesen* in particular can be very successful in either style. Many wines, though, are softened with *Süssreserve* (*see* page 92), and at their best have a fascinating tension between grapey fruit and firm, elegant acidity. They may require long bottle ageing, and mature into wines of immense complexity, or they may be made to drink within a couple of years. Either way, a wine from a top grower in a good year can be worlds away from supermarket Liebfraumilch.

As well as the wine law classifications, there are several producer groups which embrace their own sets of high standards and their identifying marks can be worth looking out for on bottles: the two most important are Charta and VDP. Charta is an organisation of Rheingau growers aimed at promoting traditional, high quality *Halbtrocken* Rheingau Riesling wines: vineyards are classified using the term *Erst Lager* (first site) and bottles bear an embossed double window symbol. The letters VDP stand for Verband Deutscher Prädikats- und Qualitätsweinguter eV, a nationwide group of top (and admirably ecologically-aware) estates, all of which use a black spread-eagle symbol on their bottle labels.

Grapes

The Riesling is Germany's finest grape, although in the warmest regions the Pinot family can actually produce finer wines. The inferior Müller-Thurgau is the most widely planted variety. The best reds come from Spätburgunder, or Pinot Noir, but only a few growers have the climate and the dedication to low yields to get the best from the grape and red wines make up only a small percentage of Germany's production. All 13 regions grow a wide variety of grapes: the most important of the others are Silvaner, Ruländer (Pinot Gris), Scheurebe, Kerner, Weissburgunder (Pinot Blanc) and the red Dornfelder. The flowery Morio-Muskat is much used to give perfume to cheaper wines.

Wines and regions

Ahr

This cold, northerly region, the second smallest of the 13 in Germany, is almost perversely dedicated mostly to the production of red wines, from Spätburgunder and Portugieser grapes. They are pale, light, usually sweetened and seldom exported. Of the whites, the Rieslings grown on slatey soil are the best.

Baden

The Baden region does two things better than the rest of Germany: one is red wines, since Baden is in the south and appreciably warmer; the other is dry wines. It faces Alsace across the Vosges mountains, and enjoys similarly balmy weather; and like Alsace it specialises in the Pinot family of grapes, here known as Weissburgunder (Pinot Blanc), Ruländer (Pinot Gris) and Spätburgunder (Pinot Noir). The soils are very varied and the hills rolling rather than steep. Most of the wines are made by the local cooperatives, which are of good standard and turn out reliable, good value wines.

Franken

Dry Silvaner is the speciality of this region, bottled in the squat, flagon-shaped '*Bocksbeutel*'. Characteristically it has an earthy taste which can be extremely attractive. Müller-Thurgau is the most widely grown grape variety, although Franken has turned with enthusiasm to newer vine crossings produced by German researchers in recent decades. They survive Franken's harsh winters, but seldom produce the best wines. The thirsty Bavarians drink most of Franken's wines, so prices are quite high.

Hessiche Bergstrasse

A tiny region that produces attractive Müller-Thurgau and good Riesling which at its best is comparable to Riesling from the Rheingau. Hardly anything is exported.

Liebfraumilch

Always a blended wine, always sweetish, usually completely bland and among the cheapest of Germany's offerings, Liebfraumilch has conquered export markets and helped to ruin Germany's vinous reputation. (Can you tell the difference between it and the Piesporter Michelsberg and Niersteiner Gutes Domtal next to it on the super-

market shelf? No, nor can I.) It must come from the regions of Rheinhessen, Pfalz, Nahe and Rheingau, and Riesling, Müller-Thurgau, Silvaner and Kerner must make up the bulk of the blend.

Mittelrhein

Another region the wines of which are seldom seen abroad. It makes good, steely Riesling, but viticulture is on the decline here.

Mosel-Saar-Ruwer

This is one of Germany's most famous regions, and with good reason: a Mosel-Saar-Ruwer wine from a top grower is light and delicate but with a thread

of steel running through it; high acidity is matched by peachy, smoky fruit, and it will live for years. The Riesling is the grape to go for, and the best wines are grown on the precipitous slate slopes of the river banks. The Saar and the Ruwer are both

(Left) The vineyards of the Mosel – often terraced to make cultivation possible – are some of the steepest in the world, but the angle gives them good exposure to the sun.

READING GERMAN LABELS

There is no pretending that German labels are instantly accessible, but, if you take them step by step, they do gradually reveal most of the vital information:

From left to right, top to bottom: Qualitätswein mit Prädikat is the broad quality category – the specific (Spätlese) comes later; the AP number is the official test number of this particular wine (all quality wine has one); the wine is in a standard 750ml (or 75cl) bottle; it has 9 percent alcohol; and it coms from the Mosel-Saar-Ruwer, one of Germany's 13 regions. Now (at last) we come to the more specific information: the vintage; the village – the word ending in er, in this case Graacher; followed immediately by the 'vineyard', in this case Himmelreich. Unfortunately this is not necessarily as straightforward as it sounds, because, while Grosslagen still exist, the vineyard can either be an Einzellage, like Himmelreich, or a much more general Grosslage. (Note also that, instead of a village, you can have the word Bereich indicating a blend from a much larger area.) Next we come to the grape variety (Riesling) and all-important ripeness level (Spätlese). Finally we learn that the wine is estate-bottled – Erzeugerabfüllung (replaced since the 1990 vintage by Gutsabfüllung) – and that the producer is Reichsgraf von Kesselstatt of Trier.

Vintages

Rhine (QmP)

1992	7	★
1991	6	★
1990	9	★
1989	9	★
1988	7	★
1987	6	▲
1986	6	▲
1985	7	▲
1984	4	▲
1983	8	▲

Mosel (QmP)

1992	7	★
1991	6	★
1990	9	★
1989	9	★
1988	8	★
1987	5	▲
1986	7	▲
1985	8	▲
1984	4	▲
1983	8	▲

Key

0–10 quality rating
(10 = top wine)

▲   must drink

★   can drink,
but no hurry

▼   must keep

(See also **When to drink**, pages 44–47)

tributaries of the Mosel, and produce wines that are yet leaner and steelier – but which soften and open out in good years. (The Mosel-Saar-Ruwer seldom makes anything richer than *Spätlese*.) These wines can never be cheap, but it's worth paying the extra for an individual grower's from a village like Brauneberg, Bernkastel, Graach or Urzig rather than settling for something less exciting. And how do you spot the dull ones? Not easy, but price should be a guide – as can the word 'Winzergenossenschaft', which means 'cooperative'.

Nahe

There are splendid Rieslings from this region, especially from the towns of Bad Kreuznach and Schlossböckelheim. The latter is the name of the village's most famous estate, as well as of the village itself; it is also the name of a *Bereich* covering half the Nahe, and *Bereich* wines are likely to be less interesting than those of the village or the estate. Generally Nahe wines come somewhere between the lightness of the Mosel and the weightiness of the Rheingau in style.

Pfalz

Until 1993 this region was known as the Rheinpfalz and in Britain it was traditionally called the Palatinate. Whichever, it falls into two distinct parts: the northern is the area of great estates and includes the Mittelhaardt with such renowned villages as Deidesheim, Forst and Bad Dürkheim; the southern part is a region of mixed farming and fewer famous names – but while standards have risen dramatically

in the Pfalz as a whole in the last few years, it is the south that is currently seeing the most changes.

The style of southern Pfalz wine used to be rich and fat, tending to flabbiness in hot years. Not now: elegance rules and the wines have become drier, leaner and more structured. Not surprisingly, they are viewed as contenders for the Rheingau's title of Germany's best. Pfalz Riesling is full and spicy, sometimes almost tropical; and Scheurebe is also excellent, particularly when in sweet wines.

Rheingau

The Rheingau has long been recognised for producing Germany's finest wine, although these days the Pfalz region is mounting a serious challenge. Rheingau's reputation rests on its Riesling which, grown on its steep river banks and on an enormous variety of soils, gives wines of weight and ripeness, balance and depth. It is warmer here than in the Mosel, so the grapes ripen more easily, and in good years can reach *Trockenbeerenauslesen* levels; *Auslesen* are relatively common. It's also a region characterised by a proliferation of aristocrats: every other property seems to be owned by a Prinz or a Graf. The best villages include Hochheim (which gave its name to the English term for all Rhine wines – hock), Eltville, Erbach, Hattenheim, Johannisberg and Rüdesheim. Assmannshausen specialises in red wines from Spätburgunder (Pinot Noir) grapes.

Rheinhessen

There are good producers here – mostly in the Rheinterrasse area, a string of riverside villages around Nierstein – but the bulk of Rheinhessen is soft, agreeable... and dull. It is one of the main sources of Liebfraumilch. The name Nierstein is used not just for the village (which has some splendid vineyards) but also for the *Bereich* of Nierstein Gutes Domtal, the wine of which is cheap and not always cheerful. Apart from Nierstein itself, the best villages are Oppenheim, Bodenheim and Nackenheim. The letters RS (Rheinhessen Silvaner *Trocken*) appear on the black and orange labels of about 80 growers keen on reviving the qualities of this traditional Rheinhessen wine, and are worth looking for.

Saale-Unstrut

Light, mostly Müller-Thurgau wines are grown here on chalky soil – but since it is what used to be East Germany, the economic problems are severe.

Sachsen

Germany's most easterly region: it used to be in the German Democratic Republic. With high produc-

(*Right*) **Assmannshausen is unusual in the Rheingau for specialising in Spätburgunder to produce red wines.**

tion costs, run-down vineyards (Müller-Thurgau is the most important vine) and all the problems of adjusting to western ways, the wines are unlikely to appear in force on export markets just yet.

Sekt
The German term for sparkling wine. Deutscher Sekt is made from German grapes; Deutscher Sekt bA comes from one of the 13 regions. The best are made from Riesling. The *méthode traditionelle* is rare in Germany; most *Sekt* is made by the tank method (*see* page 92).

Württemberg
Half the wine from this region is red, from Trollinger, Müllerrebe, Limberger, Portugieser and Spätburgunder grapes. Neither they nor the white wines are often seen abroad.

(Above) **Enjoying greater warmth and sunshine than Rhine regions to the north, the Pfalz produces fuller, riper, often more spicy wines – some of Germany's best with food.**

Italy

Italy has been a united country for less than 150 years, so it is not surprising that even today much of its thinking is still regional and that its wines developed for purely local audiences. The effects of this regionalism are to the good in that each part of Italy has evolved its own traditions and flavours, helped by a vast array of characterful indigenous grape varieties, but it also means that many wines are still little known outside their localities. They simply didn't need to travel because vines are grown, and wine is made, almost everywhere.

With such volumes and such diverse traditions, standards inevitably vary enormously, but there is no disputing that there are red wines, especially from the cooler north, to equal any in the world. Yet to some extent Italy still has a slightly tarnished reputation. This is a legacy of the seventies, when producers of some of the most familiar wines, the likes of Soave and Chianti, blotted everyone's copybook by going all out for quantity – at the expense of quality. Such high profile exports deserved the poor name they gained, but it lingers more unfairly today, for in the eighties talk – and action – turned to quality. Individual vineyards, microclimates and low yields became the buzz words. International grape varieties arrived, too – and today Cabernet Sauvignon yields some of its finest wines in Piedmont and Tuscany.

None of these developments was enshrined in Italian wine law (which was loosely based on the French *appellation contrôlée* or AC system). This recognised nearly 240 DOC (*denominazione di origine controllata*) wines which nevertheless only accounted for about 10 percent of each year's crop. In the eighties a few of these were promoted to a new higher classification, DOCG (*denominazione di origine controllata e garantita*), which in theory guar-

(*Right*) **The Tuscan hills are renowned for their great red wines, but the vineyards around the medieval hill town of San Gimignano offer a contrast – a modern white from the Vernaccia grape.**

anteed the quality of the wine as well as its origin and grape varieties. Below DOC there was *vino da tavola*: the classification regularly used by leading producers, particularly in Tuscany, whose experiments with grape varieties and French oak barrels meant that their wines were excluded from the DOC, or who felt that the whole DOC system had been devalued.

This situation, with DOC (and even DOCG) giving official blessing to wines which were all too often inferior, while the most fashionable producers ignored the law and charged stratospheric prices for their *vini da tavola*, is in theory changing. A new law has been passed and is expected to be

put into practice in time for the 1994 vintage. It recognises the existing categories, but makes some fundamental changes.

In the first place it phases out about 50 virtually defunct DOCs; more importantly, it recognises the individuality and superiority of particular areas and parcels of land and allows them to be indicated on DOC and DOCG labels, and it embraces (in DOC) all the glamorous and internationally famous *vini da tavola* (Sassicaia, Tignanello, Ornellaia, Darmagi, Grifi et al). It also introduces IGT (*indicazione geografica tipica*), a new category between *vino da tavola* and DOC which is intended to be an Italian version of *vin de pays*. Up to 60 percent of

The Wine Regions of Italy

Italian wines are expected to be classified as IGT, DOC or DOCG.

Other classifications and designations that are useful to know are Riserva, indicating a DOC or DOCG wine from a good vintage that has been aged longer than normal before release; Classico, which indicates the heartland, the best part, of a DOC or DOCG; Superiore, which usually means higher alcohol, but can mean a superior subregion; and Vigna or Vigneto, indicating a special vineyard or 'cru'.

Grapes

When it comes to grape varieties, Italy has a cast of thousands – many of them fascinating originals, such as Arneis, Favorita, Fiano, Picolit and Schioppettino, capable of high quality but entirely localised. Others such as the red Sangiovese have successfully reached most parts, though Sangiovese's heart remains in Tuscany. The white Trebbiano is similarly well spread, although everywhere could have done with a little less of it: known as Ugni Blanc outside Italy, it is one of the world's dullest grapes. The great Nebbiolo's stronghold is the northwest, but it is not alone: it shares its territory with the likes of Barbera and Dolcetto and more obscure varieties such as Freisa, Grignolino, Ruchè and Brachetto. In the northeast, there are some unusual local varieties, such as Verduzzo and Vespaiolo (white) and Refosco, Raboso and Lagrein (red) competing with happily ensconced high-class French grapes.

Wines and regions

Aglianico del Vulture

Made from Aglianico grapes in Basilicata in the far south, this can be one of Italy's finest, most complex reds. Its deep colour, smoky blackberry perfume and tannin give it admirable ageing potential. In Taurasi (Campania), Aglianico now has DOCG status.

Alto Adige

This cool, mountainous corner of Italy used to be part of Austria. And its people still sport lederhosen and, for preference, speak German. (They call their region the Südtirol.) Its 19 grape varieties, mostly white, are sold as varietals, and are light, vibrant and aromatic. Look for Chardonnay, Pinot Bianco, Traminer and Rhine Riesling, and, for the red Lagrein Dunkel: dark and fruity with a bitter-chocolate finish. Look also for red Teroldego Rotaliano.

Arneis

The Arneis grape, with its flavours of nuts, herbs and pears, produces Piedmont's and one of Italy's most characterful dry whites.

Asti

It is much-maligned, but this inexpensive, sweet sparkling Piedmont wine from the Muscat grape is low in alcohol, high in delicate, grapey perfume and perfect drunk well chilled on a summer's day – just so long as it's very young and fresh. The same applies to the very similar Moscato d'Asti. (Note that the 'spumante' – simply meaning sparkling – has been dropped from Asti labels.)

Barbaresco and Barolo

The Nebbiolo grape in the neighbouring Barolo and Barbaresco regions of Piedmont makes wines that are traditionally virtually undrinkable when young – all tannin and hidden fruit – but which mature (after at least four years) into intriguingly perfumed, complex, supple, yet always very full-bodied reds. Barolo is the more massive – described as king of Piedmont, where Barbaresco is queen – but in both regions the welcome trend is towards more approachable wines with greater fruit and riper tannins.

Nebbiolo wines that are gentler on the palate and pocket include Carema, Gattinara (now DOCG), Ghemme (blended with other grapes), Nebbiolo

(*Left*) **The tannic Nebbiolo grape, reaching its apogee in Barolo and Barbaresco, produces wines of phenomenal power and longevity.**

(*Right*) **An unmistakeably Tuscan vista, but here in Montalcino, south of Siena, an unusual clone of Sangiovese, called Brunello, gives bigger, more muscular wine than in Chianti.**

del Piemonte, Nebbiolo d'Alba and Nebbiolo della Langhe (all from Piedmont), and blends with other grapes in Lombardy and Valtellina.

Barbera d'Alba

After the prestigious Nebbiolo, Barbera is the main Piedmontese red grape (and Italy's second most planted variety). It has a herby, fruity character with relatively high acid and low tannin, and can be made to be drunk young or in a bigger style, aged in oak and left to improve in bottle for a few years – a bit like a mini-Barolo. Alba produces the fullest Barbera, closely followed by the usually slightly softer and fruitier Barbera d'Asti.

Bardolino

Made from similar grapes to those that go into Valpolicella, but on different soils around Lake Garda in the Veneto, Bardolino is a much lighter red wine – as well as a rosé. Both red and pink should be drunk very young while they still have their freshness and cherry-stone fruit, and the red (like the rosé) can be chilled.

Bianco di Custoza

On the southern fringes of Bardolino and to the west of Soave, the Bianco di Custoza DOC gives crisp, fruity whites, very much in the Soave mould – but often better and more characterful.

Brunello di Montalcino

Brunello is the Tuscan name for a good strain of Sangiovese grown in the Montalcino area south of Siena (and south of Chianti). It makes a rich, dark, concentrated red wine (heavier and more tannic than Chianti) which is aged long – often too long – in barrel, and it can usually take another five to 10 years in bottle. Despite DOCG status, it has lived on its reputation (or that of its most famous estate, Biondi Santi) for too long, and few wines are ever quite thrilling enough to justify the uniformly high prices. Rosso di Montalcino, the soft, plummy, younger version is cheaper and usually better value.

Carmignano

The small DOCG of Carmignano is an enclave of Chianti to the west of Florence that makes an exceptionally fine Sangiovese-based red that has always contained a little Cabernet Sauvignon. The wines are Chianti-like, but with greater elegance and ageing potential (Riservas need 10, non-Riservas five to eight years). There is also an attractive DOC *rosato* (rosé) and a good value, younger, less concentrated version of Carmignano called Barco Reale.

READING ITALIAN LABELS

The rise of the so-called super vini da tavola has made Italian labels more confusing in recent years, but the forthcoming new wine law should resolve this. This label is a model of precision.

From top to bottom: **The wine is a Chianti from the Classico subregion; the legal classification is denominazione di origine controllata e garantita (DOCG); and the name of the estate or producer is Isole e Olena (this may not be obvious, but all becomes clear below). Next comes vintage, followed by bottling details: the wine was bottled 'at origin' (estate bottled) at the cantina (winery or cellar) of Isole e Olena. The bottom of the label gives bottle size, company address and alcohol content; and finally, at the sides there is an exhortation, in effect, to dispose of the bottle thoughtfully and the EC lot number that now has to appear somewhere on all bottles.**

Chianti

In a dozen years Chianti has transformed itself from being one of Italy's least reliable wines to one of its most respected – which, as a DOCG, it should be. In so large a region (it covers much of central Tuscany) standards are bound to vary – and styles too – but at least it is possible nowadays to have some confidence in what you are buying.

All Chianti is made mostly from Sangiovese and has a characteristic hint of astringency, but there are two broad styles: the lighter, younger, freshly fruity Chianti, the sort which always used to come in straw-covered flasks; and the more serious, expensive type that has real depth of flavour, but also an austerity which needs time to soften (two to four years for non-Riserva and at least four for Riserva).

Most of these more serious Chiantis come from the Classico subregion (Chianti is divided into seven such regions) and they are always labelled Chianti Classico. This is the historic central area between Florence and Siena which is peppered with aristocratic estates whose owners' names read like a roll-call of the Renaissance (and now also with estates owned by rich outsiders – both foreigners and industrialists from the north). The other important subregion for top quality, long-lived wine is the much smaller Chianti Rufina. The other five tend to make lighter, easy-drinking wines, usually labelled Chianti without the subregion name.

Other Tuscan Sangiovese's to look for include the generous, minty reds of Parrina, a tiny coastal DOC, and the warm, spicy, more chunky wines of its northern neighbour, Morellino di Scansano.

Colli Orientali and Collio

These adjoining DOCs in Friuli on the Slovenian border produce more or less 20 wines (most of them varietals) apiece. Collio is renowned for the quality (and cost) of its dry whites – extraordinarily aromatic, intensely fruity and beautifully streamlined Pinot Bianco, Pinot Grigio, Sauvignon Blanc, Tocai Friulano, etc – but reds such as Cabernet Sauvignon and Merlot can be good too. Colli Orientali makes more reds – including some impressive Merlot, Cabernet Sauvignon and the local Refosco – but also some fine sweet wines (look out for Ramandolo and Verduzzo, but skip the overpriced Picolit).

Copertino

This is a robust, full-flavoured, spicy red that is inexpensive because it comes from Apulia in the unfashionable south. Often excellent value.

Dolcetto

Dolcetto d'Alba is the best known of the various varietal Dolcettos of Piedmont, but all are reliable and their vibrant cherry fruit and bitter-chocolate flavours make them one of Italy's best answers to Beaujolais. Drink them cool, but not over-chilled, and drink them young.

Est! Est!! Est!!!

The most notable thing about this simple, dry, white from north of Rome is probably still its daft name, but recent improvements are giving crisper and fruitier results.

Franciacorta

This region east of Milan accounts for most of Italy's top champagne-type sparkling wines, and the still reds and dry whites (Franciacorta Rosso and Bianco), though less well-known, are also made to a high standard.

Frascati

When good, the local wine of Rome, is fragrant and tangy, but the vast majority are soft, only just dry, and vapid – drinkable if young, but otherwise likely to be oxidised. The nearby Colli Albani DOC can be useful as a cheaper alternative.

Galestro

Galestro was devised as a way of using up the Chianti region's white grape surplus. The result is an adequate, but rather characterless, light, dry white wine.

Gavi

Gavi, the fashionable dry white wine of Piedmont, has more character than Galestro – being made largely from the citrusy Cortese grape – but it is also ridiculously expensive. Cortese del Piemonte is much cheaper and can be just as good.

(*Above*) **White grapes, especially Trebbiano, have been the bane of Chianti in the past, but here, near Panzano, the producer Fontodi is proving that more aromatic varieties, such as Pinot Bianco and Sauvignon, can be worth pursuing.**

Grave del Friuli
This is the main DOC of the Friuli region, covering grapes such as Merlot, Cabernet, Pinot Nero and Refosco for the reds and Pinot Bianco, Tocai, Pinot Grigio, Riesling Renano, Sauvignon, Traminer, Chardonnay and Verduzzo for the whites. The wines are generally well made, supple, fruity and typical of their grape variety – they are also good value.

Lambrusco
In its commercial form this is sweetened, lightly fizzy and either red, white or rosé – the vinous equivalent of cola. In its truest native form (Lambrusco di Sorbara is the best) it is deep red, refreshingly dry, crisp and juicy. Drunk young and cool, but not chilled, it is the perfect complement to the rich local food of Emilia-Romagna.

Lugana
From south of Lake Garda, this is one of Italy's few dry whites of quality and personality. Best young, it is nicely rounded, perfumed and delicately nutty.

Marsala
Sicily's famous fortified wine is now wildly unfashionable, but an old Vergine, the top quality, bone dry style, is a complex animal – like a fine old sherry, although never quite as subtle. The lesser Fine and Superiore categories may be sweetened.

Merlot del Veneto
This is just one of a huge number of light- to medium-bodied, plummy, often grassy Merlots, both DOC and *vino da tavola*, from northeast Italy. They are mostly reliable rather than exciting.

Monica di Sardegna
Sardinia's simple, soft red from the Monica grape is made all over the island and is for drinking young.

Montepulciano d'Abruzzo
The Montepulciano grape (no relation to Tuscany's Vino Nobile di Montepulciano) produces generous, ripe, spicy red wines here in the Marches.

Moscato Passito di Pantelleria
An intensely sweet, rich, apricoty wine made from sun-dried grapes on the tiny island of Pantelleria, southwest of Sicily. Quality is high, quantities small.

Orvieto
If heavily based on Trebbiano, as much is, Umbria's Orvieto is pale, dry and rather bland, but when other grapes are added, particularly in the Classico area, it can develop some nutty, peachy character; even so, it is not a wine to be kept. Abboccato is the (now) much less common semi-sweet version.

Pomino
There is a French influence in the wines from this Tuscan DOC east of Florence, with Cabernet and Merlot in the Sangiovese-based red and Pinot Bianco (Pinot Blanc) in the whites. Results are good (supple, elegant reds, creamy whites) but prices are high.

Prosecco di Conegliano-Valdobbiadene
Sparkling Prosecco (from the Veneto) can be either dry or semi-sweet. It is not a champagne copy, but a fresh, appley, affordable sparkling wine – delicious so long as it is drunk young and well-chilled.

Rosso Cònero
The full-bodied reds of the Rosso Cònero DOC in the Marches are based on the Montepulciano grape, which gives an appealing, warm, spicy character.

Salice Salentino
The impressive, long-lived, deeply fruity, chocolatey reds of Salice Salentino in Apulia can be bargains.

Sicily
Marsala is Sicily's main claim to fame, but crisp, light whites and full, spicy reds from indigenous grapes (mainly non-DOC) have recently improved greatly.

Soave
Soave, like Chianti, has been much abused and, in recent years, much improved. There is still a great deal of mass-produced dross, but from the Soave Classico heartland in the hills behind Verona it is mostly as Soave should be – crisply fruity with its own distinctive straw and almond character.

Torgiano
Lungarotti is almost the only producer in this Umbrian DOC and (for red Riserva only) DOCG near Perugia. The red is based on Sangiovese, and is like a fleshy, supple Chianti; the white, based on Trebbiano and the more characterful Grechetto, is also good. Prices are quite high.

Trentino
The southern extension of Alto Adige (*qv*) produces roughly similar wines, mostly from single grape varieties, but there are more reds and generally they are riper and broader (eg Cabernet Sauvignon, Lagrein and the almondy Marzemino). Pinot Bianco, Chardonnay and Pinot Grigio are successful whites.

(*Below*) **Close to the mountains and the Austrian border in the north, the wines of Alto Adige and Trentino are mostly made from single grape varieties – 19 different ones in Alto Adige.**

Tuscany

See Brunello di Montalcino, Carmignano, Chianti, Pomino and Vino Nobile de Montepulciano.

Valpolicella

The Veneto's best-known red varies from light-weight, simple wine – best drunk young while its modest cherry and almond flavours are still fresh – to concentrated, sweet, almost port-like Recioto della Valpolicella and equally concentrated, but more powerful, dry red Amarone della Valpolicella (both the latter are made from dehydrated, shriv-elled grapes). In between the young, light and mas-sive, end-of-dinner sipping styles there is Valpolicella Classico, which has the archetypal ripe cherry fruit and bitter-almond finish of all Valpolicella.

Verdicchio dei Castelli di Jesi

Although made from the Verdicchio rather than the ubiquitous Trebbiano grape, this is yet another of Italy's pleasantly crisp, lightly perfumed dry whites for drinking young. It comes – traditionally in an amphora bottle – from near Ancona in the Marches.

Vernaccia di San Gimignano

A nutty and honeyed or (more usually) clean, lemony and straightforward Tuscan white from the Vernaccia grape. Drink young.

Vino Nobile di Montepulciano

This Sangiovese-based red from a region to the south of Chianti was Italy's first own DOCG (though more for political than qualitative reasons). In style the wines should lie between the elegance of Chianti and the power of Brunello di Montalcino, but quality has been more erratic than it should be for a DOCG. Rosso di Montepulciano, the younger, lighter version can be good value, but has been less reliable than Rosso di Montalcino (*see* page 119).

Vin Santo

Vin (or Vino) Santo can come from anywhere, but most, and the best, is Tuscan. It is an after-dinner sipping wine, made from grapes left to dry on racks until Christmas, then fermented in barrels, sometimes for years. Intense, complex, tangy, with orange, raisin and apricot flavours, it can be sweet or dry.

Vintages

Barolo & Barbaresco

1992	6	▼
1991	6	★
1990	9	▼
1989	9	▼
1988	8	★
1987	6	▲
1986	7	★
1985	9	★
1984	5	▲
1983	6	▲

Valpolicella

(Recioto & Amarone)

1992	6	▼
1991	5	★
1990	9	▼
1989	6	★
1988	9	★
1987	4	▲
1986	7	★
1985	9	★
1984	4	▲
1983	9	★

Tuscan reds

1992	7	▼
1991	7	★
1990	10	▼
1989	6	★
1988	9	★
1987	7	▲
1986	7	▲
1985	9	★
1984	4	▲
1983	8	▲

Key

0–10 quality rating
(10 = top wine)

▲   must drink

★   can drink,
      but no hurry

▼   must keep

(See also **When to drink**, pages 44–47)

Spain

For centuries Iberia was on the edge of the known world, and Europe came to an end in a waste of barren mountains and plains cut off from France by the Pyrenees. Her more recent history, too, bred a fierce isolationism, and you can still taste this in the wines – although the demands of export markets have meant that the wood-aged character that was such a distinguishing feature of all Spanish wines (red, white and rosé) has been lessened in recent years.

Spain has more vineyard planted than any other European country, but is only the third largest wine producer (third in the world, too). Yields are low partly because even the mass-producing vineyards are not managed in the same efficient, industrial way as they are in France or Germany, but also because of the climate. Heat and aridity deprive the vines of water, and irrigation (on which most

Australian vineyards depend entirely) is banned except in rare instances within the EC. The driest and most barren part of all is the centre and most of its output is therefore bulk wine – at its best crisp, light, refreshing white, but at its worst, dull and fruitless. The north is the source of most of the finest table wines – the reds are meaty and oaky and the whites often now fresh and fruity, rather than

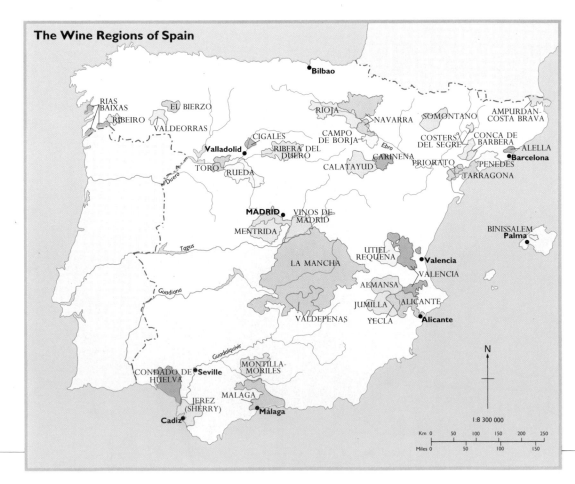

The Wine Regions of Spain

heavily-oaked and oxidised. The south produces the famous dessert and fortified wines.

Forty regions, spread across the country, are now classified *denominación de origen* (DO): the equivalent of French *appellation contrôlée*, in which the origin, grapes, vinification and maturation of the wine are carefully specified. Above them, so far, there is just one DOCa (*denominación de origen calificada*, similar to the Italian DOCG) – and that, unsurprisingly, is Rioja. DOCa does not impose any further rules on Rioja, but merely recognises that its regulations are already stricter than those of most Spanish regions.

Below DO is the equivalent of French *vin de pays*, *vino de la tierra*, and there are 61 of these, but with an increasing amount of good, inexpensive DO wine available there is little incentive for foreign buyers to import *vinos de la tierras* instead. Table wine comes under the *vino de mesa* heading and much of this is very basic, but there have been improvements on two fronts: oak chips are being used (in defiance of EC law) by some big exporters to give a creditable coconuty or vanilla-oak flavour to cheap wines; and a tiny handful of producers has followed the Italian example and is using this category to make high quality wines outside the DO regulations. As a rule, though, it is DO wines that fill our shelves.

The other significant classification for Spanish wines – especially red – is one according to age and maturation. Details vary from DO to DO, but generally a Crianza wine has been aged, partially in oak, for two years before release, and a Reserva for longer (three years for a red, with at least one year in oak); a Gran Reserva will have been aged longer again (five years, at least two in oak for a red).

Grapes

It infuriates Spanish producers to hear this said, but one of their handicaps is their grape varieties. Spain hasn't embraced the French classics to any great extent except in Penedès and Costers del Segre – and that is no bad thing – but it hasn't Italy's advantage of thrilling indigenous varieties either. The red Tempranillo is the star of a not very distinguished cast, aided and abetted by Graciano and Monastrell and by Mediterranean grapes such as red (and white) Garnacha (Grenache) and red Cariñena (Carignan). Among the whites, Albariño can be gorgeous, but is only grown in Galicia in the far northwest. Verdejo, mainly from Rueda, is the next best thing, but there isn't much of that either, which leaves Parellada, Xarel-lo, Macabeo and Airén (this last the world's most planted grape and one of its most boring).

(*Below*) **Planting vines is not always a simple matter of choosing a well-exposed slope: on the island of Lanzarote vineyards are dug into hardened lava flows, and walls around the vines protect them from wind damage.**

Wines and regions

Cariñena

The Cariñena region is southeast of Rioja, and the wine (mostly red) can, at its best, resemble chunky, rustic Rioja wines. It never reaches their classic elegance, though, largely because of the predominance of the alcoholic Garnacha grape in the blend, which only ever plays a supporting role in the better Riojas.

Cava

Cava is the name given to most of Spain's '*méthode traditionelle*' sparkling wine. State-of-the-art technology and grapes from the (relatively) cool vineyards of northern Spain (mostly Catalonia) are a promising background. Yet all too often *cava* has an earthy, rooty or apple-pips dullness. The culprits are the grapes: Xarel-lo, Macabeo (aka Viura) and Parellada just don't age well. Quality is improving all the time – and judicious additions of Chardonnay are doing their bit – but if in doubt, go for freshness by buying from a shop with a rapid turnover and drink it well chilled.

Costers del Segre

This region in the far northeast is virtually synonymous with the firm of Raimat, which makes soft, rich reds, good whites and sparkling wines from vineyards that, very unusually, are allowed to be irrigated. Classic French varieties – Cabernet Sauvignon, Merlot, Pinot Noir and Chardonnay – dominate, but there is also impressive Tempranillo.

Jumilla

There is still hefty, highly alcoholic red from Jumilla, but outside investment in this region inland from Alicante in eastern Spain has given some which are softer, lighter and often very good value, and there are also simple, appealing rosés.

La Mancha

Spain's bleak central plateau used to produce little that wasn't cheap, dull and fruitless, whether it was white (the bulk of production) or red. Most is still sold for blending, but there is a growing volume of cheap but now fresh, modestly fruity whites and even some clean, lively reds.

Málaga

A name from the past, Málaga was popular in the last century, but, like so many other fortified wines around the world, it is now crushingly unfashionable. It comes from the Costa del Sol and is almost always sweet. Its raisiny, spicy-wood character is given by Pedro Ximénez and Moscatel grapes and maturation, like sherry, in a *solera* – *see* page 128.

(*Above*) **In the north of Spain, to the north of Rioja, Navarra has made huge progress in the last decade: once renowned for its rosés, it now also has a deserved reputation for its juicy young reds – Spain's answer to Beaujolais – and for fuller, oak-aged alternatives to Rioja.**

Montilla

The DO region, which lies northeast of Jerez, is called Montilla-Moriles and the wine is like a lesser version of sherry, except that the main grape is the Pedro Ximénez which is seldom found in Jerez these days. In fact the wines are generally much less exciting than sherry, being soft where sherry is tangy and simple where sherry is complex.

Navarra

Just to the north of Rioja, grapes such as Cabernet Sauvignon and Tempranillo have muscled-in on what was once almost exclusively Garnacha territory, and Navarra's reds – both the young, fruity styles and the fuller, well-structured, oak-aged ones – are now attracting well-deserved attention as a result. The rosés, which have long been renowned, are much fruitier and more attractive than they used to be and progress is also being made with white wines, although they are not as exciting as the reds.

Penedès

Miguel Torres is certainly not the only wine producer, or even the only good one, in Penedès, but he led the way in changing its image. The wines from Torres and other top producers are semi-international in style: the grape varieties are often familiar (Cabernet and Chardonnay among them), but they are frequently blended with varieties such as Tempranillo and Parellada which give the wines their own regional character. They are not particularly cheap, but they are very good.

Priorato

Delicate wine doesn't exist in Priorato, a small northeastern DO east of Tarragona. The reds (the majority of output) are strapping, powerful wines made from Garnacha and Cariñena grapes which have to be at least 13.5 percent alcohol by law. Slightly surprisingly perhaps, they can actually be extremely good.

Rías Baixas

This DO in Galicia, the cool, rainy northwest of Spain, produces exceptional, fragrant, apricoty dry whites from the Albariño grape, easily Spain's best white variety (which, under the name of Alvarinho, helps fashion Vinhos Verdes just over the border in northern Portugal). The only pity is that Albariño is so chic in Spain that it is horribly expensive. The warmer, drier Ribeiro region to the east shows potential with whites from various indigenous varieties, including Albariño, so in the future they may be a cheaper alternative.

Ribera del Duero

It is not only in Portugal that the vineyards of the River Douro (in Spain called the Duero) produce fine wine. In northwest Spain, to the southwest of Rioja, the Ribera del Duero DO is notable for the fierceness of its temperatures (both hot and cold) and the quality – and price – of its red wines (including the legendary Vega Sicilia and its young arch-rival Pesquera). Tempranillo is the main grape and it makes, sometimes blended with a little Cabernet Sauvignon, powerful, aromatic, concentrated reds. All the wines need a few years' age and the best last 12 years or more – which gives them plenty of time to gather the sort of accolades that push up prices.

Rioja

For generations this was Spain's leading quality table wine area. It probably still is, but over the years it has gone through some disappointing phases – today it is Penedès that produces more originality and Ribera del Duero that provides Spain with its most illustrious reds. In the 1970s Rioja established itself as unmistakably oaky – the reds at the same time brimming with soft summer-pudding fruit and the whites fat and nutty. Then producers started using less and less oak (also, barrels were getting old and flavourless after the rush of investment in oak in the seventies); whites, made from a not especially interesting blend of Viura, Malvasia and Garnacha Blanco, became fresh, lemony and international in style; and the reds, made from Tempranillo, Graciano, Garnacha and Mazuelo, just became less exciting. Now things are changing again: tired old barrels have been replaced, more care is taken over the quality of the grapes themselves, and prices have stabilised.

Rioja is in fact divided into three areas, Rioja Alta, Rioja Alavesa and Rioja Baja, with the first

READING SPANISH LABELS

This is a typically traditional Spanish label: all the essential information is there, but you have to pick it out from the extraneous details. *From top to bottom:* **Vega-Sicilia is the name of the estate and Unico is the name of this wine; the vintage (cosecha) is 1979 and the denominación de origen is Ribera del Duero. Then there is a list of awards won. Then: bottle size; the fact the wine was estate bottled (embotellado en la propiedad); alcohol content; and the producer's name (Bodegas Vega Sicilia) and address. Further non-essentials follow – the number of bottles made and the UK importer.**

(Below) **In Spain growers are traditionally growers only – with traditional modes of transport! Making wine is still mainly left to the large concerns – bodegas or, as here in Ribera del Duero, local cooperatives.**

being the coolest and the last the hottest, but you do not need to know more than that because most Riojas are a blend from all three – and that's because the vast majority of *bodegas* (wine producers) buy in their grapes from growers and do not actually own many vineyards themselves.

Rueda

The Rueda region, northwest of Madrid, is understandably coming to be valued as one of Spain's best sources of reasonably-priced, reasonably characterful, dry white wines. Made mostly from the Verdejo grape, sometimes with a little Sauvignon Blanc, they are fresh and crisp, with herby, delicately nutty flavours which are best appreciated when the wines are young.

Sherry

Sherry comes only from a triangular area of chalky soil around the Andalucian town of Jerez de la Frontera near the coast in southwest Spain (anything else simply isn't sherry). It is made from the neutral, low acid Palomino grape and aged in *solera*, a system which produces highly complex wines which combine the freshness of youth with the depth of maturity (because the wines ageing in *solera* barrels are constantly 'refreshed' with younger wine: 25–33 percent of each cask is moved at a time, and at each stage the cask is topped-up with 25–33 percent of sherry from a cask at the previous, younger, stage).

The *manzanilla* style, which is matured by the sea at Sanlúcar de Barrameda, is sherry's lightest style – searingly dry, delicate and with an almost salty bite. *Fino* is similar but fractionally weightier. Both get their characteristic yeasty tang from the *flor* yeast which is left to grow as they mature in barrel*. They are the ultimate aperitif sherries, although some people prefer the fuller body of an *amontillado*, especially in winter.

Amontillado is *fino* on which the *flor* has lived, matured and died and so it is an older, darker and nuttier sherry, but one which should still have a certain tang. Sadly, short cuts are taken with the production of most commercial *amontillado* for export markets and most of it is also sweetened which blurs its character.

Oloroso is sherry which did not grow *flor*. It is the fullest and richest – with nut, fig and prune flavours – but it is still naturally dry. Again, commercial brands of *oloroso* are sweetened (and often called Cream sherry), but when the finest *olorosos* are

*Flor is a natural yeast present in the Jerez region that grows in a porridge-like layer on the surface of young fino, protecting it from oxygen.

(Above) **The solera system of ageing sherry progressively through a series of barrels means that cooperage has always been a crucial craft industry in Jerez.**

sweetened, as they are occasionally, they can make marvellous dessert wines. The rarely-seen *palo cortado* style is a sort of half-way house between *amontillado* and *oloroso*.

(Sherry is ready to drink when bottled and should be drunk as soon as it is bought. *Fino* and *manzanilla* are particularly fragile, so keep them in the fridge once opened, but preferably buy half bottles so that you can finish them in one go. And please, don't ever decant sherry.)

(Below) **Sherry has been produced for centuries and has been beloved by the English since Elizabethan times when it was known as sherry sack; sadly, though, the late 20th century has seen a steep slide in its popularity.**

Somontano

Somontano is a highly promising region in the foothills of the Pyrenees that has not been DO for long. Both local and classic French grapes are being grown in its coolish vineyards and a steady stream of attractive, fairly light reds, *rosatos* (rosés) and whites is the result.

Toro

Only Spain could have a wine region called 'Bull' — and, as if living up to the name, the Tempranillo-based wines of Toro are burly and powerful. They are also richly fruity and, though they are never as stylish and complex as the reds of Ribera del Duero to the east, they are considerably cheaper.

Valdepeñas

Traditional red Valdepeñas is an anaemic looking wine made from as much as four parts Airén (the drab white grape that covers the vast majority of Valdepeñas vineyards) to one part Tempranillo (here called Cencibel). The result doesn't bear any further discussion, but fortunately some producers are now using Cencibel on its own to make well-balanced, oak-matured red wines (Reservas and Gran Reservas) that are remarkable bargains. For the rest, there is a great deal of rather nondescript white, though the best is clean and moderately fruity, and plenty of rather ordinary reds.

Valencia

Valencia in the east produces large quantities of modern, inexpensive whites, together with some acceptable young reds and *rosatos*, but it is becoming better known in Britain for its inexpensive, sweet, barley sugar-like Moscatel de Valencia. While nobody would make any claims for complexity in these wines, they have become much cleaner and fresher in the last few years — and can be useful as a cheap alternative to Muscat de Beaumes-de-Venise.

To the west of the Valencia DO, the region of Utiel-Requena produces some surprisingly delicate, scented *rosatos* and big strong reds, but a fair amount of production slips out under the Valencia name.

Vintages

Rioja

1992	7	▼
1991	8	▼
1990	8	▼
1989	8	★
1988	6	★
1987	8	★
1986	7	★
1985	7	★
1984	4	▲
1983	7	▲

Ribera del Duero

1992	7	▼
1991	8	▼
1990	8	▼
1989	8	★
1988	5	★
1987	6	▲
1986	6	▲
1985	7	★
1984	4	▲
1983	7	▲

Key

0–10 quality rating (10 = top wine)

▲   must drink

★   can drink, but no hurry

▼   must keep

(See also **When to drink**, pages 44–47)

Portugal

Leaving aside its two most famous exports, port and Mateus Rosé, Portugal's great wine strengths are its grapes and its ability to hang onto the baby while it throws out the bathwater. Entry into the EC in 1986 gave the wine industry, especially the large cooperatives which dominate production, a much-needed boost, largely in the form of hefty subsidies. For years the co-ops only released their wines after they had first languished in worn-out wooden or cement vats – losing fruit and gaining a parched astringency. The metamorphosis involving stainless steel and earlier, more effective bottling is not yet complete, but already whole regions have been transformed, particularly the Alentejo, Dão and Setúbal which have attracted both private investment and the services of Australian winemakers.

PORTUGUESE WINE LABELS

Because Portugal's appellation system is still at a formative stage, labelling can be haphazard, but this is a crisp, clear, modern one.
From top to bottom: **the name of the producer (Vinhos Sogrape), and of the wine (Terra Franca); the regiõe determinada from which it comes (Bairrada); the colour (Vinho Tinto) – not of course an essential statement; the vintage (1987); the word 'garrafeira', indicating that it is intended to be a wine of quality and age; bottle size; alcohol content; and details of the bottler. Note that there are no claims that this is an estate-bottled wine: it is blended and bottled by the enormous Sogrape group.**

The crucial point recognised by all the new winemakers, whether native or New World, was the value of the baby – in the form of Portugal's great wealth of interesting indigenous grape varieties. Instead of grasping every opportunity to show the world that Portugal, too, could make convincing Cabernet Sauvignon and Chardonnay (which it can), they have concentrated on developing the best and most characterful of Portugal's own grapes – like the white Fernão Pires, Loureiro and Alvarinho, and the red Periquita and Baga, and port varieties such as Touriga Nacional and Touriga Francesa.

One of the areas that is still very much in a state of flux is Portugal's appellation system, partly because it has had to be changed to meet EC requirements. It is now rather complicated – not to say confused – but don't let that put you off. Briefly, the highest classification is DOC (*denominacâo de origem controlada*) and there are 13 of these regions, but producers may still use instead the pre-EC designation RD (*regiõe determinada*); then there are 44 IPRs (*indicacões de provenciência regulamentada*). There are also the merchants' brands from non-demarcated regions, and merchants' blends, among which some wines are extremely good (the description Garrafeira is a useful indicator of superior quality and age).

Wines and regions

Alentejo

This is a region to watch. In the space of a few years Alentejo, which sprawls across the south of the country, has become one of the most dynamic wine areas, producing vivid, juicy, fruity reds at very low prices. Watch out for high-profile investors, too – already the Rothschilds of Lafite are in.

Bairrada

Bairrada, to the west of the Dão region in the mid-north, began to come up in the world in the late

eighties. The Baga grape gives chunky, peppery, blackcurrant and blackberry flavours here, and the wines can be quite long-lived, although increasingly they are being made softer, less tannic and more accessible when young. White Bairrada, with its herby, fennel character, can also be good.

Dão

The ending in 1990 of the local cooperatives' stranglehold on Dão (until then nobody else was allowed to buy grapes) means that the output of dry, sinewy, stalky reds is now beginning to be challenged by wines with richer fruit and spicy flavours. Whites lag behind, but a few crisp, lemony examples are showing the way.

Douro

Under half of each year's harvest in the northerly Douro Valley is generally authorised to be made into port. The rest remains as table wine and, until recently, with the exception of Barca Velha (Portugal's unofficial 'first growth') and one or two others, no one put much effort into these. A tough port market has concentrated minds and several port houses are starting to make impressive, spicy, fruity, velvety wines.

(*Below*) **The port vineyards of the Douro are graded from A to F according to quality, but high up in the hills of the Upper Douro the vineyards are more suited to table wine, which is a growing sideline for port shippers.**

The Wine Regions of Portugal

Madeira

Madeira, one of the world's great fortified wines (and even more unfashionable today than the others), has a distinctively tangy taste acquired through a long ageing process during which all but the very finest wines are heated in large tanks called *estufas*. The best wines are aged more gently and slowly in cask.

The famous styles of madeira are named after the island's four classic (white) grape varieties,

(*Above*) **Vines and bananas jostle for space on Madeira's terraced slopes and many of the vines are the inferior Tinta Negra Mole variety, but at least in future madeira will have to be made from the grape stated on the label.**

though until an EC regulation came into force to ensure that the wines really do contain at least 85 percent of the stated grape, most were based on the inferior Tinta Negra Mole variety, and lesser wines are still made from it. The driest is Sercial, followed by Verdelho, both of which are traditionally drunk chilled as aperitifs; Bual (sweet) and Malmsey (very sweet and dark) are pudding wines or postprandials. Other terms seen on labels are 'Finest', which means the wine has been aged for only three years and is very far from fine; Reserve, which is five years old and slightly better; Special Reserve, which is at least 10 years old and should be concentrated and complex; the rarely seen Extra Reserve, aged for 15 years; and Vintage, which is rare, expensive and very good indeed. All madeira is ready to drink once bottled, though it will live almost indefinitely if unopened. It needn't be decanted.

Oeste

The large Oeste region north of Lisbon has been slower to change than Alentejo, but three of the six IPRs into which it is subdivided are improving: Arruda, with big, cheerful, hearty reds; Alenquer, with softer, smoother reds; and Torres Vedras, with lighter, crisper ones.

Port

This sweet, red fortified wine comes from the hot, dry Douro Valley where nearly 90 grape varieties are authorised (though five dominate in terms of quality) on the thin schistous soil and steep, sometimes precipitous, slopes and terraces. As seen already (page 80) the several styles of port fall into two clear categories. Vintage port – long-lived and expensive – is made only in the best years and from the grapes of one vintage only. It is bottled two years after the harvest and then matured in bottle.

Other ports are matured in wooden casks and are ready to drink when bottled. Single Quinta vintage ports, from a single property (the *quinta*), are vintage ports from lesser years – often excellent, and faster-maturing than traditional vintage wines.

Of the wood-aged ports, aged tawnies are usually of very high quality and mostly give their age on the label – 10, 20, 30 or 40 years, typically a blend of several vintages, so this is their average age. They are lighter and nuttier than vintage wines. Cheap tawny and ruby wines are of inferior quality. Late Bottled Vintage (from a single year) and Vintage Character wines are intended to have the style of vintage port at lower prices, but are mostly pretty weak shadows of the real thing (the word Traditional on the label may indicate a more authentic style). A better bet is the more unusual Crusted, or Crusting, port which throws a deposit

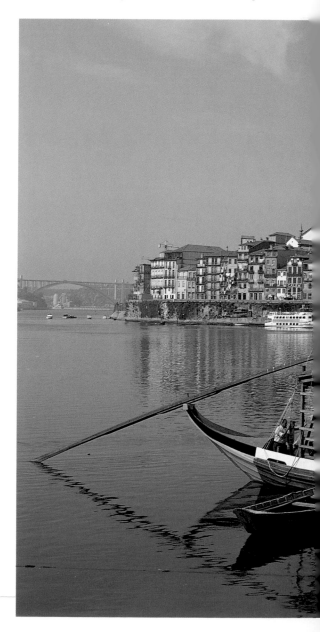

in bottle and needs decanting like true vintage port (including Single Quinta).

White port ranges from sweet to dry and is not a drink of any great finesse. It is at its best drunk well-chilled while basking in the heat of the Douro.

Rosé

Portuguese rosés, led by the redoubtable Mateus, can come from anywhere, though most big brands come from the relatively cool north. They are usually slightly sweet and slightly sparkling and, though much derided, perfectly sound and pleasant.

Setúbal (Entre Tejo e Sado)

This peninsula south of Lisbon, with its two IPRs – Palmela and Arrabida – has been in the vanguard of new wave Portuguese winemaking, with forward-looking wineries making excellent New World-influenced wines: crisp, aromatic and oaked whites, from grapes such as Muscat and Chardonnay, as well as native varieties; and alongside top quality, spicy, raspberry-scented red Periquita, there is rich, concentrated Cabernet and Merlot. Setúbal also has its own ultra-traditional wine, Moscatel de Setúbal: a fortified wine, with an orange-toffee-marmalade taste, bottled after either six or 25 years.

Vinho Verde

Over half of all Vinho Verde, from the rainy Minho in the far north, is in fact lean, tart red wine, but the wine exported is white. It is also usually sweetened, which is a shame because the bone dry versions from single estates, and preferably from Loureiro and Alvarinho grapes, have a much more mouth-watering flavour. Whatever the style, drink it young (that is what 'Verde' means in this context).

Vintages

Dão & Bairrada

1992	7	▼
1991	7	★
1990	7	★
1989	6	▲
1988	8	★
1987	5	▲
1986	5	▲
1985	8	★
1984	4	▲
1983	8	▲
1982	8	▲

Port

1992	9	▼
1991	9	▼
1990	7	▼
1989	6	▼
1988	6	★
1987	6	★
1986	5	★
1985	9	▼
1984	5	▲
1983	8	★
1982	7	★

Key

0–10 quality rating (10 = top wine)

▲   must drink

★   can drink, but no hurry

▼   must keep

(See also **When to drink**, pages 44–47)

(*Left*) **Until the Douro was dammed during the sixties and early seventies, the distinctive barcos rabelos (moored left) were used to carry pipes of port (barrels containing about 600 litres) from the port farms high up in the Douro to the lodges (cellars) by the sea at Vila Nova de Gaia.**

QUINTA DOS CANAIS

USA and Canada

In theory the modern wine history of the USA dates from the ending of Prohibition in 1933, but in practice it took another three decades to get over post-Prohibition blues and it was not until the late sixties that wine production began to spread rapidly and wine areas and growers multiplied. Today, having overtaken both Argentina and the former Soviet Union in the last five years, the USA ranks fourth in quantity among the world's producers. Only Italy, France and Spain produce more, while Australia, in fourteenth place, makes only about a quarter as much. And it is California that makes the majority of USA wine. Although most states now make _vinifera_ wine of some sort, 95 percent of it comes from California – and it was California in the seventies which first showed the world that great wines no longer came exclusively from Europe and predominantly from France.

(_Below_) **Old vines, meticulously trained younger vines and mustard on the Silverado Trail: mustard is often used by organic growers – it keeps weeds at bay and is ploughed in as 'green' manure.**

In the intervening years, while California has had to face up to the challenge of better value varietal wines being offered by Australia, New Zealand and to some degree Chile, it has taken its own top wines even closer in style and quality to the great French classics – and has come closer to them than has any other country.

That they should come so near is slightly curious, because in many ways California viticulture is the antithesis of French. In France, heavy emphasis is

given to the soil; in California, though soil is gaining credibility, especially in the Napa Valley, the accent is still on climate. Equally, each French wine has its framework laid down in the *appellation contrôlée* laws, so that an AC is a guide (if not a guarantee) of style; California (and the rest of the USA) has a widespread appellation system of Approved Viticultural Areas, but the AVAs simply define regions. Growers can grow what they want, where they want, without bureaucratic stricture (and thus, on a label, the grape variety and the producer's name are the keys to style).

Despite the freedom, the range of grape varieties, at least for premium quality wines, is not extensive. Most Californian producers choose Cabernet Sauvignon and Chardonnay. Merlot and Pinot Noir, though fashionable, are still a long way behind in terms of volume. The same, only far more so, applies to Rhône varieties such as Syrah and Viognier and Italian grapes such as Nebbiolo and Sangiovese (though all are made by mavericks to impressive standards). Sauvignon Blanc and Riesling are abundant but seldom very interesting (sweet late-harvest Rieslings being an exception); and grapes such as Colombard, Chenin Blanc and Grenache disappear into cheap, blended so-called 'jug' wines. California does, however, have one world-class grape of its own, Zinfandel. Much of this is turned into vapid pink wine (known as 'white' or 'blush') and 'jug' wine, but, given the opportunity, it makes splendid, ripe, spicy, velvety reds.

In states such as Oregon, Washington, New York and Texas, much the same applies (although often with more successful dry Rieslings), but for most other states the great standbys are North America's own indigenous (hardy, but generally low quality) *Vitis labrusca* and hybrids.

California

Mendocino

Two wine regions north of San Francisco Bay are Mendocino and the smaller Lake County to the north of Napa and Sonoma. Although they boast some of the North Coast's coolest spots and relatively long growing seasons, Mendocino also has sheltered, warm sites, and from these come soft, round, fruity Cabernets. In contrast, Pacific-cooled Anderson Valley produces first-class Chardonnay-Pinot Noir sparkling wines (the best so far from Roederer champagne's USA offshoot) and some racy whites (especially Chardonnay, Riesling and Gewürztraminer).

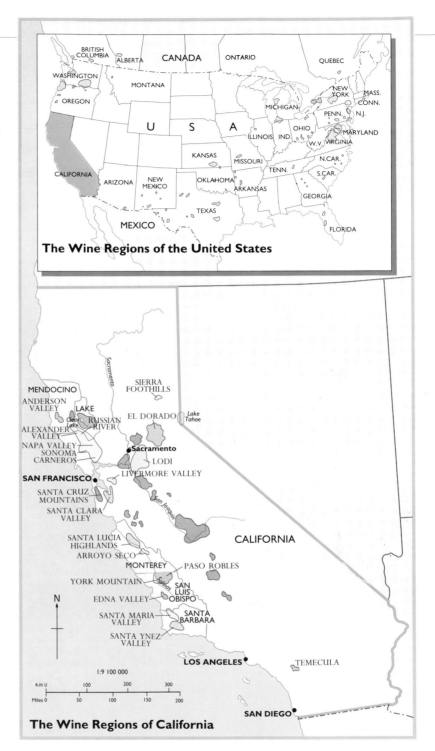

The Wine Regions of the United States

The Wine Regions of California

Monterey

Cooled by sea breezes and fogs, and with the longest growing season of all the California wine regions, coastal Monterey, south of San Francisco Bay, was originally thought too cold for vines and it was not until the seventies that it began to make its mark. The range of grapes is varied: there are both Cabernet and Riesling (especially good from Arroyo Seco), but the stars are Chardonnay and, in the San Benito AVA, superb, burgundy-styled Pinot Noir.

Napa Valley

Napa Valley, to the north of San Francisco Bay, was the first area of California to make its mark and is still in the lead, with a concentration of quality, great names and important subregions. From subregions such as Rutherford-Oakville, Stag's Leap, Howell Mountain, Spring Mountain and Mount Veeder come California's greatest Cabernet Sauvignons and Cabernet Sauvignon-Merlot-Cabernet Franc blends – powerful, full-bodied wines with the potential to age 10 years, but with a suppleness and fruitiness, too. Carneros, a cooler subregion at the south of the valley overlapping with the south of Sonoma, produces outstanding Pinot Noirs – indeed most of the best Pinot Noirs outside Burgundy. There are also some impressively crisp, elegant, yet richly buttery, complex Chardonnays from Carneros and its cool climate has attracted sparkling wine producers, including champagne houses. Napa's only problems are phylloxera, which is causing most of the valley to be replanted, and which in turn is exacerbating Napa's other problem – wine prices too high relative to the rest of the world's.

San Francisco Bay

The Bay area, especially the Livermore Valley, was one of California's first wine regions. Cabernet, Chardonnay and Sauvignon are all successful, though rarely thrilling, but pockets of exciting Cabernet and Zinfandel can be found in the rugged Santa Cruz mountains to the south of the Bay.

Santa Barbara and San Luis Obispo

Like Monterey, these two coastal counties benefit from the cooling effect of the Pacific and can make outstanding Chardonnay and Pinot Noir – in particular the Chardonnay of Edna Valley (San Luis Obispo) and Pinot Noir of Santa Maria (Santa Barbara). From the warmer areas, there is excellent rich, robust Paso Robles Zinfandel and Cabernet and good, fleshy Merlot from Santa Ynez Valley.

Sonoma

Less flashy than neighbouring Napa in its landscape, architecture and wine, Sonoma, is the other great wine district of California, with even more AVAs (among the most notable, the Russian River and Alexander valleys). Though closer to the Pacific, it produces broadly similar wines to high standards, but with an overall feeling of slightly gentler, softer textures. If Napa ultimately takes the Cabernet crown, Sonoma arguably takes the Chardonnay one, with wines that are marginally more structured and a little more refined. Its Sauvignons (Fumés), too, tend to have more vitality and cleaner flavours.

Other regions

The hot, fertile Central Valley makes about 60 percent of California's wine: the bulk is cheap jug wine, but one producer (Quady in Madera) makes some that is entrancing, exotic and sweet. Blockbuster Zinfandels come from the Shenandoah Valley in the Sierra Foothills.

(*Right*) **The cooler coastal areas of Santa Barbara produce some excellent Pinot Noir, but here in the warmer Santa Ynez Valley varieties such as Merlot flourish and give rich, velvety reds.**

(*Right*) **New vineyards in Dundee, Oregon, one of the hot spots of Pinot Noir – at least when the weather is kind.**

Oregon

Quality winemaking having trickled slowly into the state from California in the mid-sixties, Oregon, with its cool, Pacific Northwest climate, was suddenly being prematurely hyped in 1980 as the USA's best bet for Pinot Noir. There is potential, particularly in the Dundee Hills of the Willamette Valley (why else would the Burgundian producer Robert Drouhin being making wine there?), and it is beginning to be realised too, but the climate is extraordinarily like Burgundy's, which means there will always be more poor and mediocre vintages than in California.

Other varieties that do well in these chilly conditions are the aromatic Pinot Gris and Riesling. Chardonnay tends to be lean, but that should suit the recent investors from Champagne.

Washington State

Perhaps because it was on the trail of Pinot Noir (the winemakers' Holy Grail), Oregon has attracted most attention so far. Only relatively recently have outsiders come to realise that Oregon's larger, northern neighbour, Washington State, is not only more productive, but produces a wider range of high quality wines. Intense fruit flavour is their hallmark, whether from Cabernet Sauvignon, Merlot, Chardonnay, Sauvignon Blanc or Riesling (the latter including some late-harvest sweet wines).

New York State

Anyone who has sampled a New York winter will have a fair idea of its climate – harsh, with a short growing season. Most of the vines are still hybrids or *Vitis labrusca*, but *vinifera* vines – varieties like Chardonnay, Rhine Riesling and Pinot Noir – are planted round the Finger Lakes, Hudson River and on Long Island. And it is Chardonnay from Long Island that has been making waves and fooling people into thinking it is burgundy.

Canada

Vitis labrusca and hybrids rule in Canada because of the hard winters, but the growers of Ontario have founded the Vintners' Quality Alliance to raise and maintain standards of *vinifera* wines. The best wines, mostly Chardonnay and Riesling from the warmer microclimates on the shores of lakes Ontario and Eyrie, are broadly French in style. The hybrid Vidal Blanc also makes some attractive, rounded but crisp whites.

Vintages		
California Cabernet		
1992	8	▼
1991	9	▼
1990	9	★
1989	7	★
1988	7	▲
1987	8	★
1986	9	★
1985	10	★
1984	9	★
1983	6	▲

South America

Vines arrived in Chile, Argentina and Peru with the Spanish Conquistadores in the mid-16th century and almost every South American country now makes wine, but only Chile can claim to have a semi-modern industry and some claim to producing quality wines in any quantity. And even Chile is clearly not in the California-Australia-New Zealand league.

Chile

Classic French varieties from Bordeaux – Cabernet Sauvignon, Cabernet Franc, Merlot, Malbec, Sémillon and Sauvignon Blanc – so far as we know were all established in Chile in the 1850s and 1860s, and, when the rest of the world's vineyards were wiped out by phylloxera in the late 19th and early 20th centuries, Chile's were not. Phylloxera simply never penetrated the country's natural barriers – desert in the north, polar extremes in the south, the Pacific to the west and the Andes, averaging 4,000 metres, all along the east. Consequently Chile's vines do not need grafting onto phylloxera-resistant rootstock.

This is undoubtedly of historic and viticultural interest, but whether we should attribute too much to it in terms of quality and flavour of the wines is questionable. Indeed, if anything, Chile's reputation for being a grape-growing paradise – perfect, light, ideal climate, protection against disease – has been quite a handicap in the years up to the nineties. Most producers were so convinced their environment gave them perfect grapes they didn't check it was actually so. Instead they often took huge yields of inevitably dilute fruit from all varieties and continued to pass off the inferior Sauvignonasse (or Sauvignon Vert) grape as Sauvignon Blanc. Political and economic situations up until 1989 didn't help. They gave the industry limited opportunities to see and share in what was happening in places like California, Australia and New Zealand, and little chance to invest in much needed modern equipment.

But things have been moving fast in the last three or four years. Several high-profile foreign investors, including the Lafite-Rothschilds of Bordeaux, have given an enormous boost, and each year is bringing greater consistency and higher quality, especially in

Cabernet, Merlot, Chardonnay and Sauvignon, and some Riesling, Gewürztraminer and Pinot Noir.

Almost without exception these wines come from the Central Valley. Other wine regions either produce grapes for distillation into Pisco, the local brandy, or make low quality wines (mostly from the Pais grape) for local consumption. The fertile Central Valley, stretching for 250 miles parallel to the Andes, is the region dubbed the viticultural paradise. East-west valleys running from the Andes to the Pacific provide natural irrigation and the slopes rather than plains that produce the best wines.

From north to south, the four valleys whose names are most often found on labels are Aconcagua, Maipo (near Santiago, the most famous), Colchagua and Curico (alias Lontué). Those towards the south and the coast are cooler and tend to produce the best white wines, while inland and to the north, where it is warmer, there is a bias towards reds. Among newer regions are Chillan in the south and Casablanca. The latter, lying west of Santiago, nearer the cool of the coast, is already making a name for excellent Chardonnay and Sauvignon Blanc.

Argentina

Argentina is the largest wine producer in South America and the fifth largest in the world (Chile is sixteenth). The vineyards are hot and dry, irrigation is essential, yields are generally enormous, quality is low, and the local market does not mind. That said, things are beginning to stir, especially in the Mendoza region. There are some good Cabernets and Merlots, some even better Malbecs (with a spicy-tobacco character), a few respectable young Chardonnays and some interesting aromatic, floral whites made from the Torrontes grape.

Mexico

With a mostly subtropical climate, it is not surprising that Mexico comes 32nd in the world wine production league table and exports little. However, reds from Baja California are worth looking for – especially dark, chocolatey, peppery, bramble jelly-flavoured Petite Sirahs and Cabernet Sauvignons.

(*Above*) **The Andes not only provide Chile's vineyards with a natural barrier against phylloxera – they supply natural irrigation too.**

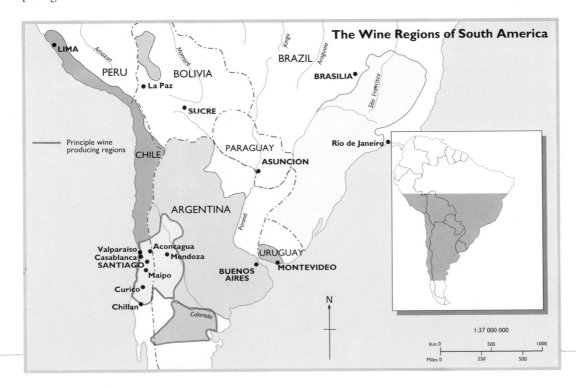

Australia

Australia is bigger, hotter and younger than most of the rest of the wine world, but what sets it apart – or rather ahead – is its sheer dynamism. Until the sixties, three-quarters of its consumption and production was of fortified wines, and for a decade or so after that the red table wines which dominated were largely the sort of brawny heavyweights that you didn't know whether to drink, eat or stir with a spoon. The first commercial Chardonnay was released as recently as 1973 (by Tyrrells in the Hunter Valley), when the white wine boom was just beginning. Yet now Australian Chardonnay is on dining tables the length and breadth of Britain (in North America, Scandinavia, Germany and Japan, too) and it is Australian winemakers who teach the world's new Chardonnay producers – in the south of France, Hungary, Moldova – how to make their wines.

It is not only Chardonnay, of course. Although Australia's vineyards are confined almost entirely to the cooler points, furthest from the equator – to the southeast and to a lesser extent to the southwest (with all due respect to Chateau Hornsby of Alice Springs and the Granite Belt in Queensland) – there is sufficient climatic variation to suit more or less any grape variety. Alongside lesser varieties such as Colombard, Chenin Blanc, Gordo (a type of Muscat), Traminer, Grenache and Mataro (alias Mourvèdre), which are largely consigned to basic blends or bag-

in-box wines, Rhine Riesling, Semillon, Shiraz (Australia's alias for Syrah) and Cabernet Sauvignon all flourish widely, although giving a naturally riper, fuller style than in Europe. Pinot Noir and Sauvignon Blanc have been typically much harder to please, but energetic and determined winemakers are increasingly finding cool, often high-altitude microclimates that favour Pinot Noir in particular.

It is also these cooler areas that are making Chardonnays, sparkling wines and Cabernet Sauvignons of greater subtlety, complexity and, it is

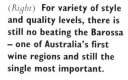

(*Right*) **For variety of style and quality levels, there is still no beating the Barossa – one of Australia's first wine regions and still the single most important.**

hoped by their makers, longevity. But we should not let the appeal of the fashionable new regions, with their inevitably more expensive, hand-crafted wines, overshadow what is still Australia's winning formula: affordable, uncomplicated, lusciously fruity, seductively oaky varietals and blends – wines made on a Brobdignagian scale, under blue skies and bright sunshine in giant high-tech wineries, by skilfully blending grapes trucked in hundreds, even thousands, of miles from any regions that come up with the right quality at the right price at harvest time.

Wines and regions

Fortified wines

Australia's most traditional style, these have steadily declined in favour of table wines, but are still worth trying. There are good port types, mostly from Shiraz and Grenache, but the flagships are wood-matured liqueur Muscat and Tokay from Victoria: dark, rich, intensely treacley-sweet with, especially in Muscat, a surprisingly attractive Earl Grey tea-like taste.

Adelaide Hills

East of Adelaide, Adelaide Hills is not a new district, but very much a rising star. The key is its high altitudes, giving cool enough climates to produce concentrated, elegant wines in a variety of styles. Its several strong suits are lime-scented (and, with age, toasty) Rhine Riesling, complex and age-worthy Chardonnay, some of Australia's best Pinot Noir and sparkling wines, and excellent Cabernet Sauvignon and Shiraz.

Barossa Valley

Colonised by German immigrants in the 1840s, whose influence is still felt in flourishing oompah bands and German names, the Barossa, northeast of Adelaide, is one of Australia's oldest wine regions, with most of the largest, oldest wineries still there. Making wines from grapes trucked in from all over South Australia, it produces a breadth of styles ranging from soft, fruity Rhine Rieslings to fat, waxy Chardonnays, rich, oaky Semillons and attractive, rounded, easygoing sparkling wines, and from inexpensive, minty, jammy Shiraz-Cabenet blends to the monumental, long-lived, Shiraz-based reds epitomised by Grange, Australia's top red.

(*Left*) **Even Grange itself is blended at Penfolds' ultra-modern Nuriootpa winery in the Barossa, but the best reds then go off to the original Magill cellars for ageing.**

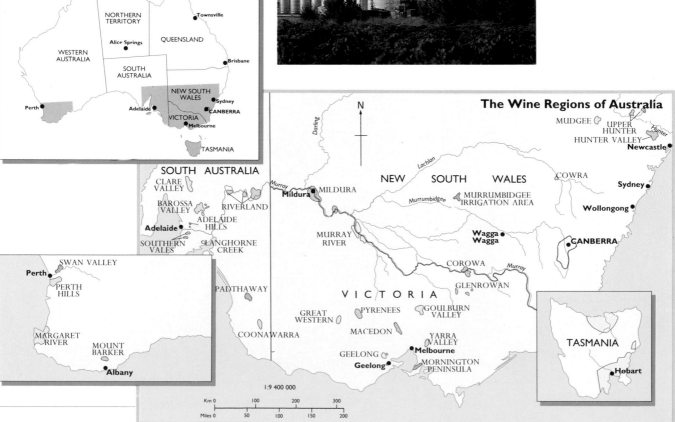

Clare Valley

Smaller than the Barossa and further north from Adelaide, the peaceful Clare Valley has a name for producing some of Australia's finest, most long-lived and intensely lime-flavoured Rieslings. The reds, from Cabernet and Shiraz, are also impressive.

Coonawarra

In southeast South Australia on the border with Victoria, Coonawarra, with its distinctive Terra Rossa soil (red soil over limestone), is perhaps Australia's best argument so far for an appellation system. Its reputation was built on its superb Cabernet Sauvignons, with their seductively vivid mint and blackcurrant flavours, but Shiraz is also outstanding, as is, increasingly, Chardonnay, and there are outposts of good Riesling and Sauvignon.

Great Western

Thanks to the Seppelt company, which still has its main winery here in central Victoria, Great Western, to most people, means a brand of sparkling wine. In fact this is predominantly red wine territory, with high quality, dense, chunky Shiraz and good Cabernet.

Hunter Valley

Hunter Valley Semillon, from north of Sydney in New South Wales, is one of Australia's unique wines. The original unoaked style can be drunk when it is young, crisp and citrusy, or left about eight years to acquire a toasted, dry honey-and-straw character; but increasingly Semillon is being made more in the Chardonnay mould, with a little oak and to be drunk young. Chardonnay itself, which is becoming more important, tends to be ebulliently fruity, fat and oaky. Reds are dominated

by broad, ripe Shirazes (which used to have the famous 'sweaty saddle' character – *see* page 16), although Cabernet, like Chardonnay, is increasingly making its mark. Surprisingly, for so warm a climate, there is also good Pinot Noir. Look out also for Chardonnays from the newly recognised (by the EC) Cowra region in New South Wales.

Margaret River

Although none of Australia's major wine companies has invested in Margaret River in Western Australia, the region's sandy soil, warm climate and sheer beauty have attracted a clutch of talented winemakers. While impressively claret-like Cabernets draw the most accolades, there are some stunning Chardonnays, good Shirazes and vibrant Semillons.

McLaren Vale

Originally a producer of the kind of strapping, heavy reds that used to be prescribed as tonics by doctors (at least in Britain), McClaren Vale, south of Adelaide, has turned to lighter wines and is making notable Cabernet Sauvignon and Shiraz, rich Chardonnay and fine Sauvignon Blanc.

Mudgee

Mudgee's high altitudes give it cool nights, warm days and a longer growing season than the Hunter

Vintages		
Hunter Valley Shiraz		
1993	8	▼
1992	6	★
1991	9	▼
1990	6	★
1989	7	★
1988	6	▲
1987	9	★
1986	9	★
1985	7	▲
1984	7	▲

Key

0–10 quality rating (10 = top wine)

▲   must drink

★   can drink, but no hurry

▼   must keep

(*See also* **When to drink**, pages 44–47)

(*Right*) **With several high-profile individuals based there, the pretty and peaceful-looking Hunter Valley has a reputation for producing five percent of Australia's wine and 50 percent of the noise.**

Valley further east in New South Wales. The result is deep, full-bodied Cabernet Sauvignons and some rich, ripe Chardonnays.

Murrumbidgee Irrigation Area

This hot, dry area miles from anywhere, in New South Wales, depends on irrigation to produce huge volumes of basic white wine, much of it for bag-in-box, but there is also a sublime botrytis-affected dessert wine made from Semillon by De Bortoli.

Padthaway

Just north of the supreme red wine region district of Coonawarra in South Australia is one of the country's greatest white wine regions, Padthaway. It is most famous for its Chardonnay, but Riesling and Sauvignon Blanc are equally good.

Riverland

The vast irrigated vineyards along the Murray River in South Australia account for about a third of Australia's annual harvest. Much of the wine is destined for bag-in-box; the rest mostly provides fresh, fruity, inexpensive varietals and blends.

Tasmania

Tasmania is so cool it's positively cold, and high winds can be a problem for growers, but the potential is there for great cool-climate wines. All sorts of grapes are being tried, and these are early days,

but the best results are coming from Chardonnay, Cabernet Sauvignon, Pinot Noir and 'méthode traditionelle' sparkling wines – all in tiny quantities.

Yarra Valley

The Yarra in Victoria, is one of Australia's most historic and now, once again, one of its fastest growing wine regions. Apart from proximity to Melbourne, producers are attracted by the way its cool climate divides into several specialised microclimates giving scope for top Pinot Noirs, Chardonnays, Cabernets, Bordeaux-style blends, and outstanding sparkling wines. (Since the latter are made by Domaine Chandon – Moët & Chandon's Australian offshoot – the Champenois don't know whether to laugh or cry.)

Other regions

In Victoria: Goulburn Valley and Bendigo for full, flavoursome reds from Cabernet and Shiraz, and equally full and flavoursome dry white Marsanne; Geelong for concentrated Cabernet and Shiraz and classic Pinot Noir; Glenrowan for muscular Shiraz (and liqueur Muscats); Mornington Peninsula for elegant Pinot Noir and Chardonnay; Pyrenees for substantial, fleshy, sometimes minty Cabernets, good Shiraz and, surprisingly, respectable Sauvignon. In Western Australia the hot Swan Valley produces good value, full, soft reds and whites, and Mount Barker is producing excellent Cabernet.

(*Above*) **From tanks such as these in the Barossa Valley come vast quantities of cheap but sound wine – much of it destined for what Australians call 'bladder packs' (alias bag-in-box).**

Vintages

South Australia (reds)		
1993	9	▼
1992	7	★
1991	8	★
1990	9	★
1989	7	▲
1988	8	★
1987	7	▲
1986	6	▲
1985	7	▲
1984	7	▲

New Zealand

New Zealand did not so much emerge as shoot onto the international wine scene in the late eighties. Having dispensed with fortified wines during the sixties and seventies and then in the early eighties with much of the Müller-Thurgau that had fuelled the transition from fortified to table wines, it produced its trump card, Sauvignon Blanc – and it was Sauvignon Blanc that reminded the world what the grape should really taste like.

Climate is the key. New Zealand is the cool-climate capital of the New World. Although it is a long country, covering the equivalent of the latitude between Germany's Rheingau and Algeria, the differences in climate are not so dramatic. The vineyards are largely concentrated in three areas on the drier eastern side of both North and South Islands where the long, cool growing season (provided it is not too long and cool) produces white wines of exceptional fruit intensity, classic varietal character and nerve tingling acidity – not only

from Sauvignon Blanc, but from Chardonnay, Riesling (both dry and sweet), Chenin Blanc and others. (Müller-Thurgau is still the widely planted work-horse grape, but is little exported.) Such is the intensity and balance of these wines that even Sauvignon and Chenin can take well to oak barrel fermentation. At the other end of the ripeness scale, the leanest Chardonnays and Pinot Noirs are being used to make some very impressive sparkling wines.

It is still relatively early days for red wines, for which the climate seemed too cool at first, but they are catching up in quality now that grape varieties are being matched to soils and climates. The most promising results are coming from Cabernet Sauvignon blended with Merlot (rounder and less herbaceous than Cabernet alone) in the warmer North Island and from Pinot Noir in the south.

New Zealand's new Regional Denomination System is based entirely on the location of vineyards, progressively subdividing the country into regions, localities and individual vineyards with no reference to quality, soil or climate.

Wines and regions

Gisborne

Gisborne, on the North Island, has been rather overshadowed by Marlborough in recent years and rather demeaned by its own reputation for making New Zealand's cheap everyday wines, especially bag-in-box, from grapes like Müller-Thurgau. In fact its Chardonnay, which tends to be richer than Marlborough's, is especially successful, and there are other good whites, including Gewürztraminer and vibrant, fruity Chenin Blanc. Reds are more variable.

Hawke's Bay

Third in size of New Zealand's major regions, this is proving to be the most exciting for red wines. It lies south of Gisborne on the North Island and is hotter than both Bordeaux and Coonawarra. From gravelly alluvial soils, come some impressive tobacco-scented, claret-like Cabernet-Merlot blends and pure Merlot; there are good Chardonnays, too – fatter and more pineappley than Marlborough's.

Marlborough

At the northern end of the South Island, Marlborough's reputation is based on its Sauvignon Blanc – much of it trucked to wineries elsewhere for vinification. Styles vary from the riper, more tropical fruit flavours of cult wine Cloudy Bay to herbaceous gooseberry-and-nettle flavours, but always with the penetrating fruit and acidity. But despite its Sauvignon fame, there is actually slightly more Chardonnay, the style of which tends to be a little leaner than that from other regions and it is often used with Pinot Noir in the increasingly fine sparkling wines. Cabernet Sauvignon, with or without Merlot, tends to have a grassy, blackcurrant freshness, rather than weight or richness.

Other regions

Martinborough, a subdistrict of the Wairarapa region in the south of the North Island, has pro-

duced New Zealand's finest, most burgundian Pinot Noir so far and also some good Chardonnay and Sauvignon Blanc. The continental climate of Central Otago (southern South Island) is beginning to bring rewards with Pinot Noir too, and with Gewürztraminer. Waiheke, an island in Auckland harbour, has some notable Cabernet Sauvignon-Merlot blends and Chardonnay. And the small wineries of Nelson (in the north of the South Island) make full-flavoured Chardonnay, classic Sauvignon Blanc, late-harvest Riesling and Pinot Noir. Auckland, more a centre of vinification than viticulture these days, still produces some interesting home-grown wines, including fat, butterscotch-flavoured Chardonnay from the Kumeu subdistrict; and there is attractive Chardonnay and Pinot Blanc from around Christchurch in Canterbury. The other wines not to be missed are New Zealand's champagne-like sparkling wines which may come from anywhere.

The Wine Regions of New Zealand

South Africa

South Africa claims to have the oldest wine tradition in the New World (though South America would dispute that), but her modern history has been more chequered than any. President de Klerk's landmark speech in February 1991, heralding the end of Apartheid, brought South African wines back to overseas markets, but the wine industry, because of its previous international isolation, has developed along different lines from the anything-goes experimentation of, say, Australia and California. And, whereas fortified wine production has fallen away dramatically in these other New World countries, in South Africa it is still very significant, even though these wines are little exported now.

Technically, South African wineries are bang up-to-date, but the red wines in the recent past often had a burnt, rubbery harshness and the more serious white wines, the oak-aged Chardonnays, were often clumsily over-oaked. Exposure to the tastes of other markets, and competition with the likes of Australia, Chile and Bulgaria, is now bringing change. The reds are becoming softer, with richness taking the place of harshness; the Chardonnays are more subtle and more complex; and the inexpensive dry and off-dry whites, whether Chenin Blanc (which accounts for a third of the area under vine), Colombard or Sauvignon Blanc, have become brisker and fruitier.

This is as it should be, since South Africa, or at least the eastern Cape, is well-endowed with natural resources. Nearly 100,000 hectares of vines are concentrated in the coastal area, in an arc of land centred on Cape Town which has an ideal Mediterranean climate and a patchwork of varied microclimates, especially in the mountain foothills of Paarl and Stellenbosch. It is also largely disease-free.

Such conditions obviously suit mainstream European grape varieties – in addition to the whites already mentioned, Cabernet Sauvignon, Merlot, Shiraz, Cinsaut, Muscat and in a limited way Pinot Noir – but South Africa does have one variety of its

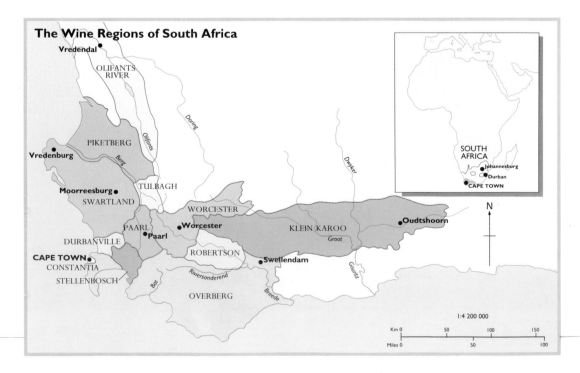

The Wine Regions of South Africa

own, the red Pinotage. A cross between Pinot Noir and workaday red Cinsaut, it gives a robust spicy-peppery character and warm berry fruit. It also has a tendency to give harsh tannin and rubberiness, but the best wines can develop some meaty complexity with age, and, if tannin is held in check, can be appealingly raspberry-scented and early-maturing.

With nearly 5,000 wine growers and just 82 single estates, the industry is dominated in quantity terms (though certainly not in quality) by the cooperatives – especially the KWV, or Kooperatieve Wijnbouwers Vereniging. This is both the largest producer of wine and the industry's policeman – although it is in the process of divesting itself of its regulatory role to concentrate more on production and marketing. The other giants are the Stellenbosch Farmers' Union (SFU) and the Distillers Corporation with its sister company, the Bergkelder.

South Africa's Wine of Origin system divides the wine growing areas into regions, districts, wards and estates, in decreasing order of size, and every bottle of wine exported carries a small black and white paper seal guaranteeing any claims regarding origin, vintage and grape variety.

Wines and regions

Constantia

The Constantia ward, close to the sea on the outskirts of Cape Town, gave its name to the most renowned wine of the Cape in past centuries – a dessert Muscat, made by leaving the grapes on the vines late into the autumn to dry. A little sweet Muscat is once again being made in this way.

Paarl

Thirty miles from Cape Town, with wet winters, long, warm, dry summers and a variety of soils, Paarl, which includes the famous ward of Franschhoek, is one of the best wine regions. Most of the main grape varieties are grown here, but Cabernet Sauvignon, Pinotage, Chardonnay, Sauvignon Blanc and Chenin Blanc are all notable.

Robertson

Together with some of the better cooperatives, there are some excellent estates in Robertson, all of them relying on irrigation in the hot, dry climate of this central region. Fortified wines still dominate, but table wines are on the increase and there is now particularly good Chardonnay and also some notable Shiraz.

Stellenbosch

Several of South Africa's top red wines come from the mountain foothills of the Stellenbosch, where there is an extraordinary concentration of fine estates (34 of the country's 82), as well as the three big companies. Most varieties do well here, but Cabernet Sauvignon, especially when blended with Merlot and Cabernet Franc (increasingly the Cape trend), can be impressive and long-lived.

Other regions

South Africa's coolest vineyard area, Walker Bay in the far south Overberg district, yields excellent, burgundy-style Pinot Noir and Chardonnay. Olifants River and Swartland are good sources of inexpensive, fresh, zesty whites.

(Below) **The years of isolation over, South Africa is now beginning to make the most of its enviable natural resources – not least in the Mediterranean climate and varied soils of Paarl's mountain foothills.**

Austria and Switzerland

Austria has emerged in the nineties as a small but outstanding producer of white wines, and yet outside its own borders its wines are little known. The lack of recognition is partly due to the enduring legacy of the 1985 scandal (the innacurately dubbed antifreeze affair), partly because it keeps most of its best wines to itself and partly because Austrian wines, at least in Britain, are commonly thought of as little more than an extension of Germany's.

There are parallels with German wines: the classification based on ripeness is similar, with *Tafelwein*, *Landwein*, *Qualitätswein*, *Kabinett* and *Prädikatswein* (the latter covering *Spätlese* to *Trockenbeerenauslese*); there is a new vineyard classification using the term *Erst Lager* (first estate), as in the Rheingau; and the two countries share several grape varieties, most notably Riesling. But Austria has significant varieties of its own, including the peppery white Grüner Veltliner (a third of the country's vines), the high-sugar Bouvier (used for sweet wines), the nutty white Neuburger, the perfumed red St-Laurent and the juicy, cherry-flavoured red, Zweigelt. Austria also does well with classic French varieties, such as Chardonnay and Pinot Noir, which

are increasingly being fermented and aged in oak barrels in the Burgundian manner.

In fact, Austria's southerly wine areas lie on the same latitude as Burgundy (its northerly ones being closer to Champagne), but they have a more continental climate, with cold winters and warm summers. The results are mostly white wines: aromatic, with steely crispness but more ripeness and alcohol and softer acidity than Germany's and a slightly lighter feel than Alsace's. Reds tend to be light- to medium-bodied, fruity and perfumed, with firmness given by acidity rather than tannin – more Beaujolais Cru than Bordeaux or burgundy, if you like.

All the vineyards lie in the east, spread over three regions. Lower Austria produces masses of lively, spicy Grüner Veltliner, some superb, age-worthy Riesling, especially from the Wachau, and light, clean whites from around Vienna. Burgenland is a mecca for sweet wine: noble rot arrives every year around the Neusiedler See in the north and produces opulent wines that are roughly Germanic in style, but fuller; away from the lake there are good, elegant, dry whites, especially Chardonnay, Traminer, Ruländer and Weissburgunder; and in the middle and south there are fruity reds of varying quality. Styria produces bone dry, fragrant whites such as Traminer and Sauvignon Blanc.

Switzerland

Swiss wines, unlike Austrian, never scale the heights of excellence – though one would never know that from their sky-high prices. Wine is made in all but two of the country's 25 cantons, but the vineyards are concentrated in the French-speaking west, in the cantons of Vaud, north of Lake Geneva, and Valais to the south of the River Rhône. The not very characterful Chasselas (aliases Fendant and Perlan) is the main grape, producing light, refreshing, modestly fruity whites. The Valais, which has more grape varieties than the Vaud, including several local ones such as Humagne (red), Amigne and Heida (both white), is planted one-third with red grapes. These include Pinot Noir and Gamay, which produce simple, light, fruity reds, whether on their own or blended together to make a wine called Dôle. The Italian-speaking Swiss canton of Ticino produces Merlot that is probably Switzerland's best red.

(*Left*) **The main wine growing areas of Switzerland are in the cantons of Vaud and Valais in the west – of the two, Valais (left) produces the greatest variety.**

Eastern Europe

Gathering half a continent under the one umbrella of 'Eastern Europe' might seem cavalier, or perhaps naive, but the former Eastern Bloc countries, adjusting in varying degrees to capitalism, share many of the same problems, the same traditional winemaking practices and attitudes. When their wine industries were nationalised, prices were controlled, quantity was more important than quality and most of the wine exported simply went to other, indiscriminating Eastern Bloc countries (especially the former Soviet Union). Bulgaria was the one exception, creating an industry more or less from scratch and targeting the West – particularly Britain. Now, little by little, whole wine industries – wineries, vineyards, state cellars – are being dismantled and handed over to private owners who need to sell to the West because Eastern export markets have dried up. Much needed European and Australian investment has begun to move in, bringing with it essential expertise to show local winemakers how wine has to be made if it is to sell to Western palates.

For the winemakers and their backers these are at the same time the most exciting and the most frustrating countries to make wine for. The raw material is there, in the form of classic French and German and worthwhile indigenous grape varieties, all growing in favourable climates, but winemaking attitudes are often as primeval as the winemaking facilities. Picking grapes at the right time and rejecting those in bad condition has rarely before been a priority; the need to protect wine from oxidation and bacteria has seldom been understood; and the widespread conviction that older is always better means that most wines have been left too long in dilapidated barrels and concrete tanks.

But the reformation has begun, progress is gathering its own momentum and there is no doubt that the next few years will see a rising tide of good wines from these countries – and perhaps not only from the five described below – so long as the political situation is stable.

The Wine Regions of Central and Southeast Europe

Bulgaria

For most of the eighties Bulgarian Cabernet Sauvignon had no competition from its neighbours' wines – and none from Australia, Chile and the south of France either. All that has changed though, and some good is beginning to come out of it for the consumer.

White wines, never Bulgaria's strong suit, are improving – both Chardonnay and cheap, flowery, grapey 'Country Wine' blends such as Ugni Blanc and Misket. And with red wines there has been a move to bottle some wines earlier, to provide Cabernet Sauvignon, Merlot and the indigenous burly, spicy Mavrud and the southern Rhône-like Melnik when they are still full of juicy, fresh fruit, rather than always leaving them to acquire the distinctively Bulgarian, spice-and-tobacco wood tones.

Privatisation should also allow regional wine characteristics to emerge more strongly, so that it becomes possible to draw plausible and consistent distinctions between Pleven, Plovdiv, Russe, Suhindol, Sliven, Stara Zagora, Haskovo and other vineyard areas.

In fact, Bulgaria's classification system recognises over 40 regions from which Wines of Declared Geographical Origin may come. Country Wine is the category below, roughly equivalent to *vin de pays* and usually a blend of two grape varieties, sometimes including one of the indigenous ones such as Gamza or Pamid. The top category is Controliran wine which comes from 27 strictly controlled zones. Reserve and Special Reserve indicate superior, longer matured wines and can apply to Wines of Declared Geographical Origin and Controliran wines.

(*Above*) **The post-communist return of vineyards, wineries and cellars to private hands in Bulgaria – and neighbouring countries – is now beginning to reap rewards in terms of new, especially younger, fresher, wine styles.**

Hungary

Hungary has the oldest wine tradition of any in Eastern Europe, based on its sweet Tokay (Tokaji), which comes from vineyards adjoining Slovakia in the northeast and is made according to a unique production process established in the 17th century (predating any comparable sweet wine tradition in France or Germany). Tokay Aszú is the most significant wine and is classed according to its sweetness, measured in *puttonyos* (*puttonyos* or *putts* are the hods the pickers use) – three *putts* being the least sweet, aged for five years, and six *putts* being the sweetest and aged eight years. Above these are Aszú Eszencia and then the almost mystical, nectar-like Eszencia. For years Tokay coasted along on its reputation, but privatisation and European investment is beginning to return it to its former glory.

On the dry wine side, too, Hungary is making huge strides with input from Australia-trained winemakers. Racy, aromatic fruit characterises the new generation of Chardonnays, Sauvignon Blancs, Muscats and white wine blends, while Cabernets, Merlots and the indigenous red Kékfrankos, particularly from the warm, southerly Villány region, are packed with supple fruit.

(Below) **Western investment has focused primarily in Hungary on modern varietal whites and on historic Tokay – but perhaps it is only a matter of time before the 'Bulls Blood' of Eger's vineyards is revitalised by outside interests.**

READING MOLDOVA WINE LABELS

From top to bottom: **This modern label focuses on the grape variety (Sauvignon) and region, Hincesti (complete with map) before giving a brief history and geography of Moldovan wine (in the box). It then gives the other, mostly compulsory, information: alcohol content; vintage; contents; producer (Vitis Hincesti) and address. (What it doesn't reveal is that the wine is the result of a joint venture between the Australian giant Penfolds and French-based 'flying winemaker' Hugh Ryman.)**

(Below) **There is still a long way to go in the modernisation of the Romanian wine industry, but the potential is considerable — for reds, dry whites and sweet wines.**

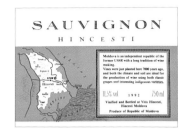

Moldova

Hundreds of thousands of hectares of vines, with no shortage of the classic French varieties and all growing in ideal climatic conditions, have made Moldova (the former Bessarabia, sandwiched between the Ukraine and Romania) a target for dynamic Western winemakers. The first whites to emerge from the new operations were simple, inexpensive Chardonnays, Sauvignon Blancs and Rkatsitelis (a soft, 'grapey' local variety). The first reds were solidly fruity, slightly rustic Cabernet Sauvignons, Merlots and Codrus (Codru is the name for a traditional oak-aged blend of Cabernet and Merlot). In addition, there are some stunning older wines — cedary, classed-growth Médoc-like in style and quality — but inevitably stocks of these are being depleted.

Romania

The main problem with Romania is unevenness of quality resulting from slovenly, unhygienic winemaking. Merlot and Cabernet, especially from around Dealul Mare, to the southeast, can be good, with quite rich, supple fruit; and peachy-apricoty sweet whites from the local Tamaioasa grape, especially from Murfatlar in the far southeast, close to the Black Sea, can be delicious in a slightly rustic way. Dry whites need to be approached with much more caution, but sporadic examples of enjoyable Pinot Gris, Silvaner and Sauvignon show potential. Pinot Noir can also be good (and cheap) but often it is simply jammy.

Slovakia

Slovakia, with its cooler climate, has a number of high quality, more individual grape varieties, particularly some enticingly lively and fragrant whites — among them musky, spicy Irsay Oliver, zesty, perfumed Pinot Blanc, spicy Traminer and peppery Grüner Veltliner. Reds are appealingly unusual, too, especially those from the fragrant yet meaty, berry-flavoured St-Laurent grape and the crisp, spicy, redcurrant-flavoured Frankovka.

Eastern
Mediterranean

The ancient world, centred on the Eastern Mediterranean, is where winemaking probably began, but an illustrious history is no guarantee of present-day quality. The climate in these countries is seldom less than hot and arid (but then so is Australia's) and old-fashioned winemaking for a captive local market predominates (which is where the comparisons with Australia end). And yet there are patches of excellence, often where Chardonnay, Sauvignon Blanc, Cabernet Sauvignon and Syrah have infiltrated.

Cyprus

It is hard to enthuse about Cyprus wines: most Commandaria, the heavy, syrupy-sweet brown wine, falls short of its ancient reputation; the sherry-style fortified wines are sound at best; and the table wines are largely flat and oxidised. That said, there are some attempts (by the huge Keo firm, for example) to freshen up the whites and give more fruit to the rustic, earthy reds. More of the native Xynisteri grape would help the whites – and perhaps some Cabernet Sauvignon would be no bad thing for the reds.

Greece

Although there is no denying that the majority of Greek wines are still either Retsina (wine flavoured with pine resin) or are dull and oxidised, a handful of large companies and individual estates is now rising well above the norm to produce lively, lemony, herby whites (from grapes such as Robola) and interesting blended reds. Among a growing number of appellations, the most reliable is Côtes de Meliton, in the north, for its claret-style and local blended reds; Naoussa (north) and Nemea (south) are good for potent, herby reds; Mantinia

(*Right*) **Picturesque as they are, these old wine jars are far from ideal containers for satisfying the modern taste for fresh-tasting unoxidised wines.**

(Left) The mountain
foothills in Cyprus
offer slightly cooler – and
therefore better – locations
for vineyards, but they
cannot make up for the
poor winemaking practices
that bedevil the wine
industry.

(south) and Cephalonia (a western island) produce some of the best dry whites; and Samos (an eastern island) is the Greek capital of sweet Muscats.

Israel

The advent, in the mid-eighties, of irreproachable kosher Chardonnay, Sauvignon Blanc and Cabernet Sauvignon from the cool, high-altitude Golan Heights region galvanised the whole of the Israeli wine industry into improvement, but the Golan Heights vineyards will always deliver the finest wines – wines with tremendous fruit intensity and fine structure, whether Cabernet and Chardonnay or cheaper dry Muscat and Colombard.

Lebanon

There are other producers, but to the outside world Lebanese wine is Château Musar, made from grapes grown high up in the Bekaa Valley. The red is world class in a marvellously individual way. An exotic, somehow wild wine, it is a blend of Cabernet Sauvignon, Cinsaut and Syrah and it tastes appropriately enough like a Bordeaux-Rhône cross – and while it is ready at seven years, it continues to evolve for 15.

United Kingdom

For a country still regarded by many as a non-producer – though not now by the Brussels bureaucracy – England has a remarkable number of vineyards. There are no fewer than 440 in England and Wales (all but a handful in England and mostly in the south) and 250 make wine on a commercial scale – even if not all of them have their own wineries. With nearly 900 hectares under vine, Britain produced over 3.5 million bottles in 1992, in a surprising array of styles – dry, medium and sweet, still and sparkling, white, red and rosé, unoaked and oak-matured.

Despite this apparent breadth, there is a characteristic style. English and Welsh wine – the major part of which is in fact white, unoaked and still – is light, crisp, aromatic and zesty, and ideal as an aperitif. The style is a reflection of the climate and of the grape varieties that are best suited to it. Germanic grapes dominate, especially crossings (led by Müller-Thurgau) which were designed to beat the cold German climate and have ended up producing better wine in Britain.

Müller-Thurgau is seldom the most exciting variety but it can produce perfectly pleasant, light, flowery, currant-leafy white and it is very useful in blends – of which there are a great many. Reichensteiner, the second most planted variety, is another useful, if fairly neutral, grape. Among the more characterful varieties, well-ripened, well-made Schönburger has a perfumed, almost Gewürztraminer-style lychees flavour; Kerner has an appley, gently spicy Riesling-like quality; and Huxelrebe can be reminiscent of elderflowers and pink grapefruit. Other varieties worth looking for include Bacchus, Faber, Ortega, Madeleine Angevine and, above all, Seyval Blanc.

(*Below*) **There are vineyards as far afield as Yorkshire and the West Midlands, but the highest concentrations are in warmer Kent (here at Lamberhurst) and Sussex.**

(*Above*) **The weather is the chief problem in Britain, but birds sometimes come a close second – hence Breaky Bottom's anti-bird netting.**

Seyval Blanc is not a pure *vinifera* strain and so it is ill-regarded in the EC, but in Britain's unpredictable climate it performs well, unquestionably giving some of the best wines – in a slightly more Loire-like than Germanic style. With age it can develop a honeyed character; it also takes well to oak and makes a perfect high-acid base for sparkling wine.

Sparkling wine is one of the new growth areas of England and Wales. Some producers have planted the champagne grapes, Chardonnay, Pinot Noir and Pinot Meunier, especially for the purpose – although one estate which has done so (Denbies, in Surrey) is so pleased with its base wines that it is also making a still Chardonnay and Pinot Noir rosé out of them.

Reds will always be small fry, but there are acceptable light reds from the hybrid Arc de Triomphe and occasional quirks like a successful oak-aged Cabernet Sauvignon-Merlot blend from Devon.

Trying to determine quality from the label has been a hit and miss affair in the past, but there is now a UK Quality Wine Scheme, loosely based on French *appellation contrôlée*, which recognises two categories, English Vineyards Quality Wine and, below it, English Table Wine. Proposals for a middle category to rescue Seyval Blanc from the Table Wine group have, for the time being, fallen foul of the EC. (British wine is something else entirely – an utterly inferior alcoholic drink made from reconstituted imported grape concentrate.)

Other countries

China

China has been making grape wine for millennia, but the best of recent times is the straightforward, fruity Chardonnay from the Shandong Peninsula, made with Western investment and expertise.

India

In the hills southeast of Bombay, Champagne technology and Indian investment have combined to produce some surprisingly good, albeit not entirely consistent, '*méthode traditionelle*' sparkling wine, from Ugni Blanc and, increasingly, Chardonnay.

Japan

Much so-called Japanese wine is blended with imported wine, but there is a handful of wineries making the real thing. The best are from Bordeaux grape varieties.

Luxembourg

Light, dry whites and sparkling wines (*crémants*) are produced along the Upper Moselle from Rivaner (alias Müller-Thurgau), Elbling, and, in smaller quantities, aromatic Alsace varieties.

North Africa

For years North Africa was a supplier of bulk wine to France, but now the vineyard area in Algeria, Morocco and Tunisia is in decline. The reds are generally fairly tough and made largely from southern French varieties, particularly Carignan. The best are from the coastal hills of Algeria. Tunisian Muscats, sweet or dry, are among the better wines too.

Turkey

Only two percent of the grapes from Turkey's 600,000 hectares of vineyards and numerous grape varieties go to make wine (the rest remain as table grapes). The quality, whether from indigenous grapes or French imports and whether red or white, is rustic.

Index

Page numbers in bold refer to main reference.

PICTURE ACKNOWLEDGEMENTS

The Anthony Blake Photo Library: Andy Collison 38 top right; Mathew Faber 33; J Murphy 36; Tony Robins 37 top left; Kieran Scott 32.
Cephas Picture Library: 93, 139 top; Jerry Alexander 83 bottom right; Nigel Blythe 73, 114, 156; R & K Muschenetz 134; Alain Proust 147; Mick Rock 42 left, 51 bottom, 53 centre, 56, 57 top and bottom, 58, 59, 71, 75, 77, 80, 83 main picture, 84, 85, 91 top left, bottom left, bottom centre and bottom right, 92, 120–1, 127, 130–1, 132–3, 136, 137, 141, 143, 149, 151, 152, 153, 157; Ted Stefanski 54 top; Helen Stylianou 154. **Robert Dieth**: 112–3. **Patrick Eagar**: 106, 109, 110, 140, 144. **Explorer**: S Cordier 52 centre; P D Forestier 89 bottom left; Hug 55 top; Francis Jalain 87 right, 108; P Lorne 96; Philippe Maille 104; Michael Plassart 83 top; J P Nacivet 102; D Reperant 63, 68–9, 98, 99, 101; Philippe Roy 41 bottom right, 89 top right and bottom right, 91 top right, 139 bottom; P Thomas 81; H Veiller 132; Patrick Weisbecker 148. **Robert Harding Picture Library** 115, 122–3; Robert Frerck 125; Adam Woolfitt 128 top. **Impact Photos**: Steve Benbow 89 top left. **Janet Price**: 142. **Reed Consumer Books Picture Library**: David Birch 35; Martin Brigdale 31; Amanda Heywood 31; James Murphy 34 top right; Ian O'Leary 34 bottom left; Charlie Stebbings 39 top; Alan Williams 126, 128–9; Paul Williams 37 bottom right, 38–9 bottom. **Scope**: Jean-Luc Barde 89 top centre, 116, 118–9, 128 bottom; Jacques Guillard 66–7, 79, 82–3, 103, 107; Michel Guillard 41 top, 91 top centre; Jacques Sierpinski 155; Jean-Daniel Sudres 86–7, 89 bottom centre, 105.
John Ferro Sims 118. **Spiral Cellars Ltd**: 42 centre, 43 bottom.

James Johnson – cut-out photography (except 26), and 14 (bottom)
Anita Corbin/John O'Grady – portraits of author
Simon Wheeler – section openers (8–9, 48–9, 94–5)

Hugh Johnson Collection – props for 18–9, 22–3, 25, 27, 28–9
Michael Johnson (Ceramics) Ltd – suppliers of all glasses, all by Riedel
Lovell Johns – cartography (part three)
Radius – locator map artwork (part two)